ENGLISH RULE

AND

NATIVE OPINION IN INDIA

ENGLISH RULE
AND
NATIVE OPINION IN INDIA

FROM NOTES TAKEN 1870-74.

BY

JAMES ROUTLEDGE

GYAN

Published by

GYAN

Gyan Publishing House
5, Ansari Road
Daryaganj, New Delhi-110002
Phone: 011-47034999, 9811692060
E-mail: books@gyanbooks.com

Distribution Network
gyanbooks.com
India, USA, Canada, UK, Australia

ISBN: 978-81-212-6882-0 (PB)
First Published, 1878

2nd Impression 2024

Printed at: Gyan Press, Delhi.

ENGLISH RULE AND NATIVE OPINION IN INDIA
Author: JAMES ROUTLEDGE

ENGLISH RULE

AND

NATIVE OPINION IN INDIA.

ENGLISH RULE

AND

NATIVE OPINION IN INDIA.

FROM NOTES TAKEN 1870-74.

BY

JAMES ROUTLEDGE.

LONDON:
TRÜBNER & CO., LUDGATE HILL.
1878.

PREFACE.

My object in this work is to try to depict some phases of Indian life as they actually are, and to make them as clear as possible to readers who know nothing practically of India. I can honestly affirm that I could with far less labour have made a work of a much more pretentious character than it has cost me to weave together this simple narrative of facts. The Indian Administration Reports alone are a mine of figures, which, with very little trouble, may be adapted to any subject, and used by any writer. No report, however, would have given me the material for the pictures which it has been my aim and wish to present. If the reader is interested with those pictures, I shall rejoice. I shall rejoice still more if I am fortunate enough to contribute anything tending to the solution of the great problems—many of them more social than political—involved in the relations of India to England.

CONTENTS.

ERRATA.

Page 103, *line* 4, *for* "Patna" *read* "Pubna."
,, 174, ,, 21, ,, "had told you that."
,, 178, ,, 14, ,, "the tow-rope."
,, 195, ,, 13, ,, "one other subject" *read* "There was one other subject which."
,, 214, ,, 5, ,, "may" *read* "might."
,, 235, ,, 6, ,, "they" ,, "were."
,, 259, ,, 1, } ,, "Greathead" ,, "Greathed."
,, 266, ,, 22, }
,, 265, ,, 4, ,, "cut off the."
,, 267, ,, 32, ,, "Gwalior's men" ,, "Gwalior men."
,, 268, ,, 21, ,, "overpouring, then" ,, "overpouring. Then."
,, 271, ,, 13, ,, "a quiet future" ,, "a great future."
,, 285, ,, 6, Quotation ends at "crops."
,, 292, ,, 24. *read* "as affording one of the best."

ENGLISH RULE

AND

NATIVE OPINION IN INDIA.

CHAPTER I.

THE OUTER PORTALS TO INDIA.

IN beginning a series of papers for *Macmillan's Magazine* in the year 1873, I ventured to claim attention, on the ground that I had had "unusual opportunities for testing, from a non-official point of view, the opinions of official men, civil and military, in India, together with perhaps equally unusual opportunities, from the same point of view, for testing the drift and tendency of native views and feeling." The papers here referred to were written carefully, and, though they were not by any means free from faults, they were as accurate as I could make them, and at least they were written without any object save that of stating exact facts, with the view of contributing something, however small, to the just interests of England and India. Since then time has passed; and in the hope that I may now approach the subject with more matured opinions I have undertaken to write this book.

That my notes will not rest on a long experience of India is fully stated in the title-page to such of them as will appear here. That they rest on exceptional opportunities for obtaining accurate information the reader may perceive in the narrative; and I can aver that no prejudice of faith or race, nor any desire to court the favour or hurt the feelings of any one, will colour or distort any record of what I saw or heard in my intercourse with any class of men in India. If I fall into the sin of egotism, I can only plead that, if there is to be any value in what is stated here, it will be in the way in which the subjects referred to appeared to myself, looking at them from the outside; not as a soldier, or a civil officer, or a missionary, or a merchant, but as a dispassionate observer, with many and varied means for testing subjects from many sides, without anything like equal opportunities for making any subject a special study.

With a view to general interest, I shall endeavour to throw my notes into a narrative form, dating from some days before the end of May 1870, when I left London for India, till the beginning of 1875, when I returned to England for the second time. My duties in the first case were to edit the *Friend of India*, and to act as Indian correspondent of *The Times*; and, in the second case, to seek for and communicate to *The Times* the exact truth as to the famine in Bengal. In India, unlike England, there are occasions when the only reliable information, even on very simple matters, is official information, and to obtain this and remain independent is often a hard problem in journalism. Happily in my own case the whole was rendered easy by the fact that the Governor-General of India was a man of such singular nobleness of character that I am certain he would have scorned to distort a fact for any purpose, and that his Private Secretary, who represented him in all cases, was characterised by like high-mindedness, and like unswerving courtesy. Apart from this invaluable courtesy, unfettered by any condition, and sometimes representing a policy which I disputed, I never owed Lord Mayo any favour. I have now a pleasure in this fact, when it may devolve on me to say something as a respectful tribute to his generous, high-minded, and honourable government.

The world into which I was about to be thrown would, I knew, differ materially from anything I had known heretofore as a journalist or a man. But I knew also that, both positively and negatively, I had some qualifications for the duties I had undertaken. I knew, for instance, that I could not easily be blinded by prejudice; that I could, and should, against any man or men, consider every subject on its merits; and that I had learned, in the best society of England, the society of the suffering poor, to feel for the weak and helpless, without at the same time thinking of the articles of their creed. In mines and mills, and shipyards, and arsenals, and schools, and literary institutions, in all parts of the United Kingdom, I had striven to know, not merely the modes of working and teaching, but the habits of thought, where thought is freest, and I believe bravest, among Englishmen.

The overland route to India in May 1870 was by Marseilles. A little later it was, as it still is, by Brindisi. In the first instance, therefore, I had the opportunity of seeing France from Calais to Paris, and from Paris to Marseilles; in the second, of twice passing through the great cities of Italy; and in the third, of making the voyage by Madras and Ceylon. It is to France, Italy, and the scenes on the Mediterranean that I refer, in using the unusual term, "The Outer Portals to India;" while of Egypt and Aden—the Red Sea and the Indian Ocean—I shall venture still further to ask the reader to think as the inner portals, or the courtyard to the kindred scenes and life of the still more distant East. This view is not put forward as a mere fancy, but as representing facts which must, I think, at some time, in some form, have influenced the thoughts, and perhaps dreams, of every Anglo-Indian. In the old days of the Cape route, the voyage involved a process of education, suited to a people who, with factories on the Indian sea-board, held, as by a proud prerogative, the ocean highways. The motley cargoes of all sorts and conditions of men and women, the long irksome voyages, the quarrels and flirtations, the "runs" on land, and the sights on sea, involved an experience never again to be lost—an experience, not merely of men of the time of Job Charnock, and Clive, and Warren Hastings, but of our own time. The Cape route is still spoken of by persons, and not necessarily old persons, whose now unvarying path to India is by the Mediterranean and the Red Sea.

The newer education may not be better—and some old Indians say certainly is not better—but at least it is different, and in some particulars it is better adapted for a fitting introduction to an empire whose relation to even the Mediterranean is much closer than some people suppose, and whose boundaries are from westward of the Indus to far beyond the Brahmapootra eastward, and from the Himalayas to the islands south of Comorin. When the traveller to India leaves the steamboat at Calais till he enters it at Marseilles, or Venice, or Genoa, or Brindisi, he is a stranger in strange lands. He changes his money to the coin or the notes current in France, Germany, or Italy; he learns to think with the men of other nations in their own languages. From the time he embarks in an English vessel on the Mediterranean till he lands at Alexandria, he is on a bit of the dominions of the Queen, and under the flag of England.

In May 1870 France was in all her glory. She was the arbiter of nations—when she was satisfied Europe was at peace. Her soldiers had that dashing military swing which comes from long years of unchecked success. I noticed a vast change in 1873, landing from Egypt at Brindisi, but passing through France. The very appearance of the men was changed. The pride and even self-respect of France had been shattered, though dancing and other amusements were unchanged, or were only changed in being wilder and less restrained. In May 1870 France was very beautiful in town and country. The boulevards, the palaces, the churches, the military displays, the pleasure-gardens and theatres, all told to the eye, as never can be told to the ear or in written words, of the splendour of a capital in some respects unapproachable. It was in the country, however, that the real charms of France were seen. The placid content on every face, the cleanliness in every cottage, the blue blouse and the white cap and apron, the fruitfulness in orchard, vineyard, and meadow, might elsewhere be sought for and never found. Of the life of Paris, and especially of that life at its lowest, the voyager to India finds many pictures in miniature at Alexandria, Cairo, Suez, and Ismailia; but the peaceful charms of the country cannot be transplanted to other lands.

From Paris a railway journey of seventeen hours would, if time were pressing, convey the traveller to Marseilles and the blue waters of the Mediterranean. A strangely ancient-looking place, it is, with churches, hotels, shops, markets, and harbour, apparently belonging, as indeed they do belong, to both East and West. It is when one looks back from, say, the Red Sea that one perceives in what Marseilles differs from Calais and Lyons, and comprehends what is meant by France possessing a Mediterranean seaboard, and a direct communication with the East. A Saturday night in the crowded streets of Marseilles reminded me at first of some familiar little English seaport towns, but when I had seen Cairo and Suez, it was not difficult to perceive in the Saturday evening market at Marseilles, in the rich profusion of fruits and flowers, in the voluble saleswomen and the easy laughing crowd of buyers, certain characteristics—slight but unmistakable—of the Eastern bazaar; indications of a border land where differences of race and custom blend—of an approach to the regions of the sun.

Early next morning, a beautiful Sunday morning, one of the Peninsular and Oriental Company's fine vessels steamed quietly out from docks crowded with men in clean blouses, and women in neat becoming white caps, and lively (you can hardly say merry) children—a pretty, peaceful, genuinely French scene. In less than three months from that time the thunderbolt of war had burst on Europe with terrific fury; the gay streets and peaceful villages of France were devastated, and the route to India was diverted to Brindisi. The excitement in Europe was carried as on the wind, and perhaps in some senses was intensified on its way to India. It was not difficult to see how in one week the very tone and character of society in many nations might reflect the feelings created by a state of war between any two portions of the virtual federation of civilised men.

From Marseilles to Alexandria is about 1400 miles as our vessel ran—between the islands of Sardinia and Corsica; then closely under Caprera; then, towards evening on Wednesday, in sight of Stromboli; then later through the beautiful Straits of Messina, with Messina itself on the one hand and Reggio on the other, in both cases lit up as in a fairy vision, while the boom of a gun over the still waters told the watchers of the steamboat company on shore that the customary "All's well" might be telegraphed to London. The traveller has before this begun to feel that he is steaming his way over the most famous of seas. He may fancy that he looks upon the very waves over which the armies of Asia were carried to uproot or submerge the fresh young civilisations of Europe, and over which the smaller but mightier armies of Europe, like streams returning to an ocean bed, were hurled against the decaying civilisations or barbarisms of Asia and Africa. It will be strange if in a Peninsular and Oriental steamboat there is not some shrewd and well-read man to tell, to those who are willing to listen and learn, of Rome and Carthage, of Greece and Sicily, of Tunis, of the Crusaders, of the Moors and their tide of conquest, and of the Turks and theirs, of the Great Desert, of the Numidian horse, of Nelson and Napoleon, of all the great past, and all the dread uncertain prospects of the lands that border on this storied sea. No vessels in the world convey so many passengers at once educated and distinguished, and a young man must be vain and foolish if he arrive at Alexandria, after his six or seven days' voyage from Europe, without having found that all that Oxford or Cambridge has taught him must be re-cast and tested by a new experience. He may have talked at one hour of the day to an officer from Peshawur, the next to a man from Madras, or from Rangoon, or from the banks of the Indus, or the Ganges, or the Jumna, or the Brahmapootra; soldiers, civil officers, missionaries, chaplains of the Established Church, Jesuits, Presbyterians, Baptists, merchants, planters. Perhaps the young voyager addresses a mild, gentlemanly, and thoroughly polite person, who he afterwards finds has been the guiding spirit of a regiment of Sikhs or Ghoorkas; perhaps plays quoits with a man who has needed all his skill and ability to avoid traps and pitfalls as the Political Resident at a native court; perhaps asks an opinion from or expresses opinions to the chief of an English regiment covered with the laurels of war, or a renowned engineer, or an able diplomatist, or a person great in knowledge of Calcutta, Bombay, Madras, Oude, the Punjab, or some far-off frontier. Each possesses some experience by means of which he can add to the knowledge of other men of whatever age or length of service; while to the young man—the new-comer to the East—there is information and matured thought on every hand. The inquirer may find also, however, that there is in some cases a vast amount of selfishness to sift away; that the chief object with many is a successful career; that some soldiers and civilians perceive only a continuous and never-ceasing battle for what are called the plums of the services. When this point has been reached the traveller may perhaps turn to the missionary or chaplain, but only to find that even here he may have turned in vain for a fair representation of those self-sacrificing qualities which England certainly does send to India. To see the deeply melancholy side of Indian life, the voyage homeward as well as that outward must be taken; the latter with its fresh or renovated life, the former with its invalids in some cases only returning home to die. Nothing sadder than some phases of Indian life can be found anywhere among persons who never are likely to need any of those comforts of life which money can provide, who would be ashamed to live in any other part of London than the West End, or to be one iota out of that great order of fashion which is interpreted and determined by Court dressmakers and tailors. The sad vein of Indian life is beyond money, or fashion, or anything that the Queen herself can give or withhold.

CHAPTER II.

EGYPT AND THE RED SEA—ADEN.

On Saturday morning at day-dawn we saw the low-lying sandy coast-line of the land of the Pyramids, of Jacob and Joseph, of early prophets, and of later scholars of almost equally enduring memory; and while the minds of some were excited by an unwonted feeling of mingled delight and awe, others were arranging a sweepstake with reference to the passing of a certain point of land—a project which gave money to the winner.

Among the second-class passengers from Marseilles there was one poor Arab whom most people had pitied, and to whom the captain had now and then spoken kindly. He had been chiefly observed lying near to the sheep-pens, a silent, dreamy, objectless man. A little before the lights were put out on Friday night the poor Arab underwent a transformation. He mounted the bridge, with his garments girt about him, and his telescope in hand. On Saturday morning he piloted the vessel into the Bay of Alexandria. The difference between the deportment of an Arab pilot on the Mediterranean, and a Hooghly pilot from the Sandheads to Calcutta, is immense, but a pilot is a pilot all the world over; and the Indian commissioner, looking through his "binocular" upon the Egyptian land, was not better fitted for the duties of his commissionership than that poor Arab was to carry the ship through those shifting sandbanks. It was but a little scene; yet it was vastly more instructive than the sweepstake.

Passengers who went onward by the next boat from Suez had a day in Alexandria, and might see somewhat of cafés and bazaars, and a varied population—Jew, Turk, Arab, African, Greek, French, English, Italian; indeed, almost every race in East and West. You perceive that there was no error of judgment in the selection of Alexandria as the centre at once of two civilisations, and of the trade of many races. You see how naturally the scholars of the East and the West would find here a common meeting-ground; how every impulse of Europe, Asia, and Africa, would make its way to Alexandria as by a common law, and with electrical sensitiveness.

Remaining behind the rest of the outward-bound passengers, and economising time, under excellent guidance, I saw much of Alexandria at its best and worst. The reader would pass through Egypt with very mixed feelings. Wandering through the bazaars, he might see openly exposed for sale "works of art" at which London would be amazed if not shocked. Entering a café at the time of mid-day rest, when every office was closed, he would find merchant-society in repose, over quiet little games of chance or skill and moderate measures of wine. Visiting the gambling dens and singing rooms at night he would witness wild orgies for which he might possibly seek in vain for a comparison. My notes are of this Saturday night, when a merchant friend guided me through all manner of scenes, illustrative of the actual life of Alexandria. How different from a Saturday night at Marseilles! Nothing worse perhaps than might be found in Manchester or Liverpool or Glasgow, but unique in its mixture of races, and suggesting a careful deportment if you would escape difficulty and indeed danger.

Of the hollowness and hardship, in a double sense, of the Khedive's government, there was evidence on every hand. The victim himself of diplomatic agents and merchants, who contracted and sub-contracted away the very life-blood of his resources, he found victims in turn in the masses of the helpless people.

A spirited young Englishman, who had been sent out

from Manchester to superintend the Government cotton estates on the Nile, found to his surprise that not one of the men, women, or children of a vast body of "hands" received any pay whatever, and only a small amount of wretched food. He remonstrated, and was met in this way: "You agree to do so-and-so if we provide labour, do you not? Very good. The provision of labour then is my business; the execution of work yours. Do not quarrel with your interest. Let us be friends. You attend to this, I to that, and so we shall avoid unpleasantness." The young Englishman, ardent for freedom and fair dealing, was powerless, and he finally left the estate in disgust. Such are some of the phases of human life which seven years ago faced an Englishman at Alexandria on his way to India. Forced labour, and taxes levied even years before due, were the prominent and all-powerful principles of a social life, in which men of wealth and European education were prominent actors.

I passed the Khedive walking with one of his sons in the fine gardens which he hardly can call his own—an intelligent, yet a bewildered-looking, melancholy man; wealthy, and yet poor. A fabulous amount of money was received in Egypt for cotton during the American War, and was lost. The viceroy had his share, the merchants theirs, the usurers theirs. Money probably was hidden to be found no more; much also went in orgies which appeared as by magic. Egypt was no richer. Twelve years prior to my visit, Alexandria had not one beer-house; at the time of my visit it had fifty, and many of them possessed "attractions" of the most questionable kind. Originating in the cotton trade, the dens increased in number year by year, till the life of Alexandria might be said to have undergone one more change, the latest, and perhaps the most contemptible, of the many changes which in the course of ages have passed over it. To be ignorant of whist, or to neglect the fashionable salute, is barbarous in Alexandria. To grind down the poor people till their life is well-nigh worn out, is fashionable and civilised.

I went to the English consular court, where a trial of some interest was going on. I was politely received, and shown to a seat, but it was immediately found that the case must be adjourned. Nothing could have been more polite, or more Egyptian. I went to the English and American schools, as I did also in Cairo (including an engineering school near the latter), and there at all events were glimpses of a nobler, perhaps a regenerating life. The railway system, too, and the cotton markets were like fresh leaves on a decayed tree. The worm much trodden upon at times turns. The merchant finds, for instance, that if he wishes to discharge a vessel there is a virtual trades union to prevent him doing so by any but his own regularly engaged men. Here, for the moment, the weak become strong. The sting, however, is only skin deep. The European is in most cases free to do almost anything. At this time he paid no taxes, save one which he had himself made for his own protection; and if he wished to vex the Government to the heart, he could begin, or threaten to begin, a newspaper, and demand his own price for its suppression. This skeleton picture might be filled up with incidents illustrative of the still-existing plague of flies, of the unending cry for baksheesh, of the ever-present donkey and donkey-boy. Of such the reader may learn much in the books of the records of many observers of Eastern life. One note, however, I cannot pass. Standing at the foot of Pompey's Pillar with my friend, who spoke Arabic, a little Arab girl drew to us, and looked wistfully in our faces. My friend said: "Do you know who made this?"—the pillar. "Yes, very well; he lives in the next village." "Go and bring him, and you shall have baksheesh." "I cannot to-day, for he is from home, but I can to-morrow." The poor little romancer received her baksheesh. She viewed the beautiful pillar as one of the gods which foolish men in black coats came to worship, and as the attraction for everlasting baksheesh.

In Cairo the scene changes to one of the most Oriental of cities. I had a letter of introduction to a gentleman, whom I found early in the morning sitting on a second story verandah, in a narrow street, across which higher still was drawn a sun-blind of many colours. He wore a pair of loose trousers, a shirt, and a pair of slippers—nothing more. On the opposite side of the street, and also on a verandah, within speaking distance, were several ladies, old and young, drinking their coffee in similarly light attire. There was no impropriety. It was custom, stronger than written law. Beneath were camels, dromedaries, donkeys, and goats, intermingled with a crowd, dense as a sea, of people of many races. A cup of strong Mocha coffee, unsweetened and without milk, is a luxury everywhere offered to a visitor in Egypt; and though its appearance is not in its favour, it is infinitely preferable to the English glass of sherry. Of the missionary schools, and the noble educational work of two generous English ladies, much has been written. Of the palace, the slave market, the petrified forest, and other of the "sights" of Cairo, I have little to say that would be worth printing. Of the dark skins, gleaming eyes, jabbering tongues, and lively costumes in the crowded streets, one might write a fairy tale; and fairy tales will be written of them while Eastern and Western life remain what they are, and while the men of the West continue to find their way eastward in the paths of these old civilisations.

One sight, however, cannot be passed over, any more than it can be effaced from the memory of especially any one who afterwards visits the Tâj at Agra. The Tâj is an Indian tomb, the part conception of a Western artist. The Pyramids are Egyptian tombs, solid, scientific, endurable as the old culture of Egypt, and significant as its embalming of the dead. After a delightful night drive, partly over what I afterwards found to be soft velvet grass, beautifully green,

I climbed the Great Pyramid at three o'clock in the morning, and waited for the sunrise on Cairo and the desert. At a little distance was the dumb Sphinx, in the face of which some have seen such remarkable expression, and in which others have declared they could find no expression whatever. The dumb, perplexing, voiceful, eternal thing! The expression doubtless depends greatly on the surroundings and on the mystery in which the story is enfolded, and this becomes apparent when one afterwards compares both with other stone faces and scenes, dissimilar in much, yet akin. From the pyramid I looked upon the minarets, fortifications, cupolas, and dark cypresses of Cairo, gradually distinguishable as the day began to dawn, and telling of a great city awakening to daily life, while the silvery Nile, glistening like a bright long line of light and life, carried the mind far away through the ruins of great cities into regions of oblivion, and to an imagined day-dawn of history. I had seen the sun rise in many different places, and I subsequently saw it rise in many more on sea and land, from mountain and plain, from palki and dak-gharry and railway carriage, and from the port-holes and the decks of ships; but the pictures of the English Bible, woven into English life, compel one to see much more than appears to the natural eye in a sunrise in Egypt. I can recollect as if it were yesterday the sudden appearance, almost with the first golden rays of the sun, of a line—about a score perhaps—of camels on the distant horizon, like a mirage in the desert, lonely, misty, almost as of ghostland, recalling stories of the patriarchs going down into Egypt, and of the flight of Joseph and Mary to save the young Child's life. No other European was present, and having silenced the clamourers for baksheesh it was easy to sit and dream. It was difficult, however, to connect the old Scripture times with Napoleon's search here for an Eastern empire, with our own highway to India, with the English names cut on the stone on which one sat, and on the stones around, or, worst of all, with an English handbill advertising English Mr Somebody's bitter ale. Bitter ale on this monument of ages! The unlucky bill jarred greatly with the glory of the patriarchs—of those times when Egypt itself was young. The drive back to Cairo was beautiful. A vast number of poor people, who were asleep on the wayside when we passed some hours earlier, now formed part of a great scene of life and labour, and one or two English parties driving out to the Pyramids seemed like elements of an altogether different creation. It ought also to be interesting to all men to know that the Khedive had at this time an opera in all its glory, to the great delight of a few Western people, and to the extreme horror of all the gravest and best old Arabs.

A night run over the desert, not now, as in earlier years, with luggage on camels and passengers in vans, but by railway, with a supper and cool claret at Zagizig, half way over, carries the traveller to Suez and the Red Sea. The voyage from Suez to Aden occupied approximately about the same time as that from Marseilles to Alexandria, and during the greater part of the time with like-recurring scenes, connected with all that is best known and all that is most mysterious in history. At the head of the Red Sea, from the Gulf of Suez, a scene of rare beauty is at times presented. The most beautiful to me was a scene at day-dawn in 1874, while approaching from the contrary direction the mouth of the canal. "Perhaps," my note, afterwards given in *Macmillan's Magazine*, said, "no day-dawn in the world surpasses in beauty that which may be seen in the passage of the Straits of Jubal into the Gulf of Suez. There are no richer tints on the heather of Scotland or Cumberland, or on the vines of Italy and France. You know, too, that the 'Sinaitic Range' on the one hand, and the African land on the other, represent a great gulf, frequently passed but never filled up so as to form a permanent highway for human life. There is no blade of grass in view; the beauty consists in the sun's magical tints on the bleak mountains, now grey, now golden; here standing out in bright relief, there deepening into shade; altogether very beautiful when seen on a still morning over a calm sea. The canal is French, but it is difficult to think so when you see the number of English flags in the Gulf and at Port Said. The forms of life, however, are those of a French colony, with an Arabian and Egyptian basis, in all probability stable as the hills, and with a mixed and lawless population, compared with which even Alexandria presents many phases of settled order." Another note says: "I wish some Englishmen who talk of human progress, of the prospects of sword being beaten into ploughshare and spear into pruning-hook all the world over, could look now and then on these dim shore-lines and the dimmer populations beyond. I asked the captain of one vessel on which side of the sea he would, in case of extremity, prefer to run ashore. He said, 'The African, decidedly.' I put the same question to another captain, and he replied, 'Well, the Arabian.' Neither had the remotest idea what would occur in either case, except that, however solitary the place might be, the ship would in an hour be surrounded by boats manned by unsparing robbers."

If we consider what the vessels on the Red Sea represent of trade and nationality we shall be carried well-nigh over the world. If we think of what the scenes represent, we may look in fancy to Syria and Jerusalem, to Medina and Mecca, and finally to Aden, and may perceive that the fibre of connected history is far from worn out as regards Arabia. A writer, referring to this year's pilgrimages, undisturbed even by the war, said: "The pilgrims will take steamer at Jeddah for the Persian Gulf, Bombay, Calcutta, Singapore, Penang, Batavia, and some to Zanzibar, for the south-eastern ports of Africa, and Capetown, while some will return to the Syrian and North African and Moorish ports"—a very comprehensive view of the intermingling of races in the East. On the other side of the Red Sea we might follow the Nile from Egypt to the interior of Africa, and by leaving it at some point for the desert, might, if we escaped a thousand dangers, emerge on the bleak sterile shore of Cape Guardafui, the extreme point to which Africa stretches into the Indian Ocean. The entire scenes are strangely mysterious to Europe. But they belong to great histories.

Aden is politically in the Presidency of Bombay. It is also the visible and real gateway to India. The steamer to India stops about twelve hours for coal, and the traveller may see those wonderful tanks which bear witness for some mighty but now dim civilisation. A British cantonment, a few European and Parsee stores on the barren shore, a strange race of wanderers—Jew, Arab, and African—and a polyglot race of expert boy divers, who never seem to grow older, comprise the elements of human life on this cinder fortress, thrown out, as it were, from the mainland, and for generations the property of the strongest hand on the Red Sea. Here, also, is the converging point of different streams of commerce, from China, Australia, Japan, and South Africa, as well as from all the ports of India. Looked at cursorily, you see the small settlement engaged in trade; the garrison, which tries to while away time in amateur theatricals, or in making shrubs to grow on hard volcanic cinder, or in watching the vessels homeward and outward, and in dreaming pleasant dreams of orders for removal to any place on the face of the earth away from Aden. You learn that the cinder fortress where the English flag now flies, 1700 feet above the level of the sea, marks the site of a city once very important in Arabia. Looking below the surface you perceive at Aden the tapping, as it were, of an unknown land, wherein feather merchants and others disappear, at stated times, to return laden with the spoils of the desert to adorn the bonnets of ladies in London and Paris. The Jew, too, is here, as everywhere; and here, as elsewhere, with all his love for gain, he keeps his holy day as religiously as in civilised and safe lands.

At this point, where the swell of the Indian Ocean

begins to make itself felt in the Straits of Babelmandeb, the traveller, who has read, while voyaging from Suez to Aden, the history, with the maps and charts, of both sides of the Red Sea, may vastly extend his range of vision. If, instead of directing the vessel's head across the Arabian Sea to Bombay, it were pointed to the northward, the voyage would be south and east of Arabia to the head of the Persian Gulf, passing the land of Oman, the scene of so many dynastic struggles of late years, the scene, too, of so many mightier struggles in ages gone. You know that if you went far enough over the land westward you might arrive at Mecca; that northward are Persia and the Caspian, north-eastward (over the gulf) Beloochistan, and further north Afghanistan; with the lines of the Indus on the west of India, from north to south. You begin now to comprehend more fully the relation that Aden bears at once to Arabia, to Persia, and Oman, to Afghanistan and Beloochistan, and to India. In India itself you will hear much of the Wahabee (the Mohammedan Puritan) sect, which has extended its teachings and influence from Arabia to the most southern and eastern parts of Bengal and Madras, and you will have no difficulty in perceiving how easily and naturally the doctrines and teachers might pass from Nedj to the Persian Gulf and to the Indus. These facts may appear more clearly in a later chapter, but they are worth noting here in approaching the last portal of the great empire of England in the East.

If, instead of keeping the vessel's head along the coast-line of Arabia, you ran southward, along the African coast past Cape Guardafui, you would come to Zanzibar. Looking, then, to the dynastic relation of Zanzibar and Oman, the ideas gathered on the Mediterranean and the Red Sea might now be aptly and naturally extended, over the sea, from Aden, southward to Abyssinia, and to where, we are told, we should find the sources of the Nile, and northward, through Arabia, till we arrived at the lands occupied by Russia in Asia.

When people say that the distances are too vast, and the deserts and steppes too dry, or bleak, or barren and desolate to be traversed, let us remember that they are so traversed continually in all directions by the men of the East; that what we call vast distances are but so many hundred different resting-places to persons who carry their homes with them. Let us remember, also, that the distances have been traversed by armies. When we hear of the ocean that separates Oman from Zanzibar, we may perceive that that ocean is made light of by boatmen ignorant of the locomotive uses of steam. Then we may see not merely what relation Aden bears to all the orders of men from the Mediterranean to the Bay of Bengal and to the Cape of Good Hope, but also how Eastern races are knit together, so that an idea thrown out in the desert or on the mountain top may extend over thousands of miles and influence many millions of men. Strangely mingled thoughts may now range over all history, from Nebuchadnezzar to Robert Clive, or from Abraham in Egypt or Moses on Sinai to the landing of Syud Toorkee a few years ago in Oman. Even such scraps of history as that the Queen of Sheba went from the ends of the earth to hear the wisdom of Solomon, may assist us to comprehend the relation of Eastern lands in old times and under very unfavourable conditions for travelling. The Queen of Sheba had some weary journeys, no doubt, but she was also doubtless a patient traveller, as behoved a daughter of the sunny East.

The importance attached by England to Aden was shown when in 1874 a Turkish force, advancing on Nedj and other parts of Arabia, approached too near to our allies the Sheikhs in the neighbourhood of the cinder fortress. A very stern mandate went from London to Constantinople, and the least hesitation on the part of the Turks would have led to English shot and shell being thrown among the invaders. Equally strong evidence of the same fact was given earlier, when by an act of sharp practice, which at one time would have led to war, an English officer seized upon the island of Perim in the very teeth of a French man-of-war sent out to make the seizure for France. Perim might have become a rival fortress to Aden, and it was not merely seized, but was also held in defiance of all diplomacy by the British Government.

If the voyager in the monsoon season is very much interested in all this, he may not observe that while the coal is being taken into the vessel by one set of men, another set are making all snug on deck and aloft for the big waves of the Indian Ocean. Better, however, to forget the waves, which may not be so easily forgotten a few hours later, than miss the lesson which the central position of Aden, and its curious relation to so many different elements of peace and war in ancient and present times, ought to suggest. I do not think this fact is commonly seen in its many-sided meaning. Every one, of course, knows that Aden is important as a coaling station. Independent of that, however, Aden has a great political significance. I do not mean for the defiance of enemies, but as a visible representation of power, on the side of peace and order, on sea and land, from the Gulf of Suez to Bombay.

CHAPTER III.

BOMBAY, AND OVERLAND TO CALCUTTA.

THE first impression received of Bombay after the voyage from England is not easy to represent on paper. The splendid bay, covered with shipping, may perhaps be entered a second time without emotion, but hardly so the first time by an Englishman. After travelling over 6000 miles through the lands and along the shores of strangers, here is English life, strong, intellectual, and self-reliant; a Government house, a fort, military lines, law courts, a custom-house, colleges, markets of uncommon excellence, European residences skirting carriage-drives open to the sea, jetties and wharves, churches and chapels, reading-rooms and libraries, clubs, cotton and other mills—everything, in fact, of all that Englishmen have accustomed themselves to term necessaries of civilised (meaning English) life. With an inland trade ever increasing as the railway system is extended, and a direct communication with England by the canal, Bombay has put forward substantial claims to become the capital of India, Calcutta being dismissed as too far away from England and as unfit for European residence all the year through, and the old capitals of the Moguls as only suited to a purely military people, possessing no basis on the sea. Nothing of all this, it is true, shakes the imperial position of the great city on the Hooghly, while Allahabad is fast becoming, if it has not become, the military capital of India. Yet there is something in Bombay that is all its own, and which at least gives it an indisputable right to be called the commercial capital of the East.

I saw Bombay under three different aspects—first, when

I was entirely unacquainted with India, while the French and German armies were approaching each other for the death-struggle; next, when I had been in India long enough to have known some representative men, and to have studied as closely as I could many subjects of the thoughts and acts both of English and native people; and again, on my way to the scenes of the Bengal famine. On the first occasion I saw the Temple of Elephanta, and I had no such favourable opportunity of seeing it again. The caves are on an island three or four miles in circumference, and from four to six miles from the Bombay shore. If the reader can imagine such an island, formed of two hills with a narrow valley between them, ending in a rugged circumscribed gorge clad with dense verdure and leading to the sacred caves, a fair general idea will be had of the approach to this ancient temple. The gorgeous rays of the sun dance outside on bush and tree; inside, the rocks drip with water, and from sombre recesses or elevations Brahma, Vishnu, and Siva in various incarnations, look down upon you with strangely human eyes, albeit eyes of stone. Years later, and after visiting many kindred places, I was still able to recall some of the faces at Elephanta, and compare them with some in the Great Fort at Gwalior—a proof of the impression made by them on at least one mind.

The missionary institutions of Bombay are almost as well known to intelligent people in England as the universities of Oxford and Cambridge; and it is curious, therefore, to record[1] that for fifty years after the cession of the island to England by Portugal (1662) there was not in the place either a church or a chaplain, and that no complete translation of the Bible into the Mahratta language existed prior to 1847. The basis of the population on this side of India is Hindoo, and largely Mahratta, but there are also numbers of Mohammedans, with Jains, Bheels, and others, and surmounting all, the able, astute Parsee—merchant, banker, scholar, millionaire, and as devout a disciple of Zoroaster,

[1] Sherring's "Protestant Missions." Trübner & Co.

and as opposed to Christianity, as ever his fathers were. "Ten papers and magazines" (Mr Sherring says, writing of 1843) "in and around Bombay, and armed with heathen learning and the most approved weapons of infidelity," were arrayed against Christianity. In many cases the Parsee is a polished gentleman, in many more a man of great enterprise and capacity in trade. I found him engaged at Aden and at the mouth of the Mutlah river, many miles below Calcutta; in all cases the head and front of commercial enterprise. I saw also at least one indication that he will occasionally do much for an English title; but apart from this, his charities are often munificent. Perhaps there are no persons in India who owe more to British rule than the Parsees, and perhaps (though they can, and sometimes with reason, be very haughty to individual Englishmen) there are no persons in India who know better the value of that rule, or who return for it a more unhesitating loyalty. Directing their energies to banking, manufacture, and trade, the Parsees preserve an unwonted degree of independence, and are in the main valuable citizens.

From Bombay to Calcutta is a distance of 1400 miles, and involves a railway journey of a little more than sixty-five hours, which a sleeping-carriage and a retiring-room, with plenty of water, are necessary to render endurable. The journey may be almost said to begin with the ascent of the Ghâts, which from first to last present successive scenes of indescribable grandeur. A fresh new picture appears at every turn of ravines that seem interminable, and in ascents and descents along the sides of rugged precipices, and into deep chasms, and on curves which are like a labyrinth. Here and there the line seems decidedly at an end. Yet still the engine goes slowly on, puffing and panting, amid such a mass of verdure as few persons can hope to see more than once in a lifetime. For more than an hour you climb and re-climb, by a sinuous path, broken by tunnels which make the scenery all the grander, till at last the giddier part of the work is done, and the line is on comparatively safe ground. I have heard that these are not the grandest of the Indian ghâts, but they are exceedingly grand.

At Jubbulpore most people stop to see certain ruins, and the picturesque Nerbudda waterfalls, and the much-talked-of marble rocks. The place for miles around abounds with objects of interest. You find, also, about here, that the scenery is fast changing to tamer hills, which long before the journey terminates give place to flat plains. Six hundred of the fourteen hundred miles have been passed, with fresh scenes of beauty by night and day. You sleep, and awake to see the dark shadows on the hills, and to feel the intense loneliness which is only broken by the bark of the jackal or the whoop of the night-bird, and by the heavy breathing of the steam-engine, wending its way through sombre gloomy districts that seem to give back silence for silence to the bright stars overhead. You sleep again, and awake with the first streaks of dawn, and watch till the grey tints broaden into amber and gold—into a myriad lines of beauty. Of the changing features of such a journey an artist might write with rapture, if indeed he could find words in which to picture what he saw.

I once watched the approach of a magnificent thunderstorm, and noted the rapid succession of changes, ending in piles upon piles of big clouds rolling onward like great mountains in motion, and with deep caverns lit up by magnificent forked lightning. A couple of hours earlier a bit of exquisite cloudland had appeared to the westward, soft, bright, and with every conceivable variety of colour, and peaceful as an English landscape on a Sunday morning in spring. In the east the black clouds were gathering grandly, and the debatable cloudland between was of a dull, leaden colour. The bright colours gradually and speedily gave place to the leaden ones, and the leaden ones to the black mountain piles. Then we had the thunderstorm, which, terrible as it was, one almost regretted to lose. To fall asleep in one kind of scenery—say a mountain district—and awake in another—say on a vast plain—is at least novel. To awake just before dawn of day, and watch for the first light in the east while the steam-engine is pushing steadily along its way, is a treat that money might fail to buy.

At Allahabad, the capital of the North West Provinces, and the great arsenal of India, the journey to Calcutta may be said (speaking generally) to have been half made. It is a city doubly sacred—to the Hindoo, because it lies at the confluence of the Ganges and the Jumna, both sacred; to the Mohammedans, because it was named by the great Akbar, Allah-abad, the city of Allah. In its old town may be found one of the most shifting, and, viewing it early one morning at a later period, I thought one of the most ferocious populations in India. The fort and arsenal are perfect for war. The European quarter, the "Station," is beautifully laid out, and admirably tended. Straight wide roads are everywhere lined with trees, interspersed with often elegant and mostly pretty bungalows. Here you may learn, more truly perhaps than in any other place, what is meant by Englishmen in India "standing on guard." Elsewhere, as Agra, Delhi, and Lucknow, there may be a varnish as of the bazaar. Here there is a clear field, and a certain something that conveys the idea of a military force polished into an unsurpassed weapon of war.

The fortress, greatly prized by Akbar, was wrung from him a short time before his death by the unnatural rebellion of his son. Then, while Clive was advancing to Plassey, Allahabad was seized by the Nawab of Oude "for the Emperor." It was afterwards ceded to the Mahrattas, Warren Hastings alone demurring in the face of his enemies in the Council. At the end of the eighteenth century it came to us by treaty, and it is not likely to again pass very readily into other hands. Wellington saw its military value with unerring certainty, and it is on record that Lord Ellenborough, who, whatever might be his faults, was pre-eminently loyal to the great duke, strove to give the view effect. The place of this city and fortress in the Mutiny of 1857 we shall see in a later chapter.

With Allahabad as a centre, many great cities of the Ganges and the Jumna may be visited, but to all save Benares we shall come in another way, and to Benares alone I shall refer here as diverging from the main line to Calcutta. At a short distance from Allahabad is the railway station of Mogul Serai, and six miles further you reach the side of the Ganges, opposite to "the Sacred City," the Jerusalem and Mecca of the Hindoos. Leaving Allahabad on a beautiful evening, I arrived at the Ganges at nightfall, and finding that the bridge had been swept away by the flood, crossed by the river boat. Here, by night or day, is a scene in many respects unique among, one may safely say, all the scenes of earth. Built on a beautiful bend of the river, Benares may be said to form a semicircle—an amphitheatre—about four miles in length. From end to end of this amphitheatre is presented a succession of temples and palaces rising from the river's bank, first by steps—bathing ghâts—then house above house, and temple above temple, each nestling in its grove or little forest of beautiful green trees, like a low-lying Alpine village, but with incomparable architecture, and such a mass of daily life as no city of Europe ever knew.

The river is literally covered with boats, as the ghâts and river banks are with boatmen, pilgrims, devotees, bathers, sleepers, bargainers, and pleasure seekers. In a boat on the river in the early morning the scene, in one respect, but with a mighty difference, is like that from the railway between the old and new towns of Edinburgh. But then the old or new parts of Benares are palaces and temples, set in frames of rich foliage, and lit up as in a sea of glory, or thrown into shade, by a brilliant sun. Commerce, religion, and pleasure intermingle beneath the monuments of faith and of ages. Within the narrow streets of the city are hosts of people carrying their offerings of flowers to lay upon the altars or to throw into the sacred wells. Wild devotees sit in silent contemplation, never changing their position from day to day or from year to year. Hosts of native beggars appear at every turn; and at every turn, too, you run the risk of stumbling against some quiet, listless, Brahminical bull, which is sacred. A small stone pillar marks the spot where a woman was burned with her dead husband in the days before Suttee was trampled down; and when you have seen one such pillar you will perceive that it is one of a host, abounding in many streets, fearful monuments of the past. The pilgrims laugh and joke beside the sacred wells, as they drop in their offerings of flowers. Women and men, old and young, laugh as they worship, and worship as they bathe. The air is laden with devotion. Rajahs and wealthy men of all castes have houses in Benares, that they may receive the blessing of the sacred city. People, rich and poor, go there and often crawl there to die. The gods are everywhere, and they are legion. A short distance outside the city there is a monkey temple, dedicated to thousands upon thousands of sacred monkeys—sacred because the great god Rama in his day of tribulation was aided by an army of monkeys. Far and wide on the roads around the temple the apes roam at will, protected by every faithful Hindoo.

Yet, close to all this strange medley of worship, there may be found native presses, and a native literature, acute, clever, and characterised by absolute incredulity where English faith is in question. Close to it, also, are powerful and effective missions; Mr Sherring, who has told a strange history in his "Sacred City of the Hindoos," and another in his "Hindoo Tribes and Castes," and Mr Griffith, who has translated the great Hindoo epic, the "Ramayana," are among the workers in Benares. And if the traveller care to climb a narrow crooked stair to a room like a garret, he will find shawls and other garments of the costliest of known workmanship. He will not, I think, leave Benares without perceiving that a very subtle intellect and a cunning power of handicraft pervade and dominate those great masses even of the apparently idle and holiday people.

Having learnt somewhat of the living Present in Benares, I went a few miles from the city to see one of the greatest monuments of the Past, the Buddhist ruin of Sárnáth, where it is quite possible to remember that "Benares," as Mr Sherring says, "has had a foremost place in Indian history for at least 2500 years," and that "when Babylon was struggling with Nineveh for supremacy, when Tyre was planting her colonies, when Athens was growing in strength, before Rome had become known, or Greece had contended with Persia, or Nebuchadnezzar had captured Jerusalem, she had already risen to greatness, if not to glory." Slowly has Europe learned, from the researches of patient and able men, that in the far-off ages of which we know so little as regards India there must have been a race that excelled in the power to work history in stone, and a race which, possessing the mighty power of letters, represented natural scenes and human feelings and knowledge in written words.

Sákya Muni, the first Budha, is believed to have "begun to turn the wheel of the law, to preach the famous doctrines of Dharma and Nirvâna at Sárnáth," in the sixth century before Christ. Long ages, however, before this the Brahmins had made Benares their sacred city, and while the Buddhists, essentially fervent and missionary, were sending out their teachers eastward, the men of the older faith concentrated their attention on the victory of their creed in India. A great war—a war of giants and of generations—ensued, and the Buddhists fell. When the crisis arrived, they buried their images side by side at Sárnáth, hoping beyond doubt for the restoration which never came. The images were exhumed not so very long ago by Western hands. The defeated religionists drifted northward to Nepal and beyond the Himalayas, but chiefly eastward to Burma and China, where a still mightier empire was in store for them. That man, by earnest contemplation, might rise into the Divinity, which has no separate individual existence, was the keystone of the faith of Sákya Muni,[1] but the success of the teaching beyond question rested mainly on the self-denying lives of the teachers. Of what was done at Sárnáth, and how life was enjoyed, or passion conquered there, we know far less than we do of the same facts in relation to Furness or Fountains Abbey; but as we know from inference that the Roman Catholic priests did endure privation even before the Reformation, and much more so afterwards, so do we know that sacrifice and conquest of self were at the foundation of the teaching of Sákya Muni. It is so to this day in Burma, China, and Ceylon; the Buddhist monk, as we shall see, the instructor of the people, not merely cannot marry, but must not even receive payment, beyond his food, day by day, for his labour. All who have read rightly the history of Buddhism will agree that its rise and progress are among the most marvellous facts in the history of men. In this way, beyond the mere comparison of dates and inscriptions, thoughts will arise at Sárnáth, of the struggles of creeds, and of men, in those far-off times, and of how great landmarks were established or removed.

In leaving Allahabad for Calcutta, the chief interest of the journey over India may be deemed at an end. Serampore is about thirteen miles up the Hooghly, on the Howrah side. Barrackpore, where the Governor General has a house and a fine park, is directly opposite to it, on the Calcutta side. It was at Barrackpore that Job Charnock made his favourite home, and to natives of India the place is "Channuk" to this day. Here also is Lady Canning's tomb, sacred to all save Vandal Englishmen, who have defaced it for relics. Many wearied chief rulers of India have driven along the road from Calcutta to Barrackpore, past the great arsenal of Dum Dum, and through

[1] Sherring's "Sacred City of the Hindoos."

picturesque villages, in search of solitude and rest. And if the road was deemed too hot or dusty, or otherwise unpleasant, there was the river, and a yacht constructed for the comfort of one who ruled over millions of men. The cantonment, with its church and schools, and its bungalows, especially pretty when in the morning or at eventide the verandahs are occupied by ladies and children, has all the advantages of Calcutta, with all the pleasures that can be eked out of an Indian country life. Vast droves of elephants, for labour in peace or war, and often marshalled by the road-side, a well-kept menagerie, and regimental bands available for amusements, fill up the picture of the outer life of Barrackpore.

There was a time when English rulers looked angrily from Barrackpore to the place over the river, where, under the Danish flag, three poor English Baptist missionaries had found a refuge from the hard laws against interlopers of the East India Company. The chapel, and college, and house of "Carey, Marshman, and Ward" remain. Their press and their newspaper were recently removed to Calcutta. To preach in India with unlicensed lips was shocking to the Company. To print, however, was much worse; and the Council at Fort William and the House in Leadenhall Street were strangely disturbed by the intrusion of these three men. The press became a real power, and the missionaries substantial facts in social life. At last the Government held out the branch of peace, and accepted the intruders as allies. Here, where the three friends laboured, they died and were buried. A little lower on the river there is an old ruined pagoda, in which Henry Martyn found rest for his ardent spirit, and a cool retreat for his studies. It is still "Henry Martyn's Pagoda." At the "Mission" at Serampore Havelock worshipped, was baptized, and was married. The old walls of the Danish forts still stand, a monument of the protection given by Denmark to English missionaries disowned and threatened by England.

A few miles higher on the Serampore side of the river is the French settlement of Chandernagore, still essentially French, with governor and "garrison," laws and customs, as marked and decided as if France were still an Indian power. When a Calcutta man seeks a very short holiday, his thoughts instinctively turn to Chandernagore, where he finds a comfortable hotel, managed by a lady (in direct contrast to Indian custom), seats by the river-side, well-trimmed walks, and all those little signs of care and supervision by which France asserts her superiority, go where she may, and which Englishmen at times affect to despise. Looking for instance at Serampore and at Chandernagore, a stranger would say that the residents in the latter had the permanent vested interest, and the former not a liferent in India. Even Barrackpore does not give the same idea of settled life that is given by Chandernagore.

Higher still on the river, and about twenty-eight miles from Calcutta, is the notable chief town of a great district, Hooghly, which may be said to include Chinsura. The history of Hooghly records some episodes of a dark kind. About 1000 Portuguese were massacred there by Shah Jehan, their fleet of shipping destroyed, and a flourishing settlement turned into a desert. At a later period the town was burnt by an English admiral, and later still it fell before the avenging arms of Clive. It is now a remarkable centre of intellectual life, both native and European, and has been the temporary home of some able Englishmen engaged in educational work. By asking the reader's attention, even thus generally, to the route from Bombay to the river Hooghly, one cursory view of certain great features of the country may, I think, have been obtained. The application of the facts will be when we view the same country from other stand-ground, as, for instance, from the line of the Ganges.

CHAPTER IV.

LORD MAYO.

In July 1870 Lord Mayo and his Government were at Simla for the hot season, after the manner of Indian Governments, and Calcutta professed to be very nearly disloyal. Why, it was asked for the hundredth time, should the Government be enjoying life in the Himalayas while merchants, missionaries, and officers civil and military, were compelled to stay on the plains all the year through? Did not Lord Canning remain in Calcutta in a crisis, as previous rulers had all the year through?—and was not this an exceptional year, financially? There is no doubt that the year was an exceptional one. A new system of finance, by which Lord Mayo rightly believed that he had put an end to deficits, included the income tax, which had been considerably increased, instead of being deemed a tax on the Mutiny of 1857, and repealed, as Mr Wilson had led people to expect it would, when once the mutiny costs and responsibilities had been met. The tax was anathematised by nearly all wealthy persons, European and Native. The injuries it inflicted on the poor had not at this time been brought to light. The Bengal landowners complained that the tax, in common with all like taxes, was an infringement of the permanent land-settlement of Lord Cornwallis. Then Mr J. Fitzjames Stephen, legal member of Council, was engaged, it was said, in making nobody knew what changes in the law. The people of India dreaded to see their old laws and customs set at nought, while Englishmen saw, in the "amendment, consolidation, and codification of the law," the absolute certainty that they would lose many "privileges of Englishmen," and be made amenable in many more cases than heretofore to the authority of native judges. All manner of sinister influences were asserted to be at work to further the ends of despotic government.

Why discuss these questions at Simla when the mercantile members of Council, who alone had any claim to be termed popular representatives, were bound to be in Calcutta? To one who had not seen the Governor General's Council, there seemed in these complaints something like the certain sounds of patriotism; and though it did appear a little absurd to think of Lord Mayo as the head and front of a conspiracy against his own Government, and as assisted by acute persons, who imposed upon him and were imposed upon by him, this was the picture one was expected to accept as a fair representation of Indian government. The popular feeling promised itself a great revenge. When last in Calcutta Lord Mayo had delighted in spending money freely, that Calcutta might rejoice in balls, dinners, garden parties, and concerts. Calcutta would this time revenge upon Lord Mayo the income tax, by refusing to attend his festivities. As if Calcutta ever could, with a female Calcutta in the background, have earnestly taken such a resolution! In the midst of all this it became known that Lord Mayo intended, before returning to the capital, to take a month's tour in Rajpootana—" delaying, you see, as long as possible, the dreaded arrival in Calcutta." Of course it was all great nonsense. The people who would have groaned instead of cheering when Lord Mayo crossed the Hooghly from Howrah, were only like the fabled fly on the carriage wheel. All reasonable people were convinced, that however the Government had erred, its aims were in the main single, and that the Viceroy's own motives, and those of, for instance, such men as Major General Norman and Mr Stephen, were beyond dispute.

That Lord Mayo was extremely sensitive no one who

watched his course of procedure could doubt. In durbar he had an imposing presence. On horseback, chasing the wild boar, he was said to be like a boy at play. In his relation to foreign chiefs he was firm and conciliatory; at his desk a downright hard worker; in his hatred of oppression and wrong-doing, inexorable; but amid it all he was, I think, very sensitive. I once heard him attempt in public to tell a funny story, and entirely lose the point of it, simply because sensitiveness (not timidity) for the moment overmastered him. Perhaps his well-known break-down in the House of Commons arose from the same cause. It was impossible to doubt, after the end of that cold season of 1870-71, that Lord Mayo really did dislike the thought of the inevitable winter residence in Calcutta. But the idea of Lord Mayo fearing anybody, or any number of bodies, was preposterous. From the day of his appointment he had given his entire heart to his duties. He began (as Dr Hunter has admirably shown) to study India in London, continued the study in France and throughout the voyage, and only ended it on that fatal day at the Andamans. It was simply that he felt, as a generous man may feel, that he had been unkindly treated where he had deserved to have his motives and acts generously construed, and that, explain as he might, there were still people to charge him with a Machiavellian policy.

With some again he had become unpopular, because he could on occasions swoop down rigorously on a man or an office whose affairs would not bear investigation. Others, who on his arrival in Calcutta had supposed him pleasantly ductile, and had found him as granite when they had attempted to mould him, discovered in him the one sin that cannot easily be stated in terms, but which can never be forgiven. Then the religious grooves in which Lord Mayo moved were different from those of Lord Lawrence. I do not say they were better. I would be ashamed even to hint or suggest a thought of disrespect towards the hero of the Punjab. They were simply different, while they were equally honourable. Lord Lawrence, who had passed through terrible scenes, inclined to persons whose devotional habits were akin to those of his own noble brother and of Sir Henry Havelock. Lord Mayo was devotional in quite another way. He took his prayer-book in his hand, and walked quietly with his wife to the English church at Barrackpore or Simla, said his prayers, and returned home. What he might have been if he had seen what the Lawrences and Havelock saw, and had endured what they endured, I do not know; but that is what he was; and one order of life may be said to have passed from Calcutta with the retirement of Lord Lawrence. Then there was a certain gaiety and festivity about Lord Mayo—an Irish gift some people called it, while they at the same time shared and enjoyed what it provided. That Lord Mayo in the Mutiny could have saved the Punjab, his best friends could hardly imagine. That he could at once have formed and led a column like Havelock's or Neill's, is, of course, equally out of the question. Under no circumstances would he have exhibited qualities like those of Warren Hastings or Clive or the Marquis Wellesley. Possibly, indeed, history may not class him among its great men. But I am mistaken if he was not a good man, generous, brave, and frank, extraordinarily clear-sighted as to facts, and while at times indolent in speech, exceedingly prompt in action, and capable both of comprehensive views and a decisive policy. I believe that if he was bitter at all it was towards some act of oppression or injustice—a quality that has always been of high repute in Eastern lands. All this a new-comer to India in the middle of 1870 had to learn; but long before Lord Mayo had arrived in Calcutta, evidence of the absolute badness of the income tax, of its unsuitableness to India, and of the cruelty with which it pressed upon the poor, was overwhelming; and I, for one, would not have defended it, come what might.

Lord Mayo went to Rajpootana to see the chiefs and

people, and to talk with the former. Most of the memoranda to which I could refer with respect to this journey relates to mere ceremonies in which no one can have much interest. Looking, however, upon these notes (taken from letters which reached me from time to time), it is not difficult to see that a decidedly practical vein ran through the entire tour. The variety of objects seems almost boundless, and also the variety of work. Of the Rajpoot line Mr J. Talboys Wheeler[1] says:

"They are the noblest and proudest race in India, and, with the exception of the Jews, there are, perhaps, no living people of higher antiquity or purer descent. They claim to be representatives of the Kshatriyas, the descendants of the Aryan warriors who conquered the Punjab and Hindostan in times primæval. To this day they display many of the characteristics of the heroes of the Maha Bharata and Ramayana. They form a military aristocracy of the feudal type. They are brave and chivalrous, keenly sensitive of an affront, and especially jealous of the honour of their women. Their chiefs, when occasion serves, are prepared to lead the lives of outlaws, like the Pandava brothers, or to go into exile with the silent haughtiness of Rama. . . . In later revolutions their seats of empire have been shifted further west and south, but the Rajpoot kingdoms still remain as relics of the old Aryan aristocracy."

This extract will supply a key to some of the incidents of the tour. An early note kindly sent to me says:

"We arrived in the neighbourhood of Jeypore on the night of the 11th of October; and camp was pitched about six miles outside the town, after a drive from Bhurtpore of about 112 miles under a burning sun. When the North West had been left behind, and the more arid parts of Rajpootana were entered upon, the country did not wear the same fruitful appearance. The roads, however, are good, many of the houses exceedingly substantial, and as far as Jeypore is concerned, all this has been done without British help, by the unaided enterprise and energy of the Maharajah. The nobles poured in from all quarters—the fine old Thakoors, followed by their wild, fierce retainers, if one may apply such a term as retainer to these motley-clad bodies of undisciplined men.

"Early in the morning the Maharajah, with a large body of Thakoors, was at the appointed rendezvous, three miles from the city.

[1] "History of India."

The procession was arrayed in a pass, formed by low rugged hills, lined with a hundred and fifty elephants in gorgeous attire. The town was in its gayest. It had for weeks been looking forward to this pageant, rare enough in one sense, for Lord Mayo is the first Governor General who ever visited Jeypore in state, though it is said Lord W. Bentinck once did so privately. What the city was at that time it would, perhaps, be difficult to ascertain, but now it is one of the most beautiful in India. Entering by the eastern gate there is a fine street eighty yards in breadth and half-a-mile long, with lofty houses of all styles of architecture and all manner of colouring, but very chaste and graceful as a rule. At the end of this street is a wide square from which other streets strike out in different directions. In the centre is the palace of the Maharajah, built of white marble or something like marble, and from it streets run in different directions, all clean and handsome, and the principal ones paved with white stone.

"By seven o'clock in the morning the route of the procession was in order—cavalry and infantry lining the entire distance; and immense crowds of people, a large number of them ladies, and in some cases very pretty, were ranged behind. The entrance to Jeypore is by an easy ascent, and the procession, about a mile long, was very picturesque. When the Viceroy's elephant entered the city the troops presented arms, the batteries fired a royal salute, and the people in the streets and on the house-tops rose as on a signal, and with an effect really imposing. At the Ajmere Gate the procession was met by a part of 'the warriors'—the Nagas—a body of men eight thousand strong, devoted to war and bound against marriage, their ranks being made up from time to time by adoption. It was a splendid guard, ready to attempt almost anything for which orders might be given. . . . The party left Jeypore on the morning of the 18th, part of the way in carriages, and part at a hand gallop to Sambhur Salt Lake. The same day Lord Mayo inspected the salt works, wonderfully primitive in the mode of operation, but interesting, and it appeared remunerative. The first part of the process is to dam off a portion of the lake, where the water is left to evaporate, the salt remaining at the bottom. The gathering of this with hands or wooden spades occupies a large number of people; men, women, and children scrambling for their share of the work. The salt is piled up in heaps, which lie for three or four years; one such heap, pointed out to the Viceroy, was valued at £7000. Several hours were spent in the inspection of this lake and the salt manufacture, if manufacture it can be called. Then a branch line of railway was decided upon. Next day Lord Mayo entered Ajmere. The road was kept by the Mhairwara Battalion, the Central Indian Horse, and other troops. The city, the streets of which are narrow but clean, was decorated with triumphal arches.

On the following morning a private durbar was held, beginning at half-past six in the morning, and ending at eleven."

In the afternoon the Viceroy opened a new part of the High School, and spoke earnestly to the boys of the value of education, and of some of the duties of life. Afterwards he visited the gaol, and reviewed the Mhairwara Battalion. Next day, Saturday, the public durbar was held, and here arose a curious difficulty as to right of precedence between the chiefs of Oodeypore and Jodhpore. When the knot had been untied in favour of Oodeypore, the defeated chief (a young man, not highly respected it was said) retired in high displeasure, and his tent among all those of the durbar alone was silent. When the poor young chief, who had evidently hoped to be called in, had fretted till he was tired, he went to the durbar. Now, however, the doors were shut, and he was ordered to quit Ajmere. I thought that this was a hard case, but the Government declared authoritatively that the behaviour of the chief had been very bad, not now merely, but generally, and that to allow him to brave the power of the Governor General would have had a most baneful effect. A fortnight later, it was stated that the Maharajah, in appealing to the Viceroy on the question of precedence, had received an exceedingly severe reprimand. The reply showed that the precedence belonged to Oodeypore, and decreed that Jodhpore should receive no more salutes or honours till the will of the Secretary of State was known. Eventually the delinquent Maharajah was forgiven, but his contention for precedence had to fall to the ground, the Oodeypore family standing exceptionally high in its claim to an ancient unbroken pedigree and unmixed blood.

In his durbar speech Lord Mayo assured the chiefs, in strong and friendly terms, that "the desire of her Majesty's Government is to secure to you and to your successors the full enjoyment of your ancient rights." In order, however, that this object might be attained, he exhorted them to evince a like care for the rights of those under them, and to see that justice, order, and the security of property prevailed "throughout the length and breadth of Rajpootana." He then with great cordiality invited the chiefs to establish a college for their sons, and pointed out in terse and forcible terms, that if the Indian Government had wished the ruling men of Rajpootana to be weak and divided, this invitation to them, now made in sincere good faith, would have been the last suggestion thought of. The speech throughout was in the same excellent taste and spirit, and was most cordially received. The idea intended to be conveyed was conveyed to the letter, and perhaps in all Lord Mayo's career no better evidence could be found of his clear-sightedness as to facts, and of his power, when unrestrained, to give effect to his perceptions in language as clear as a running brook. The school was at once decided upon, and the principle of the suggestion was, it is said, accepted cheerfully by the chiefs. From the durbar Lord Mayo went to the Nusseerabad barracks, and decided some military questions. Then he went to Agra and elsewhere, and so on the way to Calcutta. At Ghazeepore, Buxar, and Poosah, he visited the studs, evidently with delight. At Poosah, where there were eight hundred fillies, he spent a whole day in the inspection, and in making suggestions for improving the breeds. From first to last the tour was one of practical aims and unremitting work; and it may be taken as one of the prominent features of Lord Mayo's viceroyalty.

At length only the Hooghly separated the Governor General from the people who were to hiss him. He was met by the Lieutenant Governor of Bengal and a body of officials. The Calcutta volunteers, at their request, formed a guard of honour. There was no great cheering, it is true, as there rarely is under an Indian sun, unless the occasion is very marked; but though Lord Mayo had had experience of the value of that popular applause which is loud to-day and very scanty to-morrow, he was not insulted. If he had been so, the shame would not have been his. But the common sense prevailed over the nonsense of Calcutta.

I never saw any indication that Lord Mayo was not trusted for the uprightness of his motives, by any one whose confidence he would have valued. He was so free from all pretentiousness (grave or gay), so thoroughly natural in what he said and did, that in agreement or disagreement he was believed. To differ respectfully from his views never appeared to offend him; which, however, is simply to say that he was a gentleman.

Of the residence of the Government at Simla during eight months of the year, I never heard any reasonable defence. The effect of it is injurious in several different ways. It is, to native minds, an assertion that Englishmen cannot live on the plains, and hence cannot take root in India. It converts the more prominent members of the Government and their families into a series of little cliques, practically all-powerful in all cases of public employment, of honours and distinctions, and, even in social life, dividing them from the mercantile community as thoroughly as if they belonged to another race. It is also a real injustice to the lower grade of officials, who are compelled to keep two houses without any increase of salaries. A holiday, of whatever reasonable duration, would be beyond criticism. It is the habit of removing the whole machinery of the Government that is assailed. The political effect of the removal is the strongest feature of the case. The fact that the Governor General and his principal officers can only live during the hot season on the mountain tops is an ominous circumstance in view of future contingencies. The argument on the opposite side is that the Government work is better done at Simla than in Calcutta; but then the work lies in Calcutta, and, in many cases of direct influence, cannot be effectively done elsewhere.

CHAPTER V.

FOREIGN POLICY: AFGHANISTAN.

To speak of Lord Mayo's foreign policy as his own would be altogether inaccurate. It was the product of the thought of many minds, and all that Lord Mayo's friends can justly claim for him is that he gave to the policy unity of purpose, and decision, and perhaps crystallised it so that it could be better understood in England and throughout Europe. To explain fully the relation of Afghanistan to India we should first require a treatise on the geography and history of India, taking the history from very early times. When this had been accomplished the threshold of the subject might perhaps be reasonably presumed to have been crossed. All that can be attempted here will go a very short way towards elucidating the vast question of our North Western frontier policy, although sufficient may be said to indicate the general lines of that policy in past and present times. The keys to a clear idea of the physical relation of Afghanistan to India are the Afghan Passes, and the river Indus, which, rising in the Himalayas, and receiving a number of affluents during a long course of 1800 miles, falls into the Arabian Sea.

When the first English factories in India were struggling for an existence, Afghanistan and Scinde were practically beyond the range of the Company's policy. When the victories of Clive, and Coote, and Wellesley, and other of the great soldiers and administrators of India, had shown that an English empire in the East was a possibility, and might become a necessity; when the Mahrattas had been beaten, and the Pindarees all but exterminated, and the

Rohillas and the Ghoorkas defeated, the question of frontiers became an all-important one; and to comprehend and influence Afghan and Central Asian politics was a duty which could not again be lost sight of by any government of British India. Victors at Seringapatam, at Gwalior, at Agra, at Delhi, at Muckwanpoor, and at Rangoon, we may be said, during the earlier part of the governor-generalship of Lord William Bentinck, while the Reform battle which ended in 1832 was being fought in England, to have marked out in Asia limits within which no sword could again be drawn or gun fired without English permission. If we take a common map, and pass from the Carnatic over the Bay of Bengal to Tenasserim, and so along the borders of the bay to the mouths of the Brahmapootra and the Ganges, and then, passing down the opposite coast-line to Madras, go upward by the west to Bombay, we shall find that no chief or monarch whose territories rested on the coast could at this time have acted in opposition to the power at Calcutta. If the same course is taken inland it will be found that we had secured the Ganges by our victories over Nepal; and, having also interests further westward than the land of the Five Rivers, were bound to watch the Khyber and Bolan Passes, the line of the Indus, the Passes of Nepal, and the regions beyond the Irrawaddi on the east. There were vast independent territories and powerful potentates within these lines, but not one of them could lift a hand for warfare without the risk of England also taking the field.

If we look to a few general facts in the history of the North West, this may have clearer meaning. The first tangible relation of India to Western conquerors is presumed to have been B.C. 518, when the King of Persia, Darius Hystaspes, crossed the Indus, with the fatal result for India of a great increase of his revenue. From that time dates the unhappy renown of India as a land of fabulous wealth—meaning really a land which might be easily plundered. Alexander the Great came two centuries later. Marching over the Hindoo Koosh, and forcing the passes of Afghanistan, he crossed the Indus at Attock. Of his struggle with Porus, who ruled as far as Delhi, and his passage of the rivers of the Punjab, history has made great account. In the year 711 a momentous event took place. The faith of Mahomet by this time ruled from the Atlantic to the Persian Gulf, on both sides of the Red Sea, and throughout Persia and Cabul. It had been in a fashion established among the Afghans half a century earlier, and had put forth its terrible feelers in different directions without much success. In this year (during the Heptarchy in England) India was invaded by the Arabs from Bussora. The Rajpoots were defeated, and Scinde conquered by a force of not more than 8000 men. Forty years later the Arab Mohammedans were expelled by the Rajpoots, and Arab rule in India closed.

Next came the series of invasions from Afghanistan, from Ghuznee, where a dynasty famous in Indian history was founded in blood about the middle of the tenth century. Mahmoud of Ghuznee, who called himself "the image-breaker," invaded India ten times, and undertook twelve or thirteen distinct expeditions of fearfully cruel import. On the last occasion he carried away the sandalwood gates of Somnâth, which 800 years later, after the victorious operations of Sale, Pollock, and Nott, Lord Ellenborough recovered,[1] or believed he recovered, for the Hindoos. Mahmoud's cruel and barbarous expeditions engaged him from A.D. 1001 till about 1025. He died in 1030. It should be observed that he reigned from Ispahan, on the west, to Lahore, which 120 years after his death became the Afghan capital. Nearly all the difficulty Englishmen may have in comprehending the disputes of Dost Mohammed and Runjeet Singh and our own relation to them would be removed if these few simple facts were borne in mind. We are apt to think of Afghanistan as having natural boundaries, the same yesterday, to-day, and for ever. History, it will be seen, has no such lesson.

[1] Appendix, Note I.

The Afghan (Ghor) dynasty (from Ghori in Khorassan) succeeded in 1186, and though the dynasty only lasted twenty-six years, its greatest chief, Mohammed Ghori, is accepted as the real founder of the future Mohammedan empire. The cruel tide of conquest again swept over the quiet cities of the Ganges, which were not merely plundered as before without mercy, but were also annexed. The Slave Kings of Delhi ruled from 1205 to 1239. Two other dynasties, which may for convenience be termed Afghan, followed, and continued till 1398, when Delhi was sacked by Timour the Tartar. A curious incident of one of these dynasties—the Toghluk—was an attempted invasion of China by the passes of the Himalayas in 1337. A force of 100,000 men actually penetrated to the Chinese frontier. They were, however, met by a Chinese army, and forced back to the Terai of Nepal, and are said to have nearly all perished. The same monarch (Afghan, let us remember) subjugated the Deccan, conquered and annexed as far as Chittagong eastward, and raised 370,000 horse for the conquest of Persia.

Next came the Moguls. The founder of the dynasty, Ghengis Khan, believed, at least, that he had an empire from the Caspian Sea to Pekin, and there can be no doubt that his victories and annexations ranged over all this immense territory, though there can be quite as little doubt that, when he turned his back in any direction, there his rule ended. His son Timour invaded India, and laid the foundation of the Mogul line. His conquests in Syria, Bagdad, on the Caspian, in Asia Minor, and in India, are a still further proof that the vast distances, and the deserts and steppes of Asia, never yet barred the way to India, if India could not bar the way by its own strong hand. Timour died in 1404, on his way to invade China.

It was not, however, till the time of Baber, the sixth in descent from Timour, that the empire was established by the victory of Paniput. Humayoon succeeded in 1530, but was ignominiously driven from the throne. During his flight westward, a girl of his harem, and said to have been beautiful, gave birth to a son, who was named Akbar. Humayoon never stopped in his flight till he reached Herat. He returned from Cabul to India for the recovery of his throne in 1555, and succeeded, but died in the following year. Akbar, a boy of thirteen, ascended the throne, and established his rule by another great victory at Panipur. He reigned fifty-one years, from 1556 to 1605—one of the most glorious reigns in the history of any land. Of his greatness and magnificence no special mention can be made here; but it is quite within the scope of this chapter to observe that among his conquests were the Punjab, Bengal, Orissa, Cashmere, and Candahar. That is, not only was Afghanistan within dominions which extended to the east of India, but Akbar held also in Cashmere the highway to what we now call Kashgaria.

Of Jehangir and his Noor Jehan ("Light of the World"), of Shah Jehan and the beautiful wife for whose tomb he built the Tâj, and of Aurungzebe, much that would illustrate passing events might be told. But it is chiefly to our purpose to note that now the Mahrattas and Sikhs rose against the Mogul rule, and that Delhi itself seemed on the point of falling before Bajee Rao, the Mahratta Peishwa (prime minister), in 1737, when another tide of invasion swept through the passes of the North West. The Persians, under Nadir Shah, carried all before them, captured and plundered Delhi, and bore off to Afghanistan the Koh-i-noor and the Peacock Throne. The Mahrattas, under Bajee Rao, but also with devastating forces under Holkar and Scindia, now made havoc of the carcase of the Mogul empire, when again a mightier power interposed. Ahmed, the successor of Nadir, appeared east of the Indus, and swept all before him with almost unrivalled cruelty. Twice again he led similar waves. On the second of these occasions (Afghan invasions), a third great battle was fought at Paniput, and the Mahrattas crushingly defeated.

Ahmed then returned to Afghanistan, leaving the Mogul empire for ever.

If the reader will observe these facts, I think they will supply a better clue to our frontier policy both eastward and westward, than could possibly be had by taking the facts for granted, and referring at once to Dost Mohammed and Runjeet Singh. It will be seen how little account was made of vast distances and natural obstacles; how Afghanistan was not a frontier, or barrier for a frontier, but actually the centre of great empires. Observe also that in the year in which Ahmed sacked Delhi, Clive won Plassey. The first step was taken in stemming those terrible waves of conquest which had only plunder and cruelty for their object. No persons anywhere comprehend this fact more clearly than the really educated readers and thinkers of Bengal.

It is very easy from this point to take up the threads of the North Western policy of the Indian Government. From early in the century till 1839, two representative men seem to fill the entire range of vision in the North West—Runjeet Singh, the Lion of Lahore, and Dost Mohammed, the Afghan. Runjeet Singh succeeded to the throne of the Sikhs in 1792, and began with singular ability, even while a boy, to consolidate his power and increase his dominions. In return for assistance to the ruler of Cabul, he received back the old capital of the Punjab—Lahore. He perfected his army with the help of able European officers till it was one of the finest in India; and he was prudent enough, when to all appearance about to spring on Sirhind (lying between the Punjab and the Sutlej), to stop short of the spring, when General Ochterlony, the hero of Nepal, appeared with an army. Then there came a crisis for England. The Governor General, Lord Minto, having decided, in view of Russian and French advances,[1] to send embassies to Persia, Afghanistan, and Lahore, Runjeet Singh received his embassy, and agreed to a treaty which was signed at Amritsur in 1809. The embassy to Shah Sujah, monarch of

[1] Appendix II.

Afghanistan, found him at Peshawur, but all that he could understand of the business was, that he ought, in virtue of a treaty, to receive help against his internal enemies. The British Government did not quite see this, and Shah Sujah's affairs went from bad to worse, till at last he was a fugitive over the Indus. He sought refuge with Runjeet Singh, and was robbed, by that accomplished gentleman, of the Koh-i-noor, which Nadir Shah had stolen from India. This collapse of the Afghan monarch's affairs was in 1814. He then crossed into British territory, and was pensioned. The Sikh ruler meanwhile pursued his inexorable way; at one time defeated, then victorious, but in the end sacking Peshawur, and defeating the Afghans to the Khyber Pass. In 1831 Lord William Bentinck and Runjeet Singh met at Roopur, the latter attended by 16,000 chosen men, the Governor General by a small retinue. The pomp of this meeting was the theme of many pens; the practical result of it was the protection of Scinde from the grasp of the Sikh. In 1833 Shah Sujah made another attempt for his throne, and was defeated by Dost Mohammed. A little later he returned hopeless to British territory.

This brings before the reader the second of the two remarkable men to whom reference has been made. While Dost Mohammed was engaged with Shah Sujah (whom all Englishmen who knew him contemned), Runjeet Singh seized Peshawur. Dost Mohammed proclaimed a religious war for its recovery, but the address and intrigue of the Sikh were too much for him. His army melted away before his eyes; and he was compelled to return, a defeated man, to Cabul. When Lord Auckland arrived in India (1836), the Afghan chief appealed to him for mediation, and Lord Auckland, contrary to the advice of all who knew best the state of the North West, answered the request by resolving to restore Shah Sujah to the throne—a design naturally enough supported by Runjeet Singh. Dost Mohammed, in dread of the English and the Sikhs on the one hand, and of the Persians and Russians on the other, had no alternative but to appeal to the latter powers; and Russia sending an embassy to Cabul, Lord Auckland began his ill-fated war. A splendid British army set out for Afghanistan in December 1838, and was everywhere successful. Ghuznee and Cabul were captured, and Candahar occupied. In August 1839 Shah Sujah re-entered his capital after thirty years of exile. Sir William Macnaghten (then knighted) was appointed envoy at his court, with Sir Alexander Burnes as his assistant. Lord Auckland was created an earl. The commanders of the expedition were thanked by Parliament. Wellington, Lord William Bentinck, and others had, it is true, discountenanced the expedition, and every British officer concerned had spoken as highly of Dost Mohammed as they had spoken deprecatingly of Shah Sujah, and doubtfully of Runjeet Singh. Here, however, was the endorsement of complete success.

In June 1839 Runjeet Singh died. In November 1840 Dost Mohammed, after a gallant struggle, surrendered, and was pensioned in Calcutta. A year later Sir A. Burnes and his brother were murdered in Cabul; and a fierce insurrection under Akbar Khan, son of Dost Mohammed, bore down all before it, till Macnaghten consented to treat on the basis of evacuating Cabul, Candahar, Ghuznee, and Jellalabad, and restoring the family of Dost Mohammed to the throne. On this understanding Akbar Khan agreed to himself conduct the British through the passes on their way to India. Up to this time there is no reason to believe that the disgrace to our arms was to have been accompanied with massacre. At this critical time, however, Sir William Macnaghten was detected by Akbar in undoubted intrigues with the Ghilzye and other tribes, to detach them from the Afghans. The fate of the English in Cabul was then sealed. Macnaghten, invited to a conference, and Captain Trevor who accompanied him, were shot by Akbar himself on the open ground.

The British troops, eager to avenge the murder, of the real cause of which they knew nothing, were held back by their chiefs. Another treaty was made, and on the 6th January 1842 the fatal march of about 4500 soldiers and 12,000 camp followers began. On the 8th they entered the Khoord Cabul Pass, lined with the Ghilzyes, and were massacred in detail. On the 10th the army numbered 50 artillerymen, 250 men of the 24th, 150 cavalry, and about 4000 camp followers. On the 13th the force, drooping and disheartened, numbered 20 officers and 45 men. Finally one man, Dr Brydon, the sole survivor of the army, arrived at Jellalabad. With these events and what followed them every Englishman ought to be acquainted. The defence of Jellalabad by Sale, and of Candahar by Nott; the glorious concerted marches of Nott and Pollock, and their gallant and soldierly assumption of the responsibility which Lord Ellenborough threw upon them; the march into Cabul, and the rescue of the English ladies who were threatened with slavery beyond the Hindoo Koosh, are among those features of our history that never can pass away. The subsequent restoration of Dost Mohammed is the pivot-fact on which all Afghan affairs since then have centred. His reign continued till his death in 1863.

It is necessary also to observe, that while our and Shah Sujah's struggle with Dost Mohammed was going on, the Persians, assisted openly by Russian officers, invested Herat, from which, after a siege of nine months, they were driven (1838), mainly by the courage and capacity of a young Irish officer, Eldred Pottinger. This important event, and the fact that many names, afterwards very memorable, came first into note at this time—Outram, Havelock, the Lawrences, Durand, John Nicholson, and others—may properly close up one stage of this summary. All these elements, Afghan, Persian, Russian, and Sikh, must be taken into consideration, together with the turmoil in Beloochistan, Kelat, and as far as Oman, if we would see the real character of the policy which once more has its pivots in the passes of Afghanistan. That the expedition of Lord Auckland was a huge error, and that

Lord Ellenborough did not essentially redeem the error, wise men saw then, and all men see now. In advancing the story another stage, the following table of the family of Dost Mohammed will be found both interesting and useful—a key in fact to all that has passed on the North West frontier for the last thirteen years.

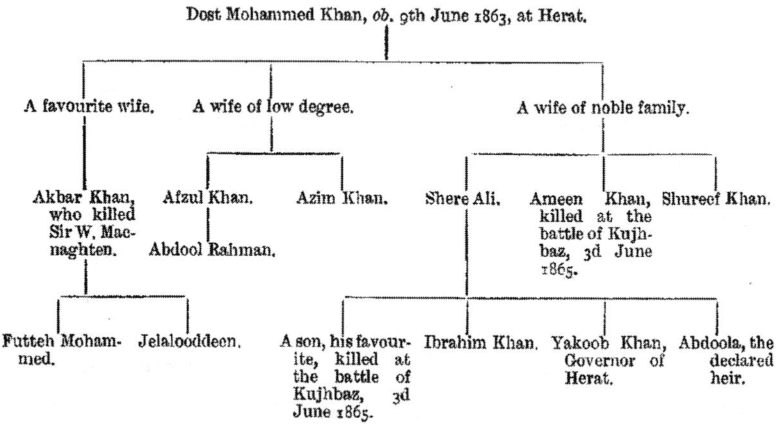

When Dost Mohammed died, the succession was by his will declared in favour of Shere Ali, to the exclusion of his two elder brothers, Afzul and Azim. In 1864-65 the elder brothers rebelled, and Afzul was captured and imprisoned. His son, Abdool Rahman (one of the main factors in the present state of affairs), found refuge with the Ameer of Bokhara, whose daughter he had married. In the same year Ameen rose in rebellion. He was defeated, but with the loss to Shere Ali of his favourite eldest son. In the same year Rahman again crossed the Oxus, and was joined by his uncle Azim. Cabul was wrested from the Ameer's son Ibrahim, and the Ameer himself was defeated, near Ghuznee, in May 1866. Afzul was now released and declared Ameer. Shere Ali fled with his son Ibrahim and his nephew to Herat, where his son Yakoob, of tried courage, commanded. In May 1867 Afzul died, and eventually Shere Ali won the position he has ever since retained, and won it in a great measure by the warlike capacity of Yakoob. Abdool Rahman again fled beyond the Oxus, where he was pensioned by the Russians.

During the governor-generalship of Lord Lawrence the apprehension of Persian (covering Russian) interference was so great, that when in 1868 a British expedition was sent against the Afghans of the Black Mountain (influenced by the Wahabees), it was difficult to persuade people that beneath the nominal object a great deal more was not hidden. In referring to this subject in the House of Lords this year (June 15th), Lord Lawrence said: "It was now twenty years since he made the treaty which still exists between the Cabul Government and the British Government. Since then the reigning Ameer had been our prisoner, and by Lord Ellenborough magnanimously restored to his country. Before his death that Ameer warned the British Government against supporting the conflicting pretensions of either of his two sons, and advised us to let them fight it out, and to steadily refuse to support either party until one got the better of the other." In March 1869 Lord Mayo and Shere Ali met in splendid durbar at Umballa, the Ameer accompanied by his youngest son, Abdoola Jan (son of a favourite wife), while Yakoob was left behind—"in the cold," some, including M. Vambery, said; in high trust and command, others maintained. Yakoob seems to have agreed with the former. Abdoola was acknowledged the heir; and though Lord Mayo did not support, or beyond what was possible to withhold, countenance the Ameer's succession policy, there cannot be a doubt that Abdoola was present for a specific purpose which Yakoob never could forgive.

In September 1870 news arrived in Calcutta that Yaboob was in rebellion, and fast collecting a powerful force. Three weeks later there was talk of a proposal, favoured by the Indian Government, to give up Candahar to Yakoob. The allowance of Abdool Rahman was about the same time reported to have been stopped by the Russians—a token, it was held, of good faith. Early in the year a letter, without date, had been found, inviting Rahman to Samarcand, where he "would find friends." In December the rebellion was reported nearly at an end. The Ameer's commander-in-chief, Feramoorz Khan, and Aslum Khan, the Ameer's half-brother and great favourite, were pushing Yakoob hard; and as Persia made no sign in his favour, his cause was deemed hopeless. In January 1871 Yakoob was reported on his way to Cabul, a suppliant for his father's mercy. A few days later he had broken from his escort, and was again at large. At the end of June Feramoorz and Aslum were beginning fresh operations. In July a telegram reported the murder of Feramoorz, and the suspicion that Aslum was the murderer.

Telegram after telegram now recorded the changing phases of the drama. Aslum, the Ameer's favourite, had been sent prisoner to Cabul, where Yakoob had, with dire intent, preceded him, and made peace with the Ameer. Aslum and Yakoob were bitter foes, Aslum having favoured the succession of Abdoola Jan. The official account of the murder stated that Aslum, Alum Khan, Feramoorz Khan, and some others, were sitting in a tent playing backgammon, when a gun was fired from the outside, and the commander-in-chief fell, shot in the back, and died in a few minutes. The army at once attempted to take vengeance on Aslum, whose differences with the dead general were known; but Alum, second in command, and now commander-in-chief, stepped before Aslum, Koran in hand, and demanded that the rights of justice should be left to the Ameer; and the troops agreed. Early in August Aslum was taken into the city in irons, Yakoob meanwhile reported to be in high favour. On October 18th news arrived that Aslum had been murdered in prison by two of his brothers. He had, it was said, confessed his guilt, and his brothers having obtained access to him, attempted poison, and, that failing, fell back on the unerring rope.

What passed in that prison no one ever will know. If Aslum had succeeded he would have carried his brothers up with him to fortune. As he failed, his brothers sent him down to the grave. Such is the state of affairs on this stormy frontier.

From that time to this Yakoob has been more or less a prisoner. The Umballa policy, it was said, was at an end; and while some people maintained that Lord Mayo was bound to defend the Ameer against the rebel son, others held that the son, without whom the Ameer might have been a fugitive at Samarcand, or perhaps in the grave, ought to have been defended against the father. The truth is that the policy of the durbar was the policy of the passing hour, and could not be otherwise, so far as individuals were concerned. All that is enduring is that England shall support Afghanistan in its own choice of ruler, and interfere as little as possible in Afghan affairs. Of late (1877) there has been a rupture, which may end in anything on earth without causing surprise to any one who has watched the affairs of Afghanistan. The Ameer, it is said, is discontented, and Yakoob, for the first time for many years, has become "all English." Englishmen, where so much is uncertain, may differ in much; but will they differ as to there being in these facts a cause of disquietude beyond this North West frontier?

If the object of this chapter has been attained, it has been shown that all the conditions, save one, of the wars of Mahmoud of Ghuznee, and Ghengis Khan, and Timour, and Nadir Shah, and Ahmed, exist to this day. All beyond the Indus westward is the same. The distances are no greater. The steppes and deserts are no more difficult than of old. Human life is of no greater value; and plunder and massacre are no less fashionable. The one single new fact is the strength of British power east of the Indus. All who hate wars and bloodshed, and wish to see civilisation advance, may well pray to God that the rule may be as wise and good as it has been strong.

CHAPTER VI.

THE PERSIAN GULF—PERSIA, BELOOCHISTAN, AND KELAT—BURMA AND YARKUND—THE LOOSHAI.

THE vexed questions of the Persian, Kelat, and Beloochistan boundaries, although little heard of in England, apart from statesmen, geographers, and merchants, are of a nature to excite lively apprehensions among persons whose duty it is to watch and divine each half-developed turn of the drama, and every new impulse of strangely impulsive races.

The story of the dynasties of Oman was told some years ago to the Hakluyt Society, in a translation of an Arabic work, by the Rev. Dr Badger, and was introduced by him in an "Analysis," which was in fact a distinct work. About the same time a Bombay administration report (foreign affairs) took up the story where Dr Badger left off. Dr Badger's work tells the story from A.D. 661 to A.D. 1865. The Bombay report begins at that year, and brings down the narrative to the time of Lord Mayo's administration.

Syud Said, beyond whom it is unnecessary to go, died in the year 1856, after a reign of fifty-two years—seventeen conjointly with his brother, and the rest alone. He left fifteen sons to scramble for the succession, and three of them at the time of his death ruled over the three chief districts under his sovereignty: Thoweynee (the eldest) at Muscat, Toorkee (the third) at Sohar, and Majid (the fourth) at Zanzibar. The geographical position of Zanzibar is worth remembering here. The Wahabees, who had long been a thorn in the side of Syud Said and his family, appeared on the outside, with ominous movements, which had when necessary to be restrained. What Syud Said's true will was nobody can exactly say, but Thoweynee and Majid agreed to retain their respective governments, the latter paying tribute, while Toorkee, in fact, claimed independence. In a little time Majid also discontinued his tributé, and Thoweynee was preparing an expedition against him when the British Government interfered. In 1862, the dispute having been referred to British arbitration, Syud Thoweynee's authority was confirmed in Oman, with a guarantee of tribute from Zanzibar. At the same time, however, Zanzibar was in its government declared independent, an important separation of the dominions of the Syuds in Africa from those in Asia. Toorkee alone of the three was dissatisfied. In dealing with the danger which his enmity created, it is curious to observe that Thoweynee opened negotiations with the Wahabee Ameer, re-opened a long discontinued intercourse with Nedj in Arabia (claimed by the Turks, but held by the Wahabees, as the cradle of their creed), and promised a subsidy, which was to be termed a contribution to the Shereef of Mecca. I mention these facts to show still further how swiftly and far an Eastern impulse may spread.

In 1864 the Walli (ruler) of Er-Rostak, Azzan-bin-Ghias, revolted, and offered to transfer his allegiance to the Wahabee Ameer; and Syud Thoweynee was preparing, with British countenance, to put down the rebellion, when (1866) he was murdered by his son Salim, who had also shut up Toorkee in Sohar. The British resident in the gulf, Colonel Pelly, suspecting the true fact, proceeded to Sohar and set Toorkee free. Of the murder by Salim there was believed to be no moral doubt, but as there was assumed to be no legal or decisive proof, Salim ascended the throne, the British Government concurring, and so effectually opposing the pretensions of Toorkee, that he was altogether foiled in an enterprise which for a time had bade fair to depose the murderer. Toorkee retired to Bombay at the end of 1867, resigning all territorial claims in consideration of a payment to him of 7200 dollars a year by the Syud. A year later Azzan-bin-Ghias again took the field, defeated Salim, and was proclaimed ruler.

Toorkee could now consider himself free from his engagement, but he saw no chance of success till, in 1869, Azzan captured El-Beraymee, the great Wahabee outpost and stronghold. The Wahabee lieutenant had brought the disaster upon himself, by entering into league with Salim, but that was a mere side issue to Toorkee, who at last saw a fair chance of success while Azzan was at war with the Wahabees. In 1870, after some joint attempts with Salim, Toorkee landed on the pirate coast, the Indian Government warning him not to break the peace of the gulf. Money to a limited extent he received from Zanzibar, but his followers were few, in the face of a ruler who had at least shown great military capacity. For about two months the position of the invader was most critical. Azzan, with a powerful ally, the Aboothabee chief, who held Beraymee, was carrying all before him. Toorkee attacked this chief and was defeated, but in the very moment of defeat he caught and attacked Azzan himself in one of the passes, and was victorious. At this critical time, however, his supplies were cut off by the death of his brother, the Sultan of Zanzibar, and there was again for him a dark time of suspense.

Early in January 1871 intelligence reached the Indian Government that Toorkee was marching on Muscat, and that the "Hugh Rose" (English steamer) would keep a sharp look-out to prevent operations by sea. Up to this date the Government had stood altogether aloof from Toorkee. On February 8th news came that Ibraham-bin-Ghias (Azzan's brother, ruler of Muscat) had been killed, and that Toorkee was on a fair way to capturing Muscat. In April the Government learned that the chiefs were submitting to Toorkee, who had already farmed the customs revenue of Muscat for thirty thousand more dollars than Azzan had obtained for them. Beraymee also had surrendered. In

July Toorkee's success was assured. In August his position was acknowledged; and he was formally recognised by the British Government as ruler of Muscat. Then he received with ceremony the political agent, the senior naval officer on the station, and the officers of the "Bullfinch" and "Constance," with a number of English residents. The day was kept as a holiday. The vessels in the harbour were dressed, and the "Bullfinch" fired a royal salute. Never, perhaps, in the world's history was there a series of more interesting and curious instances of the proverbial slip between the cup and the lip, than these operations exhibited to the looker-on. To the Indian Government, however, the interest was intermixed with some anxiety. The master of Muscat had always been the real master of Oman, and Toorkee held Muscat. His victories too had been sharp and prompt, but so also had been Azzan's; and Toorkee's competitors for the throne were no fewer than thirty, with, in many cases, titles as good as his own in all save that of the sword. The situation for months was critical, but with Toorkee remained the victory. From July 1870 I had taken notes regularly of these curious events.

Then what was done in the Persian Gulf must of necessity be taken in connection with affairs in Afghanistan, with the disturbing elements in Persia, and with the curious invasion (referred to in relation to Aden and the Red Sea) of Arabia by the Turks. In May 1871 it was placed beyond doubt that Nedj was to be attacked for the Porte, and there was a strong impression on the minds of Indian, and also I think of English diplomatists, that if this succeeded the armed claim would be extended to Muscat, Mekran, and elsewhere, on the ground of those rights of conquest referred to in the previous chapter. Here was indeed a momentous issue—an attempt to re-weld an empire from the European side of the Bosphorus to beyond the passes of Cabul. England hardly comprehended what was passing, but Russia and Persia did so fully. In June it was known in India that the first infantry detachments of the expedition had been afloat in April, and that artillery and cavalry were on their way overland from Amurah and Bagdad, while guns and stores were being sent by boats. The Mountific Arabs were to supply a thousand horsemen, and other tribes in the neighbourhood contingents of horsemen and matchlock-men. All this, it will be observed, had been arranged and carried into effect without causing a ripple on the sea of European diplomacy. It was not till November 1873 that England was startled, as shown in the earlier chapter, by intelligence that the invaders were threatening our allies the Sheikhs in the neighbourhood of Aden. Then the English Government stepped in, and the expedition collapsed. Who would venture to say, however, that some similar impulse, under some more favourable conditions, may not any day lead to a like exigency?

At the same time there was going on under Colonel Goldsmidt a difficult arbitration with respect to the boundaries of Persia, Afghanistan, Kelat, and Siestan, with such other side issues as these huge questions involved. The Government of Persia, chiefly concerned as a claimant, had the reputation of being one of the most shifty in the world, and the most difficult to fasten to an engagement. Occupying a position between Russia on the one hand, with the Khanates and other wild territories intervening, and India on the other, with Afghanistan, Beloochistan, Kelat, and other districts, also wild and lawless, intervening, Persia seems by its very position marked for intrigue. The refuge of fugitives from west and east; the heir to a great name and an ignoble reality; looking back to a history of conquests, yet chained to an existence more and more circumscribed every year, it could hardly be expected that such a Government would materially assist the arbitrator of England to arrive at a just conclusion. Moreover, it could not be denied that the losses of Persia in her Caspian provinces, and even at her very doors, were enough to sour more patient spirits than she had for many ages possessed. It was not unnatural that as she was cut off from her dominions westward, while Russia crept on to the Oxus and the Turks evinced designs on Arabia, she should put forward claims—not clearly invalid if read by a certain kind of historic light—eastward in the direction of Kelat and Mekran, if not of Cabul. That the negotiation was in terms, and to some essential degree in fact, successful, was allowed; but again it must be said that, as in the case of Afghanistan, no such treaty is worth the paper it is written upon any longer than the power to enforce it exists. What Colonel Goldsmidt had to do was to check the progress of chronic disorder. The disorder itself he was powerless to remove.

Reference may also be usefully made to the light thrown on frontier affairs by an outbreak of a tribe of Wuzeeree mountaineers, the Mohammed Keyls, on the same frontier. The tribe, numbering in all about 3000, of whom only 300 were fighting men, had been for years settled on British territory, migrating to the hills in the hot weather and returning when they pleased. In some sort of panic difficult to account for, they fell upon and cut up a detachment of British troops, and a costly and imposing expedition was sent out to punish the outrage—so costly and imposing indeed that the Wahabees and not the petty tribe of Mohammed Keyls were supposed to be the real object. On the 21st September 1871, the whole tribe—men, women, and children, with horses, cattle, and sheep—arrived at Edwardesabad and surrendered. People said that a steam-hammer had been put in motion to crush a fly. The reply was, that no one knew what was in the background; that England cannot now afford in India to risk a repulse, and that the fly was dangerously near to uncaged tigers.

Turning to the eastern frontier of India, we find immense difficulties in connection with the King of Burma, whose caprice was as perplexing as war. Now he was our friend, now our enemy; at one moment encouraging English enterprise with enthusiasm, at another endeavouring to open up negotiations avowedly against that enterprise with some other European power. One day, again, intelligence reached Calcutta that the king was for free trade—not a half-and-half freedom, a mere "free breakfast table," it was said, but absolutely unrestricted commerce. "Why not?" he asked; and Indian merchants echoed his question. Next we heard that the king was about to turn shopkeeper on the largest scale, and required for his purpose a general monopoly. It was difficult to see what might not occur from the whims of such a king.

Major Sladen, Captain Strover, and other public-spirited men, had striven hard to re-open the old trade routes to Momein and Western China, and Lord Mayo very sincerely favoured their projects. It was reported also that the Panthays at Momein and elsewhere ardently desired the routes re-opened, and only dreaded the adoption of some route that would cut them off from the expected benefits. Here again his Majesty of Burma appeared like an evil influence. There were three roads, Major Sladen said, all of which he deemed practicable, and a great trade might easily be opened if the King of Burma could be made to stand aside. As yet, however, this has not been accomplished. The deeds done on that frontier had long been appalling where known, though Europe had heard little of them. At one time the Mohammedans proved successful, and butchered or circumcised and enslaved every Buddhist or follower of Confucius whom they could capture. Then the Chinese prepared themselves for a great fierce effort, and swarming over the frontier when least expected, paid back their enemy in kind. Women and children, old and young, frequently disappeared in one huge merciless massacre. This was, and is common life on the western borders of China—life which Lord Mayo strove to influence from two different directions, by way of the north-east through Burma, Bhamo, and Momein, and to the north-west by Cashmere and Yarkund.

In the latter direction a mission was sent in 1870, under

Mr, now Sir T. D. Forsyth, to Yakoob Beg, Ameer of Kashgaria. Mr Forsyth had previously been entrusted by Lord Clarendon with a kind of informal mission to Russia with reference to the Afghan and Yarkund frontiers, and had elicited an informal statement which, though not put in writing, was deemed satisfactory. Early in 1870 Yakoob Beg sent an embassy, ostensibly for commercial purposes, to Calcutta. Mr Forsyth's was a return mission, arranged to overtake and join the Yarkund people at Leh in Ladakh. It also was declared to have a purely commercial object, while, however, expressing to Yakoob Beg and his people amity and goodwill. This declaration was almost certainly true, but it probably was not so accepted by the Russians, who read it in connection with the fact that on the high land of Asia, where Russia was steadily approaching on the one hand and the Chinese ceaselessly encroaching on the other, this Yakoob Beg—a man of lowly origin but of proved capacity, both in administration and war—had placed himself at the head of a veritable "Mohammedan revival," which might become no one could say what. The order for the embassy was dated April 1870. In November the same year Mr Forsyth was again in Calcutta. Yakoob Beg was away, with his army, at some great distance from Yarkund, fighting the Tungani, and Mr Forsyth having strict orders to return before the passes closed for the year, the main object of the mission—an interview with the successful soldier—was lost, though some important subsidiary objects were gained. It was, I think, seen afterwards that the decision to return was the only practicable one, and that it would have been impolitic to sacrifice too much to the dignity of Yakoob Beg.

Mr Forsyth was accompanied by two scientific men—Dr Henderson and Dr Cayley—and by a skilful trader, Mr Shaw. The two latter met him at Leh in Ladakh. On the 7th July the start was made from Leh for Yarkund. The notes of this journey made by Mr Forsyth and his colleagues were in many parts very interesting, and depict marvellous changes of scenery. Thirty marches over an almost uninhabited country; a long journey by the banks of the Indus; then by a pleasant valley to the foot of the Chang La Pass, 17,000 feet high; then, on the other side, by pleasant villages and valleys rich with trees and foliage; then by a long dreary desert, and another higher pass, over brown and barren mountains, to a pass higher still, the high land of Asia. The scenery was described as grand, though often for vast distances not a shrub or blade of grass could be seen. One of the curiosities of this desert was a large soda plain, with dust or spray offensive to taste and smell. On entering Yarkund territory the envoy was met by the fact of the Ameer's absence, and he resolved to return to India. Yakoob Beg's representative, the Dadkhwah (so called), however, pleaded hard for delay, and the embassy remained long enough to make many inquiries as to the manner of life in Yarkund, and to collect valuable scientific facts.

There was found considerable industry, good cultivation, trade with Russia and Cashmere, and a Russian outpost eight days' journey from Kashgar, the capital of Yakoob Beg's dominions. The old trade routes between China and Central Asia were closed by the war, and part of the Chinese had fled to Russian territory. Of the Tungani Mr Forsyth wrote: "Whatever the origin of their name, the Tungans were Mohammedans when they were first removed to China, and, though they have insensibly fallen into Chinese habits and customs, they adhere to the laws of the Prophet, and observe strict rules of life, abstaining from drink, opium, and even from tobacco." These are the people who had been mainly instrumental in wresting from the Chinese a vast amount of territory, and were on a fair way to establishing an empire, when Yakoob Beg appeared and massacred both them and the Chinese. Little more need be said of this mission than that it returned to India, and that it supplied the material for subsequent negotiations, and led to the appointment of Mr Shaw to a post from which he could watch for any openings that, from time to time, were presented for trade.

A rumour of the death of Yakoob Beg (this year), and of preparation by the Chinese to assail his dominions, gave fresh interest to a wide political question involved. It was hardly likely that another such man would appear in this generation. Mr Forsyth's description of the Dadkhwah gives one the idea of a mere though a skilful farm bailiff.[1] Yet it became necessary to mark afresh the relations with Yarkund, and "a retired officer, who knows the frontier well," protested strongly in *The Times* of July last against England mixing herself up in the affairs of Kashgaria and China. "Russia alone," he said, "is concerned; she is watching the course of events, and in due time will use her influence for her own purpose." Wiser words than those of this letter have not been written on the subject; always premising that the object of our missions was anything beyond obtaining accurate intelligence, and opening up highways for trade. I do not think, however, that Lord Mayo had any more remote object. Certainly he did not dream of a military demonstration beyond the passes of Cashmere.

Another phase of frontier policy was the despatch of an envoy (Mr Edgar) for the second time to the Looshai tribes, a dangerous, and so far untamable class of gentlemen on our north-eastern frontier. Mr Edgar's instructions were "to fix a boundary line from the borders of Munipoor to Hill Tipperah, where ordinary British jurisdiction would cease, and beyond which the tribes would be held responsible for the peace of the district; to endeavour to open up bridlepaths over the Cachar and Chittagong frontiers, and to use his utmost endeavours to convince the Looshai chiefs that while the Indian Government wished to live in peace with them, and assist them to push their trade and open up new veins of wealth in their own districts, any recurrence of the old raiding practices would be sternly repressed and punished." The plan was settled in

[1] Appendix III.

December 1870. Mr Edgar was to be met on his way by a deputation from a noted chief's (Sookpilal's) village, and at the same time two other envoys, Major Graham and Major Macdonald, were to start with a like object on a visit to the chiefs of the south. At the end of January 1871, intelligence arrived that a fierce attack had been made on some Cachar tea plantations by a portion of the Looshai tribes, at the very time that Mr Edgar was engaged with Sookpilal, and indeed almost while that chief (one of the worst raiders of 1868-69) was accepting Lord Mayo's terms. Lord Napier of Magdala went at once to the scene of the outrage, but the rains were so heavy that even intelligence could not for a time be obtained. The Government meanwhile expressed doubt that the raiders were Looshais. The tea merchants of Calcutta laughed scornfully, and said, "Not merely Looshais, but directed by Sookpilal." In the latter case, however, it appeared they were mistaken.

The attack had been made on 23d January by different bodies of raiders. The coolies fled in all directions, and the marauders having plundered and destroyed property to their hearts' content, and life where it came in their way, retired in safety, as they thought, to hills which never as yet had been invaded. A little girl, the daughter of a planter, Mr Winchester, who had been killed, was taken away, but after an apparently not unpleasant sojourn with her captors, was recovered by the men of the military expedition which was speedily resolved upon. Nothing could be done till the cold season at the end of the year. By that time Lord Napier's plans were arranged in his usually complete way. The force was to consist of two columns, which were to start on the same date (20th November), the one from Chittagong under Colonel Brownlow, and the other from Cachar under General Bourchier. The date was afterwards altered, but the plan was carried out in its main features. These steps were not taken without uneasiness. The difficulty was to know where and how to strike. If houses and stores were burnt, they would almost certainly, it was said, be those of the wrong people, and while the raiders escaped, persons altogether innocent would be killed. Yet that the tea gardens should be abandoned to these ever-recurring raids could not for a moment be endured.

The war—really a return raid—is not one that need be dwelt upon. Major General Nuthall, Political Resident at the court of the Rajah of Munipore, and in command of a contingent of Munipoories, was first in action; in consequence, he said, of an attack upon his men at the post assigned to them by General Bourchier; in consequence of his having advanced beyond that post, General Bourchier affirmed. At all events he beat back the assailants.

After this, the war, mainly with rockets, shells, and the rifle, progressed sharply. Early in May 1871 the reports of the generals of the two columns were published in the *Gazette of India.* The expedition was at an end. In fighting men and camp followers the Cachar column had lost about 500 men, and the Chittagong column about 150; but in both cases the losses were chiefly under the head of died, not killed; the real foe was the climate. So ended Lord Mayo's one war, avoided by him as long as possible, and undertaken with unfeigned regret. He had no ambition for the laurels of war, and least of all for those of such a war as this; but before the expedition was concluded, Lord Mayo was no more. The tribes were subdued and humbled. How greatly they suffered, the innocent with the guilty, will never be known, though it is known that when the troops of the expedition turned their faces Indiaward, they left cholera and other diseases incident to war behind.

These facts of course present but a meagre view of the causes of disquietude beyond the frontiers of India. The aim has been, as far as possible, to show in this bare general outline of some among many ever-recurring causes of disquietude, the nature of many more. Indeed the subject of the Wahabees in the chapter that will follow this, with special reference to "causes of disquietude within," has an even greater relation to causes of disquietude beyond the frontier, though it was as a fact within India itself that Wahabeeism was grappled with during the years more especially considered in these pages. If I were asked what Native India thinks of our foreign policy, I would say that Native India, on the whole, is critical; is not displeased to see us checkmated in our great designs; is rather glad indeed when events remind us that we are mortal. Men like Ameer Shere Ali the Afghan, and Jung Bahadoor of Nepal, and even the King of Burma, are reminders to India that there still remains for her the last dread appeal in case of dire necessity. I believe that the "mildest" Bengalee is glad to know that India and Afghanistan can produce soldiers like Yakoob Khan and like Scindia, and that it is comforting to him to reflect that the Magistrate Sahib, and even the great Lord Sahib in Calcutta, might any day or hour be called upon to face real peril. But I believe also, and on sound and reasonable grounds, that Native India would not wish to, at any rate, exchange English for Russian rule, although the latter might provide for India careers in life which the former in fact refuses.

CHAPTER VII.

CAUSES OF DISQUIETUDE WITHIN THE FRONTIERS—THE WAHABEES—AMEEROODEEN—AMEER KHAN—JUSTICE NORMAN—LIAKUT ALI—A PRETENDED NANA SAHIB.

If the real truth as to the Wahabees in India could have been as clearly seen in 1870 as it can be in 1877, a very different course might have been taken by the Indian Government. Seven years ago it was believed that a Mohammedan uprising on a large scale might any day be one of the facts of Indian life. That it would be sharply conquered when once seen was not among the subjects on which Englishmen allowed themselves to doubt. For though Mohammedanism in itself was now native to the soil of India, Wahabeeism not only never had become so, but was, on the ground of its extreme purism and severity, as hateful to many well-to-do Mohammedans, as it was to all Hindoos. Yet confidence in the power to conquer did not imply confidence that there would not be great destruction of life, and the Wahabees were undoubtedly dreaded. The Government had evidence that a propaganda, issuing from Sittana, beyond the North West frontier, and from Patna, one of the most famous and excitable cities on the Ganges, had been carried to every part of India. Skilful detectives had sought in all directions to discover the presumedly deeply-laid and widely-spread plots. Men who had studied frontier questions and the remote origin of that inflammable material which, after smouldering long, would often burst into flame in a moment, and in many places at one time, among Mussulman races, believed that the signs of a storm were in the air. The smoothness of the surface of the general life was counted for little by persons who remembered the sense of security that preceded the Mutiny, the ease with which the conspiracy had then been carried from place to place, and the rapidity with which it had spread. Of the origin and progress of the Wahabees Dr Hunter says:[1] "About a hundred and fifty years ago a young Arab pilgrim, by name Abdool Wahab, the son of a petty Nedj chief, was deeply struck with the profligacy of his fellow-pilgrims, and with the endless mummeries which profaned the holy cities. For three years he pondered over the corruptions of Mohammedanism in Damascus, and then stepped forth as their denouncer. He rendered himself peculiarly hateful to the creatures of the Constantinople court, accusing the Turkish doctors of making the written word of no effect by their traditions (Sanat), and the Turkish people of being worse than the infidels by reason of their vices." Driven from city to city, he at length "formed a small Arab league, and raised the standard of revolt against the Government of Constantinople, and of protest against her corrupted creed."

He became, in fact, an extreme reformer, and a denouncer of sin; and as the Soonis, themselves puritan, were numerous in India, and fierce in certain districts, the Wahabees had a clear field for their propaganda, so long as moral and not political aims were avowed by them. The Wahabee leader died in 1787, after an extraordinary series of victories over his more easy and orthodox co-religionists and the races that bowed to the once all-powerful sway.

"It was Mehemet Ali, Pasha of Egypt, who succeeded in arresting the victorious advance of the hated puritans.[2] In 1812 Medina was taken from them by storm. Mecca fell in 1813; and five years later this vast power which had so miraculously sprung up, as miraculously vanished, like a shifting sand-mountain of the desert. The Wahabees, now a scattered and a homeless sect, profess doctrines hateful to the well-to-do classes of Mohammedans. In formal divinity they are the

[1] "Our Indian Mussulmans." [2] *Ib.*

Unitarians of Islam. They refuse divine attributes to Mahomet, forbid prayers in his name, and denounce supplications to departed saints. It is their earnest practical theology, however, that contains the secret of their strength. They boldly insist upon a return to the faith of the primitive Mohammedan Church, to its simplicity of manners, its purity of morals, and its determination to spread the truth, at whatever expense of the blood of the infidel, and at whatever sacrifice of their own lives."

In directing attention, however, to the Wahabee camp on the frontier, and to the propaganda within, Dr Hunter insisted also on the sad condition of the Mussulman population of India. Where English rule, he said, had existed longest, there the Mohammedans had sunk lowest. They could acquire wealth, but save in exceptional cases they could not be induced to accept English education, and the glory of their race had gone. This was a very fair, as it was a very painful, statement of the case; and it was strengthened by some pictures fearfully startling of the decay of old Mohammedan families of high position. The book is well worth reading. A thousand facts went, and still go, to prove that if a great orthodox leader appeared in the name of the Prophet, we should have to face a huge danger. But the Wahabees are heterodox—the Tenth Monarchy men of Islam—and there cannot be a doubt that but for English interference in Arabia in 1873, the Porte would have striven hard to exterminate them. In 1858 Sir Sydney Cotton, with 5000 British troops, stormed the camp of the Wahabees at Sittana, and razed the villages of their allies.[1] After this for a time the fire smouldered, and seemed to be extinguished; but it again burst out, and in such a way that the Government decided to attack the propaganda in India itself, from whence there was no doubt that money in large amounts was sent to Sittana.

In the year 1870 a tedious trial at Malda ended in the conviction of a man named Ameeroodeen, a man whose principles and efforts were strongly brought out in an official report of great pitifulness, by Mr Reilly, district

[1] There was a second expedition ten years later.

superintendent of police, and an able officer. The Wahabee propaganda began, he said, in Malda, about twenty-five years previously, in the preaching of Velayut Ally of Patna, a Kalifa or lieutenant of the Wahabees. He visited the district, and appointed as Kalifa Abdool Rahman, who opened a school, and taught children, and preached the jehad—the holy war against infidels. Among his leading supporters was Ruffeek Mondul of Narinpore, the father of the Moulvie Ameeroodeen. Ruffeek Mondul devoted his son to the priesthood, and in due time Ameeroodeen was made Kalifa, and began those labours which were so fatal to him. Ruffeek Mondul, at the time the story was told (1871), was seventy years of age, and in his dotage; and though the fire of enthusiasm still broke out, in view of the principles to which he had devoted his life, he could hardly be counted dangerous. There were those, however, this report said; who remembered the old man as foremost in the indigo disputes, and spending both time and money in opposition to the exactions of the planters, fighting every battle to the bitter end, even in the High Court and before the Sudder Revenue Board of Calcutta, and never yielding a foot of ground while he was able to maintain it. The rent laws were put in force against him; the Ganges overflowed its banks and swept away his property; he was brought to the verge of ruin. Once, at the funeral of a Mondul, where hundreds of people had assembled, Ruffeek Mondul stood upon a white ant hill, and denounced another Mondul, rich and influential, as unworthy to take part in the ceremony. The accused demanded an explanation. Ruffeek Mondul boldly asked him if he had not taken usury from his co-religionists contrary to the precepts of the Koran. The question was a charge. Witnesses were present to prove it, and the accused was not restored to communion with his sect till he signed a bond renouncing for ever the sin of usury. When Ameeroodeen was condemned, the fine old man embraced him, and bade him keep firm to the faith. This is an abridgment of the story told by one of the enemies of the Wahabees. If such a story had been told of Greece or Rome, or any nation or race that had lived hundreds of years ago, it would have been among the lessons of Oxford and Cambridge —a story termed classical. That the history will some day be read with just pride in India, when India knows its own most honourable records, I take to be among the certainties of life. Can any one, whatever his views, help feeling for those two men, father and son? Is there an Englishman anywhere who would refuse to petition the Indian Government, or the Government at home, beseeching them, if Ameeroodeen still lives, to find some means for his release? We may be bound, for the safeguard of society, to punish rebellion, whatever its cause or justification; but are we not also bound by the highest laws to admire such heroism and self-sacrifice as these men evinced? Tried, and condemned, in a dusky little court, under circumstances of which even Englishmen in India knew little, and Englishmen at home nothing at all, I think the name and fame of Ameeroodeen, and of his gallant old father, will not readily die.

While this drama was being played to its end, a number of other persons were imprisoned, or kept in imprisonment, on a charge of Wahabeeism; and among them two notable men, named Ameer Khan and Hashmadad Khan, whose trials attracted general attention. A petition at the end of 1870, presented to the Judicial Committee of the Privy Council, stated that the petitioners, aged men living in Calcutta, "were in July 1869 suddenly arrested by order of the Government, and could not ascertain the charge. They applied to Mr Justice Norman for a writ of *habeas corpus* in order to be released, and under the Bengal Regulation III. of 1818, and of the Indian Acts 34 of 1850 and III. of 1858, he refused to grant the writ. An appeal was to be made to the Supreme Court, but as the vacation was at hand and the applicants in gaol, the present petition was lodged. After the petition was presented information had been received from India that the appeal had been heard and dismissed." This new phase of the question necessitated an amendment of the petition, but indeed the action of the Judicial Committee has little place in this narrative. The case remained with the Indian law courts; and in them the drama was played out, at an enormous cost to the prisoners. Mr Chisholm Anstey, then practising in Bombay, since dead, made the application to Mr Justice Norman, and made it in speeches so fiercely denunciatory of Lord Mayo and his Government, that it was difficult to believe he had the slightest hope of the writ being granted. The standing counsel, Mr Paul, having eulogised Lord Mayo as a nobleman who had left ease and comfort at home to give his services to India, Mr Anstey "hoped his learned friend would for that glowing panegyric be rewarded in the next world as he was sure to be in this." Of a claim which he held Lord Mayo was making to irresponsible power, he said: "Finch and his atrocious crew, in their endeavours to put down the just rights of the people, used the very same language. 'Who shall command the king?' said Lord Finch. 'Why,' replied those glorious old Puritans, 'the law shall command your king.' So if my learned friend asks, 'Who shall command Lord Mayo?' I say, the law shall command Lord Mayo. He cannot be irresponsible and remain a British subject." Mr Anstey was assisted very zealously by two gentlemen of the Calcutta bar, and assuredly every effort was made for the accused; but on the 24th August Mr Norman gave an adverse decision, and in September the Supreme Court rejected the motion for permission to appeal. Mr Anstey meanwhile had moved for a writ of *mainprise*, that the prisoners might be admitted to bail. That too had been refused.

Late in December or early in January the prisoners were set free from Alipore gaol, but while they were marvelling at their good fortune they were re-arrested at the prison doors. It had been discovered that their apprehension six months earlier had been on a Governor General's warrant, about which there was some question. The cup of hope was held to their lips and then dashed away. They were re-arrested on a magistrate's warrant, and were eventually tried before a civilian judge (Mr Prinsep) at Patna, where the offences were alleged to have been committed, and were sentenced to imprisonment for life. In August 1871 an application was made for a suspension of the sentence pending an appeal, and the case was to be heard in September before Mr Justice Norman, whom the Mohammedans, in consequence of the position he had been compelled to take as the Acting Chief Justice, considered their undoubted enemy. Before passing to what, I fear, was a terrible consequence of this belief, a few facts in relation to the chief, because the wealthier, of the two prisoners, Ameer Khan, may be interesting.

He was a Mussulman banker and money-lender of a kind well known in India, and was beyond doubt very wealthy. A highly-honourable European merchant in Calcutta told me that he once, having business to transact with the old man, found him seated luxuriously in a sort of state, on a dais which the visitor was told he must not approach without taking off his shoes. Of course he declined to do that, but the fact shows the manner of life of Ameer Khan. I by chance saw the old man some months after his sentence, picking jute or oakum in the great gaol of Calcutta. He never, I was told, spoke to any one from morning to night, but incessantly muttered something to himself, and glanced, as we saw him glance, furtively from under a very contracted forehead. The contrast of the two pictures was painful. I believe he was guilty, either as a principal or as an agent, of supplying money to the propaganda, and I never heard anything in his favour at all like what has been stated of Ruffeek Mondul and Ameeroodeen. But the long imprisonment without trial, the re-arrest at Alipore, and the removal from the jurisdiction of the highest courts of law to the court of a civilian judge, able and respected though he was as an officer, did not give one the idea of that impartial dignity of the law which is one of the best claims of England to her supremacy in India. Nor is it easy to escape the belief that Lord Mayo, by whatever advice he acted, was in this case primarily to blame.[1]

About eleven o'clock on the morning of September 20th, Mr Justice Norman was murdered. He had driven as usual to the High Court, where he was to hear appeals, and had turned round at the top of the great stair to give some direction to his servant, when a man rushed from one of the doorways and stabbed him deeply on the left shoulder. Turning, with a faint cry, to defend himself, he was again stabbed; and, it was stated in evidence that the blows in both cases were given with the unerring certainty indicative of a man who had probably studied the art of murder. Utterly helpless, the poor judge ran down the steps, followed by the assassin, who brandished his knife and dared any one to approach him. After some little time, however, he was struck down by a native workman, captured, and committed for trial. Mr Norman lingered for some hours in great pain; then he fell into a merciful unconsciousness, and died at about one o'clock in the morning. The door of the house to which he had been carried was all this time surrounded by his friends, and the grief for his sad end was, I am sure, both general and sincere. He had been known as a kind and humane man, as well as an upright judge; the idea of any prejudice against the Mohammedans influencing his decisions was everywhere dismissed as preposterous. He was buried on the following evening; the coffin was carried by six English sailors; the service was read by Archdeacon Pratt (a distinguished clergyman, since dead); the city was in mourning; the cemetery crowded by men of all races and creeds known in Calcutta; the minute-guns booming from Fort William. And it was told, amid all, how the judge when suffering most, had desired the Lord's Prayer to be said with him, and had paused

[1] The prisoners were released on the proclamation of the Queen as Empress.

and twice repeated, "Forgive us our trespasses, as we forgive them that trespass against us"—a lesson not without value in India.

I was present at the trial of the prisoner, and noted certain peculiarities in his appearance and conduct. He was short and strongly built, and his countenance seemed to me of a Jewish cast. His head rose, from a rather low forehead, to a cone in shape like a sugar-loaf inclining backward, or a Parsee's hat. His eye was cold and glassy, and though at times fierce, was never bright. The manner in which he questioned the native witnesses was extraordinary. The questions, "Where was I?"—"Where was Norman Sahib?"—"Where were you?"—"Is that (pointing to the table) the knife?" startled people by their defiant audacity. The knife, a long, tapering Ghoorka weapon, seemed to interest the prisoner much in the way that a new specimen might interest a scientific man. The Advocate General, Mr Graham, conducted the prosecution, as he had conducted the Wahabee trials, with a temper and dignity which were highly spoken of by both Natives and Europeans. The *Hindoo Patriot* said: "Nothing could be more impressive than the stern rules of an English court of justice, which would not deny a fair and open trial to the basest criminal. The man is arrested by the police and taken before the coroner. He is allowed every opportunity to cross-examine the witnesses and prove his innocence. He is again brought up before the magistrate, where the same form is observed. At the High Court he is allowed to challenge the jury, and to examine the witnesses to any length he likes. The Advocate General, who conducts the prosecution, exhorts the jury to dismiss from their minds what they had heard outside, and to bring in their verdict without bias and in good conscience." Here also was a lesson of great worth.

The prisoner when first arrested had answered in some Oriental jargon, such as, "The earth is sunk below the waters; the men have gone to the skies; the dog is eating the wall"—probably under the influence of bhang. Then he became silent; but from first to last nothing further was elicited from him. The Advocate General wisely confined his questions to proving the murder, and abandoned, if he ever had entertained, any hope of discovering the motive for the crime. That a very uneasy feeling prevailed throughout India is certain. People saw in the murder the beginning of a system of warfare in which one man of a body of Thugs of a new order would draw a lot which would condemn him to give his life, if need be, to destroy that of some distinguished Englishman. Looking at all the circumstances of the case, with many notes before me, I have no doubt that the cause of the murder was the Wahabee trials. That the prisoners Ameer Khan and Hashmadad Khan were concerned in the act, their friends held to be to the last degree improbable, since such a deed was sure to remove, as it did remove, their last hope of mercy. There is not much perhaps in the argument as applied to such impulsive races, but at all events no one had any right to even hint at the criminality of these men to the extent of participation in this murder. The idea of the new order of Thuggee passed away, but it was revived a little later by the murder of the Governor General.

About the same time another strange story was made public. In July (1871) the police had apprehended, at the Bombay railway station, a man who had for some time been watched as a preacher of treason, and who was then about to leave for the North Western Provinces. Treasonable documents were found in his possession, with a bamboo staff filled with small ingots of gold, in value about £200, and a bag of money. In a little while he was found to be the notorious Liakut Ali, who had proclaimed the King of Delhi at Allahabad in the crisis of the Mutiny. He was described as a good-looking man, proud of his looks, eager to be photographed, and quite easy as to the danger of his position. It was as late as May 1872 before the Government ventured to bring him to trial, but then the evidence against him was overwhelming. The charges were: "That you are accused of complicity in the rebellion of 1857; that during the month of June 1857 you held a court and camp at the Khoosroo Bagh, Allahabad, and headed the mutineers; and that you subsequently took the field against the troops of Her Majesty." The prisoner was advised to plead guilty with extenuating circumstances, and he did so, apparently with the same coolness with which for fifteen years he had roamed about India.

"I acknowledge," he said, "having been a leader of rebels in June 1857. I also acknowledge having had a camp in the Khoosroo garden. I was engaged in a fight with the British troops. I wish to say that beyond engaging in fight I did not cause any further loss. I saved the lives of gentlemen and ladies. I saved the life of a lady at Cawnpore. Owing to fear of the Nana I clothed her in Hindostani clothes and pretended she was my sister. When the Nana Sahib was defeated I went to Furruckabad. The rebels sent two cannons and two companies after me to kill me and the mem sahib (the lady). I sent her off on a doolee as soon as I saw the soldiers coming, and myself went towards them. They arrested and took me back to Furruckabad. Their officers held a court on me, and decided to blow me away from a gun as a loyal subject of the English. Some of my men explained to the Mussulman sepoys that I was not a well-wisher of the English." "Did you consider yourself under the orders of any one?" he was asked. "I considered myself subordinate to Bahadoor Shah, King of Delhi."

Doubtful as part of this at first seemed, it was substantially confirmed by witnesses. The woman referred to by the prisoner said, that in May 1857 she with her mother, stepfather, and five brothers and a sister, removed from Lucknow to Cawnpore for protection, and that they were in the intrenchment till the surrender of General Wheeler. They then attempted to escape in boats, but she was seized by a native and forcibly carried off, just before the boats were fired upon, and was barely saved from the massacre.

She was taken before the Moulvie, Liakut Ali—the prisoner, she believed, though he was not then grey; and a little later she heard the firing which was the death-knell of her friends. Having exchanged her European dress for a native one, and received a little blanket-tent for her residence, she remained there till the British approached, when she was hurried away with the retreating rebels. She was removed from Cawnpore to Bithoor, and then further up country; but the party returned on hearing of the fall of Delhi. At Futtehghur she was told that she was to be blown from a gun, and she escaped at night with a sowar who had her in charge, but, she felt confident, with the connivance of the Moulvie, whom, however, she never had seen again till she saw him then on his trial.

For ten months this woman was carried about from place to place, and at last was handed over to her friends at Allahabad. Her evidence undoubtedly saved the life of the Moulvie, who was sentenced to transportation, and sent to the Andamans. Here then had this man, with a capital charge hanging over him, been wandering over India from 1857 to 1870. What, it was said, is there unreasonable in supposing that the Nana himself may have been similarly engaged. False Nanas indeed had sprung up, and the cry of wolf had so often been raised that the fashion had long been to say authoritatively that the Nana had died in the Terai of Nepal; and though the assertion when examined was found to have no basis whatever, beyond the belief that he could not have escaped so long with such a reward offered for his capture, the words still passed from lip to lip as a popular faith.

I was about leaving India in 1874, when a telegram informed me that the real Nana had at last been caught at Morar, and that besides confessing himself the Nana he had been identified by the Maharajah Scindia. I saw Colonel Mowbray Thompson, one of the four heroic survivors of General Wheeler's force in 1857, and found that he had been summoned to Morar to examine the man who had claimed the dangerous title; and for Morar I also at once started. On the 28th October I saw the presumed Nana, and a man who had been captured with him, sitting on their haunches in a sort of cage, in the lines of the 26th Cameronians—two miserable-looking beings, gibbering and talking incessantly, and calling gods and men to witness the hard usage to which they were subjected. The only hardship I saw was in the savage looks of the sturdy Cameronian guard. The pretended Nana, however, seemed to have a perpetual laugh on his lips, and he hardly for a moment ceased protesting: "I am not the Nana. How can I lie?" He had, it was stated, arrived at Morar as a fakeer, among many fakeers, for the Doorga festival; and having been addressed as the Nana by some of Scindia's troopers, had confessed that they were right, and thereupon had written as the Nana to Scindia, and claimed his protection. The Maharajah, the account ran, immediately ordered out a body of cavalry, and surrounded the pretender. The letter had stated that the writer, after wandering in the jungles in great wretchedness for many years, had at last determined to throw himself on Scindia's protection ("lay his head in Scindia's lap"), and would do whatever he was bidden. All this seemed very straightforward.

It was necessary, however, for several reasons, that Scindia should act with caution. In the first place, the real Nana, if he lived, was head of the Mahrattas, as the representative of the late Peishwa of Bithoor, Bajee Rao, and in that capacity was the head of Scindia's own race. If the Nana was dead, no one living could take precedence of Scindia in the claim to the coveted headship. In the former case, however, and granting that this was the real Nana, it was by no means a small matter to Scindia how his impulsive warlike people would view the surrender by him, a chief of the Mahrattas, of a Mahratta who by right of rank claimed his fealty. When the two met, Scindia said, "Do you know me?" and the fakeer replied, "Yes, you are Scindia." "Can you," he asked further, "tell me anything whereby I can be assured you are the Nana." The man said he could, and thereupon he related particulars of a private, and, as I gathered, sacred ceremony, in which when the two were young men, Scindia had presented the Nana with a tulwar (sword), in acknowledgment of the higher rank of the latter. These facts the Maharajah Scindia himself stated to me, Colonel Willoughby Osborne kindly interpreting. The Maharajah also repeated the expression of his belief that the prisoner was, as he professed to be, the real Nana. The surrender had been made to Scindia at his palace of Lushkur, to which reference will be made hereafter, and the prisoners were sent to Morar. Colonel Osborne, the Political Resident, accompanied the escort to the cantonment, where the two men were handed over to the general in command. I was also present at two examinations, which were at least curious.

Sahib Apbey,[1] a Gwalior noble in Scindia's service, and from sixty-five to seventy years of age, stated that his son married the daughter of Bajee Rao Peishwa, and that the Nana, who had been adopted as the son and heir of Bajee Rao, was held to be brother to the Peishwa's daughter. That the prisoner was the veritable Nana he had no doubt; and he had, he said, been in daily intercourse with the Nana for about a month and a half during the marriage ceremonies which took place in the palace at Bithoor during the Hoolee festival in the year Sumbut, 1913—month Phagua, corresponding to March-April, 1856. Witness, although he had not seen the Nana either before or since that time, professed to have at once recognised a scar on his forehead. So positive was he that, when appealed to by the prisoner, he simply smiled and said, "But you are the Nana."

Unnâ, a Brahmin, son of Narain, otherwise termed Baba Bhut, "the Nana's own brother," identified the prisoner as his uncle, who had been adopted by the Peishwa, Bajee Rao, as his son and heir. This witness

[1] I have some doubt as to the spelling of this name.

stated that he last saw the Nana at Bithoor before the Mutiny, when he himself was about ten years of age; but long as that was ago, he could testify that the prisoner was beyond all dispute the same man. Colonel Mowbray Thompson, after some preliminary remarks as to the official directions which had led to his journey to Morar, said: "I stated that if he was the man, I should recognise him by a scar on the forehead. Captain Wolsely, brigade-major, said, 'He has such a mark,' and asked me on which side of the head it was. I replied I had forgotten that. I must say, on first seeing the prisoner, notwithstanding the presence of the scar alluded to, I did not think him the man he was said to be. He was so changed—being much thinner, well bearded, with long unkempt hair — appearing a most disreputable fellow, cringing and humble, and utterly different to what I remember him in his glory at Bithoor. I asked, however, that he might be shaved and dressed in the clothes of a Mahratta gentleman. This was done, and of course changed his appearance materially, and made him strangely like what I remember of the Nana of Bithoor. Still I cannot go so far as to swear he is the man. All I can say is, the likeness is extraordinary, and the presence of the scar a most strange coincidence." Dr Barnard said: "I entered the cell of the prisoner supposed to be the Nana Sahib, and carefully examined him from head to foot. I don't know that I ever saw this man before. I saw the Nana twice or three times during the summer of 1856 at Cawnpore, but only in his carriage at the band, or on the mall in the dusk of the evening; and I have no recollection of him, excepting that he was a young-looking man, of the ordinary lightish-brown complexion of the better class of natives of Hindostan. I know I could not recognise him now."

Indisputable evidence that the man was not the Nana was given by Dr Tressider, a medical officer, who had attended the Nana professionally, and in the operation of cupping had left an indelible scar, no trace of which was on the prisoner. In a few days the impression was general that we had made another error. The question was, what did it mean? Some doubted the good faith of Scindia—an ungenerous and unfair view, and one that Lord Northbrook promptly and unhesitatingly evinced was not shared by the Indian Government. Some thought that the imposition was a stratagem to test Scindia, and that if he had said, "Yes, I will protect you," the true Nana would have appeared. Others again, returning to the "undoubted death of the Nana in the Terai of Nepal," held that the whole affair rested on the passion for notoriety of a silly fakeer, drunk with bhang. Of Scindia's good faith it was hardly possible to entertain a doubt, after fairly considering all the facts. If, however, I had had such a doubt, it would have been removed by a conversation I afterwards had at Agra with Scindia's loyal adviser in the Mutiny, Sir Dinkur Rao, "the honourable and true man—the man of his word"—of the Mahrattas. He did not of course say anything definitely as to a person whom he had not seen, but he expressed an unhesitating opinion that the evidence at that time—before Dr Tressider's statement was known—was immensely in favour of the view that we had caught the Nana.

I cannot help thinking that the second of the views stated above may some day be found to have been the correct one, and that a man in some respects not unlike the Nana was induced to personate him for the purpose either of privately securing the protection claimed, or of leading Scindia into a pitfall. I shall not readily forget the way in which the old man, "Sahib Apbey," put on his spectacles and said, with a triumphant grin, "You're the Nana." The effect of the Nana's name on the people, I believe, was for a few days almost magical. I had taken from Calcutta an intelligent Mohammedan servant, who teased me hourly with, "Sahib, can't I *now* see the Nana?" At last I said, "Dear me, yes; come, and I will ask for permission." We obtained the permission, and saw "the Nana," but the man's disappointment was woful. He shook his head gently but firmly. "No, no, sahib," he said, "*he* not the Nana." I have narrated these facts chiefly in their relation to the story of Liakut Ali; but apart from that, they have their own significance. The first impression of satisfaction in all English minds that the murderer had been caught, gave place to a strong suspicion that there was more in the affair than appeared on the surface. That this suspicion was warranted by the circumstances of the case, I still believe, though before I reached Morar I had reason to conclude that whatever was signified in the man's mock confession, the one thing not signified was that we had caught the real criminal. I can see nothing in the least improbable in the Nana still being alive in a land where the seclusion of households is carried out to such perfection; and I do not think it is from any mere spirit of revenge that sensible, not to say humane, Englishmen would have rejoiced to know that the great criminal had been caught. Subsequently, in Calcutta, a Hindoo gentleman of high character and honour said to me jocularly: "How dreadfully eager you all are to catch the Nana. Cannot you, after all this time, dismiss him from your minds, and commit the Mutiny and all its belongings to history?" That, however, cannot well be unless by a miracle of some kind. If Tantia Topee had escaped, few Englishmen would have felt very bitterly towards him; but as a matter of simple fact, the feeling towards the Nana can only pass away when this generation is gone. Yet if the Nana lives, no one need envy him his lot since 1857. It can hardly, even under the best circumstances, have been other than a living death.

CHAPTER VIII.

INDEPENDENT CHIEFS—SCINDIA AND HOLKAR—SIR DINKUR RAO—MOHAMMEDAN OPINION—GWALIOR AND JHANSI.

WHILE the identification of the pretended Nana was in question, I availed myself of the opportunity of seeing and learning a little of the great country of the once dreaded Mahrattas. The Gwalior territory, watered by the Chumbal, the Nerbudda, and the Taptee, comprises large tracts of land naturally fertile; but either because the population is too sparse to provide the necessary labour, or too warlike to brook peaceful pursuits, comparatively little of it is cultivated. The Political Resident at Morar informed me that Scindia had offered to lease land on terms which would at once have made a poor cultivator wealthy, but that in few cases had the offers been accepted. The Bengalee, who would have instantly perceived the value of the inducements, was too much wedded to Bengal to throw in his lot with the Mahrattas, while Scindia's own subjects were first of all soldiers. In the middle of a vast plain, not unlike a lion recumbent, the Great Fort of Gwalior appears by its very form and position to have been created by nature for the dominance it has so long maintained. At the foot of the rock, under the very nose of the silent stone lion, are Scindia's old and new towns of Lushkur. The cantonment of Morar is about six miles distant, in the contrary direction, nearer to Jhansi. It was at Lushkur that the Ranee of Jhansi, one of our most terrible and inexorable enemies during the Mutiny, died on the battlefield, fighting us, like the indomitable woman she was, to the last. In the far distance are the Jhansi hills, terribly suggestive to an Englishman.

The origin of the chieftains, Scindia and his neighbour Holkar of Indore, was lowly enough, judged from a Western standard, and in India has only been counterbalanced, not altogether redeemed, by great capacity, which always stands below pedigree. It should never be forgotten, if we would understand the mainsprings of difficulty and danger in India, that there is no right of Hindoos more sacred than that of adoption. The Nana Sahib was the adopted son merely of the head of the Mahrattas; but his title to headship was nowhere disputed. Neither Holkar nor Scindia, though direct heirs, had the same title which the adopted son of Bajee Rao had, though they have pedigree sprung from undoubted courage and skill in perilous times. Mulhar Rao Holkar was the son of a herdsman, who, about 1730, rose to power under that Bajee Rao who himself had risen, though with caste on his side, from the rank of prime minister to supreme ruler among his warrior race. This is referred to in an earlier chapter. Holkar was a man so swift and terrible in war that territory was allotted to him, and he became a chief. Ranajee Scindia, though said to be allied to noble families in Rajpootana, was a menial servant; but being faithful, courageous, and able, he too was made a chief and a ruler of many villages. Dr Russell, writing from the scenes of the Mutiny in 1857, said:

"When the mutinies broke out, Scindia and Holkar, whose territories are conterminous and closely adjacent to the disturbed districts, remained faithful to our cause; and the former, by far the more powerful of the two, displayed considerable judgment as well as loyalty in the policy he pursued. In virtue of the arrangements subsisting between him and the British Government, he maintained from the revenues of his principality a compact and well-disciplined force as a contingent available in aid of the Bengal army. This force, now so notorious under the name of the Gwalior contingent, was organised and officered exactly like our own sepoy regiments, and proved true to its model in all respects by joining in the Mutiny at a very early period. . . . In June 1858 the commander-in-chief notified in a general order his 'high gratification' that the town and fort of Gwalior had been conquered by Major General Sir Hugh Rose. On the 20th of June the Maharajah Scindia, attended by the Governor General's agent for Central India and Sir Hugh Rose, and escorted by British troops, was restored to the palace of his ancestors, and was welcomed by his subjects with every mark of loyalty and attachment. It was on June 1st that the rebels, aided by the treachery of some of Maharajah Scindia's troops, seized the capital of his Highness' kingdom, and hoped to establish a new government under a pretender in his Highness' territory. Eighteen days had not elapsed before they were compelled to evacuate the town and fort of Gwalior, and to relinquish the authority which they had endeavoured to usurp."

This is very satisfactory, and England's debt to Scindia, among other chiefs, is not overstated. Yet twenty years after the Mutiny we still keep possession of the Fort of Gwalior. Scindia has, it is true, the palace, which, however, he declines to use, and his flag flies from the flagstaff, and salutes are fired on his birthday and *fête* days; but the garrison is British. Sir Dinkur Rao, in speaking on this subject, made no secret of his conviction that we had not kept faith with India. The remarks of the great old statesman were kindly interpreted to me by the Commissioner at Agra, Mr Drummond. My object was simply to know and learn from Sir Dinkur Rao; but there was a distinct understanding that I should state whatever I deemed of public usefulness; and on this understanding I wrote on the subject in *Macmillan's Magazine* in 1875. I said that Sir Dinkur Rao, though now perhaps best known in England as one of the judges of the Guikwar of Baroda, has for twenty years stood foremost among his people as a man both of ability and probity; that his character might partly be judged from the fact that he learned the English language in eleven months, with no text-book but the "Wealth of Nations;" and that his views on many subjects might be divined from the fact that he gave up his use of the English language on the avowed ground that Englishmen had ceased to do justice to his country. He is a man short, slender, and now aged, with an extraordinarily quick eye, and a grave, calm, kind face. He spoke slowly and carefully, apparently weighing every word, but with the utmost decision, and with a noble scorn of secrecy. His loyalty is unquestioned. In the Mutiny, as we have seen, he cast the die for himself and Scindia, and again and again the lives of both were in extreme peril in consequence of this decision. Lord Canning said of him: "Of all the men I have met, no one has impressed me more with a sense of natural ability;" and I think a distinguished living witness to the same effect could be found in Lord Lawrence. Mr Drummond said, "He is the Nestor of India; every word he speaks is pregnant with wisdom." And again, "In the Mutiny he was deemed the Englishman's friend. When the mutineers of the Gwalior contingent had murdered their officers, they rushed into Scindia's presence waving their bloody swords, and called for Dinkur Rao to be given up to them as the firm friend of the English Government. Scindia was firm (Dinkur Rao was sitting behind him), and said, 'No, he is my servant, and no one shall touch him.' Dinkur Rao then at once sent out the fiery cross (pukar) to the Rajpoots, whom he had made his firm friends by his justice, courtesy, and good revenue management, and he was answered by the appearance of 10,000 Rajpoots of the fighting clans, who told him that 10,000 more were ready at a word. Armed with matchlock, sword, and shield, they were a match for the rebels." The people honour Sir Dinkur Rao with a great honour, as the wise man of their race.

The good old man spoke somewhat mournfully and sadly when he depicted what he deemed a great change for the worse in the character of English rule in India. "You are not now," he said, "true to your word. Once your word was as if it were written on a stone tablet with an iron pen. Now I speak of it as a promissory note. You promise and do not fulfil." I thought then, and for some time, that the reference was to Gwalior; but I have since been led to believe that it had a much wider range, and related, amid much else, both to Gwalior and the confiscations in Oude. I could say much more of Sir Dinkur Rao than my space will admit, but as it is, his name will recur again in another chapter. Between him and the Commissioner at Agra (a man who showed his confidence in the people by remaining outside the fort with his family during the Mutiny) there seemed to be a fast friendship, honourable to both. I met also in Agra a well-read Mohammedan gentleman who had visited England, and he courteously gave me, in quite a pile of papers, his view of public affairs, especially with reference to the hardships of the people in the North Western Provinces and Oude.

Do not, he said, "believe that the educated people of India of any race or faith undervalue the benignant rule of the British Government; but England, too, has advantages from the union, and ought to accept the duty of looking to the happiness of the people placed under her protection by the Almighty God." He maintained that the confidence between England and India had diminished, as their intercourse had increased. India, he said, was yearly becoming poorer, and under the Queen's government had lost many of the advantages it possessed under that of the East India Company. In Oude annexation meant the sudden resumption of pensions, granted, in some cases, ages previously, by native rulers; and many persons, who before annexation were wealthy, were now old and infirm, begging in the streets of Lucknow, while many had "died off in indigence and wretchedness." There might, he granted, be sound political reasons for resuming some pensions; but so many persons, once in affluence, and now in poverty, he held, inflamed and disturbed the minds of the people, and destroyed all hope of permanent loyalty. The competitive examinations, this gentleman also maintained, were sending an inferior class of Englishmen into India—"men not to be compared with the Lawrences, Montgomery, M'Leod, and Durand. Yet while the men were inferior, their power was greater, and appeal from their decisions was all but impossible." One case was given of property having been confiscated on the ground of participation in the Mutiny, in the direct face of a recorded legal verdict of not guilty. These and like statements made in this memoranda passed the eye of an English officer of high rank, and were revised by him. The great allegation of all, however, in the statements of this Mohammedan gentleman, is that the Government have no machinery whereby to test the real feeling of the people. We have nothing now, he said, that answers to the judgment-seat of great rulers like Akbar, who dispensed justice in person, and checked interested judgments on the part of the officers employed.

I give these statements as the views of an educated, and, I have reason to believe, honest man; and they will, I think, have additional interest if the reader will bear them in mind as a key to some facts yet to be stated with reference to the Mutiny. In 1858 Lord Stanley wrote a despatch on the measures necessary for the pacification, after the annexation of Oude, and in particular recommended conciliation and a strict regard for those very interests to which my Mohammedan friend says there has not been paid any regard whatever. One of the bitterest and commonest complaints I found in my intercourse with Native India, was that Englishmen in these times seem to have no conception, as Englishmen of old had, of the existence of such persons as Hindoo and Mohammedan gentlemen. The traditions of the Company were of at least an outward and visible regard for native forms of life. This rule, it was said, exists no longer. Often thoroughly polite themselves, the gentlemen of India are shocked to find, that while the forms of English life are more exact in India than in England, the forms of native life are often trampled under foot. I do not think it may be out of place, in view of this opinion, to refer incidentally to the fact, which no one travelling through India can well overlook, that the little groups of English people, men, women, and children, scattered over the country, are every year becoming more numerous, and of necessity more isolated, as trade increases, and railways are extended. Is it not becoming more and more necessary, even on this ground of pure self-preservation and comfort, that there should be reminders that Native India thinks we are falling off from the best features of a Company which was very far from being altogether good?

I drove from Morar to Lushkur and Gwalior on a beautiful morning a little before day-dawn, along a road lined with trees, and even then crowded with people. Lushkur, a purely Mahratta city (the term signifying camp or army), was in old times to the fort of Gwalior what the village was to the feudal castle of old in England—the villagers were both the vassals and retainers of the lords of Gwalior. Within what appears but a stone's throw from the fort, but really 600 yards from our No. 1 Battery, and entirely commanded by it, is Scindia's new palace, at the time I saw it very nearly finished, and likely to be one of the most luxurious and beautiful buildings in India or anywhere. In general outline it gave one at first sight the idea of the Tuileries, but with all that provision for coolness, quietude, ease, the luxury of baths, and the charm of flower-gardens, carried to such a high art in Pompeii in the days of the most luxurious of the Romans. Within and without were flower-beds, and ingenious plans for defying the heat of the sun, for amusements suited to every season, for receptions, and indeed for whatever the heart of man could desire to make life pleasant under an Eastern sky.

The road from Morar lies under the guns of the Great

Fort. The people I met on the road seemed haughty and self-reliant. The women, who wore petticoats of Manchester or other cotton, not the intricate but graceful garment of Bengal, looked up bravely, if not saucily, and in very few cases hid their faces, as a Bengalee woman with the least pretension to respectability always does on the approach of a stranger. Women or men, however, young or old, they impressed one with a pleasant sense of dignity. The Mahratta boy is proud of his horse, and is in fact a born soldier.

Approaching Lushkur "City" the scene varied at every turn. The fine road became narrow and crooked, and branched off in all manner of directions in a series of curious curves, connected by equally crooked bridges, along the sides of miniature quarries or ravines, alive with people. Every road or street was lined with shops and crowded with workers, whose laughter and talk never ceased. Here and there the scene was varied by a temple with its many worshippers. This was the old bazaar, a labyrinth of huts, such as a mole or an Esquimaux might burrow in, only beneath a sun which makes life bright and cheerful. The same road led to the new bazaar, and then to Scindia's grounds, where many servants (who, in my case, steadfastly refused baksheesh) were ready to point out what was to be seen, and to do so most obligingly. I did not care to see the inhabited palace, about which there was sure to be some natural difficulty incident to Indian life. The horse on which Scindia escaped from the mutineers might, I was told, be seen there; but not much more. The new palace, however, and the older ones, unused, in the Fort above, were quite sufficient for the object I had in view, and for the work of the cooler parts of two days.

Approaching nearer to the Great Fort, one perceived in it still more the appearance of a huge beast of prey, with jutting peaks and deep indentations which might pass for natural curves, and dwarf foliage not unlike shaggy hair. Ascending on elephant back, by a narrow, rugged, and unpleasant curved path, 600 yards long, and with a gradient at times of as much as one in five, might under ordinary circumstances be the reverse of pleasant, especially if the elephant insisted, as elephants will insist, upon walking on the very edge of a path which in the grey morning seems like the border of chaos. "A slip?"—but elephants never slip, people say; and at all events there was soon before the eye a panorama the beauty of which drove all other thoughts away. In the far distance were the Jhansi hills, dimly defined, but forming a fine background to a picture which the sun was now tinting with the first streaks of day—the territory, no one is likely to forget, of the once indomitable Ranee, now held in the name of Queen Victoria. Beneath was Scindia's city, awaking to daily life. Far and near, here in cultivated beauty, there in wild waste, and as if untouched by the hand of man since the creation of the world, was one vast expanse of foliage, dense as a forest, varied with every imaginable colour, and relieved by lofty trees, and bamboo huts and red tiles, and by the signs of a busy human life which is truly teeming in the immediate neighbourhood of Gwalior. Above, on strange sentry places, were men of gallant regiments, whose colours bore the records of many days of mortal struggle. Every fresh curve brought to view a fresh sentry, till at last, having passed through five fortified gateways, the path opened on the plateau, where a man might halt, and feel thankful that friends and not enemies had been above him during the ascent.

The hill has an upper surface a mile and a half long and three-quarters of a mile wide, and commands every spot of ground on every side, save one hill 2000 yards distant. At the end nearest to Lushkur are Scindia's uncared-for palace and storehouses. Nearer to the other end are the barracks and storehouses of England; the garrison of four hundred infantry and a battery of Royal Artillery, eighty men strong. The proper garrison in war ought not, I was assured, to be less than 11,000 men, and in native hands was probably 20,000. Of course we have the cantonment close at hand; but if we remember that the nominal British force in all India is only 60,000 men, and the real force, excluding depôts, much smaller, it will be seen that the faith of race and destiny must be strong when a man can look cheerfully upon those gallant little garrisons.

In the centre of the hill there is a strangely-rugged gully—deep, I suppose, as the base of the hill, and formed of a series of chasms and quarries, covered in every part with the thickest of thick foliage. This is the "Happy Valley," and I have no doubt it well deserved its name when held by some of the old conquerors of India. The position must in those times have been impregnable; the capacity for storage is practically unlimited, and in addition to several serviceable wells in the Fort, every rock in the gorge drips with water. As on the outside, so to this Happy Valley there is one rugged path; and the two are alike in the fact that from top to bottom they overhang awful precipices. The entire valley is filled with images—not fewer than 20,000, I was informed. In all manner of leafy recesses, in nooks and corners, at every turn of every curve, there is a god, with a slightly broken nose, or a chipped forehead, or a broken finger or toe—the work of iconoclastic Mussulmans, but in few cases sufficient really to impair the work of the artist. Enough for the iconoclasts that there was no longer a perfect idol. A similar story in stone exists in a fine Jain temple in the Fort. Elephanta, compared with Gwalior, is voiceless as to the history of India. How clearly and distinctly one may read of the happy Hindoo in his Happy Valley—his impregnable home. Then of some dark time when the home changed hands, and the cherished idols were mutilated. Tide after tide of invasion rolled around Gwalior, till at last we English came as a race born out of due time, and garrisoned the fort with five hundred men, whom Major Gordon now commanded for Queen Victoria. This in brief terms is the story of the cities of Scindia, and of his Great Fort of Gwalior.

That Jhansi road, too, along which the Ranee, Luckshmee Bye, marched to her death at Lushkur, has a grim story. To the Ranee reference will again be made. It need only be said here that when her husband the Rajah died in 1853, leaving an adopted heir whom Lord Dalhousie refused to recognise, her husband's private property (horses, jewels, and furniture included) was sold, to be invested for the family it was said, but in any case for a mere moiety of its value. When the Mutiny began, the Ranee cast in her lot with Tantia Topee. On June 4th she besieged the English garrison; on June 8th she massacred it, sparing neither young nor old, male or female. In December Sir Hugh Rose, with the Bombay column, arrived at Indore. In January 1858 he began the operations which were to relieve Saugor, capture Jhansi, and secure the great road by Calpee. Jhansi was invested, Tantia Topee defeated, Jhansi taken by storm, and no quarter given by the maddened soldiery. For three days the streets, the palace, and the private houses ran blood; only not, it is said, the blood of women or children. The Ranee and Tantia fled, first to the Fort, then from the city. They made a stand, and were defeated in a fierce battle. They stood again at Lushkur, whither Sir Hugh Rose pursued them, first, however, reminding his men at Calpee, in words of the nature of those which have made ordinary men heroes, that they had already marched 1000 miles, forced passes, and trampled down every enemy that had appeared. Near to where Scindia's new palace now stands the last of the Ranee's battles was fought, and she fell like a heroine, on a spot yet pointed out by the people with unmistakable pride. It is a story known all India through.

Of Scindia's military organisation I was told that it is formed on the plan of that by which the Prussians checkmated and finally defeated the first Napoleon. That is, that while Scindia is bound by treaty to maintain only 10,000 men in arms, he could in an emergency bring six times as many men into the field. He is, I should say, a fine soldier. He rode into Morar on the occasion on which I saw him at the head of about a hundred splendid horsemen. When he was about to leave the Residency and had put his foot into the stirrup, a hundred other feet were put into stirrups at the same moment. The next moment they were away like the wind; or like what they were—Mahrattas. Now and then we caught a glimpse of them among the trees, but as a gleam of light merely. I expressed a wish to see the camp, but the Maharajah hesitated, and I saw that it would be improper to repeat the evidently unwelcome request. Yet Scindia appeared to me a gentleman as well as a chief and a soldier. Intending to refer to the scenes of the Mutiny as a whole, I tried to forget those scenes in relation to this beautiful country. Thinking of the rich tints on the foliage, of the busy workers, and the lively roads, how pleasant it would have been to escape a word of the horrors of war! But the facts will come, here as everywhere, journey as one may on the blood-stained soil of India.

I desire especially here to guard myself against being supposed to advocate the giving up of the Great Fort at Gwalior to Scindia. It would be simply absurd in a civilian to give an opinion on the subject. The importance of the Fort from a strategical point of view, and the fact that the men of the Gwalior force fell away in 1857, might again represent questions of life or death some day. We hold the Fort, at best, by no other right than the law of self-preservation; but that, for aught I know, may in this case be the paramount law. I should not like to say more, in view of what any year may bring forth. At the same time, I wish we held Gwalior by a better title.

CHAPTER IX.

HINDOO AND MUSSULMAN FEUDS — EXECUTION OF KOOKAS — THE SANTALS — AGRARIAN RIOTS — OUTBREAK IN A GAOL—RIOTS IN BOMBAY.

FROM the very nature of the Mohammedan and Hindoo creeds, there is a standing feud between the Mohammedan and Hindoo races. Not merely are the festivals of each an offence to the other, a case which might be provided for, but the peculiarities of the creeds run into the necessary acts of everyday life. To the Hindoo the cow is a sacred animal—the "mother and milk-giver of the family," while the Mohammedans not merely kill cows, but, in the spirit of their image-breaking forefathers, insist upon doing so publicly, and sometimes in the very street. This is beyond measure distressing to the Hindoos; while Englishmen, partial to beef, and scornful of the idea that a cow is sacred, too often take the side of those from whom the offence cometh. Nor is it in the mere killing of the cow publicly that the Mohammedan butchers transgress; they too often are dreadfully cruel in what they do; and from one cause or another the grievance never ceases. Englishmen say, "But how absurd." Well, it is so; quite as absurd indeed as some of our Orange and Catholic feuds; but at least the Hindoo's faith involves the sacrifice of his interest. He could sell his cows for slaughter, and often refuses. Herein surely is some title to respect.

In the middle of 1870 several Mohammedan cow butchers were murdered in the Punjab, under more than ordinarily suspicious circumstances, from the fact that the crimes were almost simultaneously committed in different parts of the country, and appeared to be induced by a new Sikh sect known as the Kookas, pre-eminently defenders of the cow. Several of the Kookas were summarily executed, and an impression was created that the roots of the uprisings went deeper than merely the defence of the sacred cow. On the 30th August, a native judge of the Small Cause Court at Lahore gave judgment against a Kooka, a goldsmith. The man waited till the court closed. Then he met the judge, who was on his way home, and killed him. The man was tried and executed, and the sentence was made more terrible by the executioner being chosen from the Mehter (of the lowest, sweeper,) caste, whose touch is pollution.

While the disquietude from these causes was increasing, an Englishman, Mr Bull, secretary to the municipality of Lahore, was murdered by a Mohammedan fakeer, who said as he struck, "Your watch is over, your raj is gone." These two facts were put together as showing a concerted plot of Sikhs and Mussulmans—a by no means improbable union, considered simply by the light of history, but exceedingly improbable when it was remembered that the Kooka outbreaks were primarily against the Mohammedans, among whom this fakeer was a fanatic. None of the conditions of the proposed union of Dost Mohammed and Runjeet Singh existed, and I never saw any reason to believe that the presumed union was not a mere fancy. Nearly at the same time there was a strange panic among the Europeans at Allahabad, who believed that they were about to witness another mutiny. The Wahabee trials also, in the case of Ameeroodeen and others, were proceeding at Malda; and a few weeks later Sir Henry Durand was thrown from the back of an elephant and killed on the Punjab frontier. The fact that Sir Henry was a soldier of high reputation, and that the accident, as we shall see, was of an altogether unusual character, assisted to create that feeling of alarm which had been growing on different hands. Was it a plot to rid the Punjab of its military head in view of an uprising?

The evidence went to show that the calamity was an accident; but this was not seen at the time.

In June or the beginning of July 1871, a Mohammedan butcher at Amritsur wantonly threw a bone into a Hindoo well. There was an instantaneous rising and some loss of life; and the spirit of Hindoo revenge spread rapidly to nearly all the chief stations in the Punjab. The wildest proposals were made and applauded. A Hindoo vernacular paper begged the Government to stop all slaughter of cows. "Such outrages on cows," it said, "we can no longer bear." A little later a Mohammedan alleged that a Hindoo had sold him a mango fruit filled with pigs' bristles. On examination it was found that the Mohammedan had put the bristles there himself, and he was sentenced to a month's imprisonment.

A number of exactly similar facts show clearly and indisputably that what the Government had to contend against was not a union of Hindoo Sikhs and Mussulmans, not in fact a political impulse at all, but a deadly religious feud of the two races.

About the middle of November judgment was given in the case of a murder of butchers, committed nearly six months previously by Kookas at Amritsur. For some time there had seemed no hope of bringing the murderers to justice; but at last a man, under sentence of death for another crime, offered to lay the whole circumstances bare if his life were spared. The Government reluctantly accepted the offer; and it was then found that the conspirators, ten in number, after two attempts to commit the murder had been foiled by the murderers missing their way to the butchers' quarters, succeeded in their attempt on a dark night in June. The butchers were in several cases caught in their sleep. Four of them were murdered and three wounded. One of the murderers escaped. The first informer and another were accepted as evidence. Four were executed, and two transported. What came of the tenth has somehow escaped me. The

Punjab was in this unsettled and really dangerous state in 1870-71; and Englishmen, unable to see below the surface of native life, were free to give full play to their imagination. This should be remembered in view of a still more startling proceeding.

In January 1872 there was a deed done which made the ears of nearly all who heard of it to tingle. On the 16th January tidings arrived in Calcutta to the effect that an attack had been made on what was known as the Malod Fort, in the small native state of Kotla, in the neighbourhood of Loodiana, and 235 miles from Delhi, where Lord Napier of Magdala was in camp with a splendid force of 16,000 men of all arms. Nothing more absurd ever was known in the history of rebellion. The one idea in the minds of the "rebels" (numbering perhaps 300, including women) was that at the Malod Fort, owned by a chief not favourable to the Kookas, arms might be seized; but to what purpose the arms, if seized, were to be applied, seemed a problem. The wildness of the attempt was abundantly shown. Ram Singh, chief and prophet (Gooroo) of the Kooka sect, had warned the Government that some design was on foot. Lord Napier was at hand with a force powerful enough to march through India. And finally the rebels—who had tried to fasten with cords, instead of killing the people they attacked—after being driven away from the fort, went rambling about the fields, without an aim or a leader, till they were hunted down by the men of the neighbouring chiefs, Puttiala and Nubha, and by the police. The remnant of these "desperate fanatics," in many cases wounded, were led away in a body to prison. The attack on the fort was made on the 15th January, and was repulsed, with the loss of about three men killed and wounded on the side of the defenders, and about six on that of the assailants. On the 16th January all was at an end. Ram Singh, and others, unconcerned in the outbreak, were quietly apprehended at their homes. Another body of Kookas, who had taken arms, hastened to disperse. A force from Lord

Napier's camp at Delhi was stopped on its march, and ordered to return to camp. These are the bare leading facts of the Kooka outbreak in January 1872. That there was no fear of the prisoners being rescued, or of the riot spreading, everything testified.

On hearing of the attack, Mr Cowan, deputy-commissioner at Loodiana, went at once, with the district superintendent of police and the district surgeon, to the scene of the disturbances. On the 16th he telegraphed to the Punjab Government for permission to summarily execute four prisoners—Mr Cowan not himself having power to take life. Mr Forsyth, commissioner at Umballa, who possessed power of life or death, wrote to Mr Cowan, directing him to send the prisoners to Shirpore—Mr Forsyth afterwards said he added "for trial." Mr Cowan said that the letter contained no such words as "for trial;" the letter itself was lost. On the 17th, before the answer of the Punjab Government arrived, Mr Cowan had, without any semblance of trial, begun at Maleir Kotla, to blow forty-nine prisoners from the cannon's mouth; and the execution was carried out to the bitter end. One man had been cut down in advance. Fifty in all were killed. In the midst of this carnage, the details of which were heart-rending, a letter from Mr Forsyth arrived, directing procedure according to law. The executions, however, were continued. On the 18th Mr Forsyth wrote his full and unqualified approval of what Mr Cowan had done, and also approved of some like acts of the Kotla officials.

The Indian Government, however, took a different view of the proceedings. After a long investigation, a masterly minute, which recapitulated the facts of the case with judicial exactness, declared Mr Cowan dismissed from the service, and Mr Forsyth removed from the commissionership of Umballa, and incapacitated from again exercising jurisdiction where human life might be in question. The order was made public on May 9th, 1872, after the death of Lord Mayo, by the temporary Government of Lord

Napier and Ettrick, but the decision had, I believe, been come to previously. At the same time the order fully admitted Mr Cowan's previous good services, and in particular his humane care for the people in a time of great distress. Mr Cowan's case remains as it was. Mr Forsyth was soon afterwards sent by Lord Northbrook on an important embassy, and was knighted—to my view a political error of the first magnitude.

Early in the same year a disturbance which threatened to have disastrous results broke out among the Santals. The causes of discontent had been simmering for many years, and for a period of about six years had been met by a Santal ryots' association—a remarkable step for the uncultured race which supplies the unclothed coolies of Calcutta. The mountaineers held a meeting to discuss their wrongs, and to complain to some person or persons possessing the power to redress those wrongs. A second meeting was held two years later, and two more meetings of "representatives" a year later still. The whole proceedings indicated great patience on the part of the poor people. At the end of 1871 a final meeting was held, and the language of some of the leaders was so indignant that the men were imprisoned. The complaints were not in any sense political, but purely social. It was asserted that fair and just measures taken to protect both landlords and tenants, after the outbreak of 1858, had been systematically evaded by the former; that the Bengalee landlords, assisted by an iniquitous race of Mahajuns (money-lenders), who charged an appalling rate of interest for money which the owners of the land virtually compelled the tenants to borrow, had made the lot of the people worse than slavery. They alleged also, amid much else, that the landlords in addition to just rent levied unjust fines, and that a tenant who appealed to the law-courts was inevitably defeated, by cross-examinations in a language he did not understand, and often before the trial was entrapped into signing some deed which invalidated his case. In May 1872 a "Regulation" was published in the *Gazette of India*, defining the rights and duties of the Santals. It was decreed:

First, that no money-lender should be permitted to take interest at a higher rate than two per cent. per month, in spite of any agreement to the contrary, or to take compound interest arising from any intermediate account. The total interest on any loan or debt was never to exceed a fourth of the original sum, if the period were not for more than one year, and the interest was not under any circumstances to exceed the principal, as it often had in very considerable amounts. Large powers were placed in the hands of the lieutenant governor for the settlement of land, for inquiry into landed rights, for the record of rights, for the demarcation of land, etc. An attempt was also made to let bygones be bygones as far as the village headmen were concerned. Then—and most important—any ryot who either himself, or through persons from whom he inherited, could show that he had held fields for a period of twelve years, was deemed to have occupancy right in such fields. Any ryot also who held fields by an equitable claim at the end of December 1858, and afterwards lost them, might claim to be reinstated; and any ryot who had exchanged fields in the same village had his occupancy right legalised. In fact, this remarkable decision gave to the settlement officers power to make a complete revolution in the affairs of the poor Santals.

This Regulation was one of the good things of Lord Napier's government, but it is not difficult to recognise in it the bolder hand of the Lieutenant Governor of Bengal; and if Sir George Campbell had done nothing more for India, this alone would have entitled him to the gratitude of at least the poor. I do not know that the tenants were altogether right, and I am sure the landlords were not all tyrants in league with unjust Mahajuns; but that there were great wrongs no one can doubt, and to meet those wrongs this trenchant order was issued. We shall see more of the Santals later.

A year or so after the final outburst of wrath among the Santals, the equanimity of Bengal was upset and the Government alarmed by tidings of an agrarian rising in the district of Patna. The magistrate of Serajgunge, Mr Nolan, in reporting on the riots, said that while the root of them undoubtedly lay in the enhancement of rents, the law itself was not faultless, since it allowed a landlord to increase his rents, even when reasonably high, if he could show that higher sums were obtained for similar farms in the neighbourhood. These riots were very little heard of in England, but they were characterised by pillage and loss of life, and in the end assumed so serious an aspect that the Governor General (Lord Northbrook) called upon Sir George Campbell for explanations. Sir George replied:

> "As regards the specific questions asked by the Government of India, the ryots have not generally shown a disposition to refuse all rents, but, on the contrary, generally offer rents which the zemindars consider inadequate, and have in many cases deposited these proffered rents in court. Our officers seem to think that, as might have been expected, while the zemindars ask too much, the ryots offer too little. The combinations to resist the payment of all rents are merely attempts to bring the zemindars to terms by keeping them out of all rents till they settle the question in dispute."

This paragraph may perhaps lead the reader to suspect that there is a landlord's as well as a tenant's side of these disputes, and also that the tenants are not in all cases quite so helpless as some people suppose. The sympathies of many English officers almost invariably go with the poorer side, and I know that in the case of the Santal disputes, as also in the income tax appeals in different parts of India, missionaries interfered with very marked effect on the side of at least the poor Christians. I think, indeed, that it will not be overstating the case if I express a belief that part at least, not of any new-born sense of security against oppression (for that the rudest races have when the limits of endurance have been reached), but of rights within the law, have their origin in the teachings and influence of the missionaries. At the same time, I do not wish to lead any one to suppose that the law should be strained any more in favour of the poor than in that of the rich; and I do not think it can be done so without danger.

An outbreak in Bareilly gaol in September 1871 affords an example of a race and creed outbreak, resting, as was believed, on a strange union of the highest caste Hindoos and the most fanatical Mohammedans. It may not be known to every reader that the Brahmin wears suspended, in a long loop falling over one shoulder, a thin common-looking thread, which is the badge of his high caste—of a nobility to which princes may bow. The superintendent of Bareilly gaol was led to believe that, by virtue of this thread, high-caste prisoners secured unauthorised privileges, including immunity from punishment, no warder caring to inform against a Brahmin; which probably was the fact. Relying, therefore, on a prison rule which authorised in certain cases the taking away of prisoners' clothing, Dr Eades removed the threads, the direst injury short of death that could be inflicted on a Brahmin. The rage of the Brahmins was extreme, and a number of Mohammedan prisoners fanned the flame to white heat.

At length an outbreak was determined upon. Means were found to cut off rivets and remove a door, and about eleven o'clock on the night of September 6th (a very dark night), forty-seven prisoners rushed into the yard, knocking down sentries, and making their way to where some portions of looms had been stored. Armed with these, they attacked the watchmen and guard; how desperately may be judged from the fact that thirty-seven of the prisoners were wounded, and twenty-one of the number with clubs, while only sixteen were disabled by gunshot wounds. A stern inquiry followed and resulted in an equally stern decision on the part of the Lieutenant Governor of the North Western Provinces, Sir William Muir. Dr Eades was removed from his post, and was informed that he had done a double wrong, first to the individual in taking away his thread, and secondly to the empire in forgetting that the principle upon which British power in India rests is religious toleration. Certainly if any one had ventured to do on a larger scale what Dr Eades (no doubt with the best intention) did in Bareilly gaol, there had been another mutiny in India.

One other outbreak may be worth the reader's attention as illustrative of causes of disquietude within our frontiers. Early in 1874 it was known in both official and unofficial life that the Mohammedans of Bombay and the regions generally where Gujeratee is spoken had become greatly excited by the publication in that language of Washington Irving's "Life of Mohammed," construed into an attack on the Prophet. The publisher was a Parsee, and no more seemed needed to direct upon the whole Parsee community the vengeance of the Mussulman fanatics. On the 13th February the explosion came. The houses of the Parsees were sacked, the property destroyed, and the people cruelly abused. For fully two hours in the middle of the day the rioters worked their will without any police interference. Elegant houses were wrecked to desolation, and life destroyed, while some Englishmen, it was said, reproached the Parsees with having caused the disturbance. For several days the riots continued, the Parsees, now, at times leading, the Government apparently at its wits' end. A number of Arabs who landed from the sea were supposed for the moment to have come by invitation. The Mussulman Mohurrum festival, too, was beginning. Altogether there was reason to fear the worst. At last troops arrived, and the rioters rapidly disappeared. Here was another powder magazine which a spark had ignited, and not for the first time. If the area had been extended, and sparks carried to other magazines, the loss of life might have been great, even though no political crisis involving a race mutiny had resulted. It will be observed that in none of the cases here referred to was there a political motive as against the Indian Government. In none, perhaps, was there serious political danger. In all there was serious danger to individuals, and in all also there were issues which required to be met with firm but calm and forbearing statesmanship.

I think the reader will conclude also, after considering these facts, that there is such a thing as "Native Opinion in India." I do not mean by native opinion the great power of a united popular will, kindred to that which I think is much more clearly seen in Manchester and Birmingham than in London. I do mean the power of great bodies of people to perceive a fact from some common stand-ground, and to make that fact the basis of united action. That is, I am asking the reader to view Indian life by the light of facts which came under my own observation and by the light of history before English rule in India began, as well as by that of the hundred and twenty years since Plassey. It is a history of action resting on opinion. The application of these facts, in their broad and general importance, will pertain more appropriately to a later chapter. Here, however, independent of anything the Government can do, or avoid doing, are elements both of disquietude and danger.

CHAPTER X.

THE NORTH WESTERN PROVINCES AND THE PUNJAB—SIR HENRY DURAND, SIR WILLIAM MUIR, AND SIR JOHN STRACHEY.

THE three names at the head of this chapter represent not merely three distinct orders of men wielding almost irresponsible power, but also three distinct kinds of government in India. In the cold season of 1870-71, Sir Henry Durand and Sir William Muir went away on tour through their respective provinces, the North Western Provinces in the case of Sir William Muir, the Punjab in that of Sir Henry Durand. The latter had a very short time previously been appointed to the lieutenant governorship, and his career had been so marked by honest speech, as well as by meritorious action, that his appointment was generally spoken of as an honour at once to an able soldier and administrator, and to the Governor General who had appointed him. I never saw Sir Henry Durand, but he had contributed to the journal I edited (a fact made public at his death), and while on this tour he sent me two articles entitled, "The Life of a Soldier of Adventure of the Old Time." It was the story of Colonel Gardiner, an American of Scotch and Irish parentage, who, after long journeyings in the East, from 1813 to 1819, at length made his way through Persia to Cabul, and secured the friendship of certain able foreign officers, Allard and Avitabile among others, who so materially influenced the fate of Dost Mohammed and Runjeet Singh. By the aid of these men Gardiner was made chief of artillery to the Maharajah of Cashmere, and in Cashmere he very recently lived.

The daring adventures of this really remarkable soldier seemed to have an especial charm for Sir Henry Durand; and if the opportunities for work had not suddenly been cut off, there can hardly be a doubt that the literary treasures of the Punjab would, in such hands, have afforded material for throwing light upon some other strange careers; such, for instance, as that of Avitabile, of whom old Anglo-Indians with experience of the North West never tire of talking, but of whom also the mass of even well-read Englishmen know nothing.[1]

On Saturday evening, the last day of 1870, Sir Henry was entering Tonk, a town near to Dera Ismail Khan, on the extreme frontier of the Punjab. His, of course, was the loftiest elephant and the tallest howdah of the procession, and the ruler of Tonk sat by his side. On approaching the gateway the elephant was driven more rapidly, and the howdah and its occupants were thrown to the ground. The seat had been higher than the gateway. The chief escaped. The lieutenant governor was lifted from the ground insensible. On Sunday morning he recovered consciousness. On Sunday evening he was no more. He was buried at Dera Ismail Khan, and was mourned by a large number of people as men mourn for a friend. Many years previously he and another warrior of a different stamp, Dr Duff, had made their first voyage to India together, and whether it was from the influence of that voyage or not I cannot say, but Sir Henry Durand was noted throughout his life as a God-fearing man of the grave and not ostentatious kind. From the time when in 1839 he carried the powder-bag to the Cabul gate at Ghuznee, scraping the hose with his finger-nail to ignite the powder, till he left the Governor General's Council for the lieutenant governorship of the Punjab, his name had stood exceptionally high. As Resident in the court of Scindia, he had learned the intricacies of the Mahratta politics. As Resident at Indore in 1857, he committed the serious error

[1] Appendix IV.

of deeming Holkar disloyal—an error which led to great loss of life. Yet throughout all, and in spite of a pen and tongue which knew no compromise of principle, his ability and courage were his passport to confidence. The life of India, however, does not admit of long seasons of mourning, and in a few days the subject seemed to pass away. Mr Davis, chief commissioner of Oude, succeeded to the Punjab, and General Barlow to Oude. The sea of passing events went on as before.

Sir William Muir was unlike Sir Henry Durand in much, but like him in a sense of duty, and in a belief, not a convenient figment, that God really did make of one blood all the nations of men, Hindoo as well as Englishman. Sir Henry would probably, apart from military affairs, have been noted chiefly for his stern justice to the people of India. Sir William Muir was noted as their helper, their counsellor, and friend. In season and out of season, in kind and conciliatory speeches, he attacked the people of the North Western Provinces on such all-important subjects as education, marriage expenses, and infanticide; and his words remain like dew in a parched land. Infanticide, some people suppose, has gone, like Suttee and Thuggee; but the supposition is an error. As late as 1868 the secretary to the Government of the North Western Provinces said: "Investigation affords sufficient evidence that since the inquiry made in 1856, there has been no perceptible change in the barbarous tendencies towards infanticide which stigmatise certain branches of the Rajpoot family. The crime indeed is shown to be so prevalent in some villages as to leave no doubt that wholesale murder is perpetrated of every female born into the world." Mr Hobart, joint-magistrate of Bustee, wrote: "I believe that the returns of certainly 180 of the 216 villages visited are as correct, with regard to numbers and age, as they possibly can be. . . . Nearly all spoke of the crime as one of the past. I regret that I cannot think the crime obsolete or even diminished. It is practised with greater secrecy perhaps, but it is certainly most extensively practised. . . . The Soorujbunses of the Bharut Dwaj clan are the highest caste of Rajpoots in the district, and are the most addicted to infanticide. The Baboos of Bhudawur Kalan live in ten villages, in seven of which I found 104 boys and one girl, who, luckily for herself, was born and bred at the house of her mother's family, and who has not been permitted to come to her father's house. Their other villages are said to contain two girls. They admit that for ten years there has been but one girl married in all those villages. Next come the Baboos of Nagpore, who live in twenty-seven villages. In fifteen of the villages no marriage of a girl has taken place for a decade. In their three remaining villages there would appear to be three girls. The Baboos of Asogpoor preserve their old reputation. They have twenty boys and no girl, and no girl has ever been married from among them, or known in their village."

To this dreadful state of things Sir William Muir directed almost unremitting attention. In a beautiful spirit he implored the people to reduce their ruinous marriage expenses, to educate their children, and to lead upright lives. How beneficent the influence was, and how great the power for good or evil of an Indian governor is, may be judged from the fact that the Government of Bombay about the same time actually laid a graduated tax on marriages in lieu of one previously proposed on native feasts. Of course a tax on marriages, dividing the marriages into classes, graduating according to the tax paid, could not fail to bring revenue to the Government in exactly the proportion that it brought ruin to the people. At a time when the Brahmists were nobly striving to promote widow marriages, and men like Sir William Muir were labouring to induce a curtailment of expenses, this absurd and baneful proposal was put forth. I believe it was given up, but I am not quite sure. To Sir William Muir's minute on the outbreak in Bareilly gaol reference has previously been made. To his administration generally a long chapter might easily be devoted. Among other parting words to his officers when leaving India in 1874, he said: "He trusted his young friends especially would excuse him if he urged upon them to cultivate sympathy with the natives of the country, to understand and feel with them in their trials, their joys, their griefs, and to understand and bear with them even in their prejudices, and it might be their superstitions. Indeed this was essential if we were to fulfil the golden law of doing to others as we would that they should do to us. The natives of India were, he well knew, susceptible of kind and grateful feelings towards those who thus felt with and loved them; and, indeed, if we were not to make this our object, he did not see what good our coming to the country was at all. He trusted his young friends would bear with him in these observations, the result of a long and careful study of the people and our treatment of them." In all this the reader will see a man who had framed his policy on models which only obtain respect where the aim is pure and single. I am writing from public records purely; I never saw Sir William Muir.

The next lieutenant governor was Sir John Strachey, now Finance Minister. Of his statesmanship there are various opinions. Some speak of him as one of the ablest men in India; some say that in ability and strength of character he overtops all his fellows; some maintain that he has been the evil genius of the Indian Government in his time. That he has acquired a character for cynicism is undoubted, but there are instances in which it has been a courageous cynicism, raising him above the meanness of pandering to sentiments popular with bodies of men wielding great influence. If, for instance, any religious society invited Sir John Strachey to take the chair at one of its meetings, it would do so with the full consciousness that his sympathies were not with the objects of the meeting, and that he had no wish to be differently considered. I have heard people say,

"He has always some plot in his head," and I have heard others ask in reply, "Well, what plot can you give us as as instance?" a question I never heard answered with the "instance." That he was the moving spirit in much that was done by Lord Mayo's Government, every one knows who knows aught of that Government; and there certainly are unmistakable instances in which, when the work was done, he stood aside—cynically it may be—and cared nothing for the credit or applause. When he succeeded Sir Richard Temple as Commissioner of the Central Provinces, his eulogy of Sir Richard's administration was as hearty and generous as it was simple and manly. It was either the testimony of a man who knew that if he lived he would have no need to borrow any one's laurels, or of a man who despised the laurels so long as he possessed the power.

In the Council Chamber he had the air of a man who was content to be unobserved, but who knew that he was not unobserved, especially when, with his head inclined to one shoulder, he glanced sidewise, and with a comical expression of face, at some speaker of more than ordinary fervour, and appeared by his look to say, "Don't you know now that all this is sad fustian?" When Lord Mayo was murdered, Sir John Strachey became Governor General, pending the arrival of Lord Napier and Ettrick, and people knew that a strong hand held the helm. When he succeeded Sir William Muir in 1874, one of his first acts was to visit the "Famine Districts"—the parts of his province adjoining Bengal—and after a personal inquiry to close the famine works. He could, he said, meet every requirement of the province by ordinary means. This step was taken at the very time that Sir Richard Temple was preparing for a second year's famine, and when England had insisted that no lives should be lost. How far it was the right step cannot easily be determined; but it shows the will of the man. That he cares much for the people of the country I would scarcely suppose. If they asked for education, I think he would give the education, as he would give justice in a law-court, simply because it was the proper course in sound administration, not from any other motive. In extreme danger he would be one of a few men in India who could not be overlooked. In ordinary times he is a man who may be of real service to India and England, especially if India can learn to trust him, and to comprehend his proud if not perverse individuality; and if he, on his part, can convince people that he has some abiding principle, and does not act merely with regard to the exigency of the hour. That is, he is one of the foremost of administrators. He might, however, if he pleased, be also a notable statesman. An administrator may attain high place without rising above an exact performance of passing duties. Sir John Strachey aims higher. He would impress his character on his time. To achieve the higher success he only lacks—if he does lack—sympathy. I see no proof that he esteems that essential element of high statesmanship at its true value.

Of the North Western Provinces generally it may be said that they were formed into a separate presidency by an Act of 1833, during the government of Lord William Bentinck, and that their first ruler was Sir Charles Metcalfe, who, a little later, as provisional Governor General, did India the great service of setting the press free. The Punjab was annexed in 1849, after the series of fierce battles which ended with Gujerat; a war in reality—that is, a standing state of war, with only intervals of peace—continued from the time of Lord Auckland's fatal expedition to Cabul till the Maharajah Duleep Singh sat for the last time on the throne of the Lion of Lahore, when the Kingdom of the Five Rivers became part of the dominions of England. Our enemies for so many years, the men of the Punjab became our firm allies, and assisted to save the empire in 1857. In this annexation at any rate Lord Dalhousie will be more than justified by history.

There is a fact, or at least a substantial belief, which

may properly be mentioned here with reference to the Sikhs. It is said that after the Mutiny a very little encouragement by England would have gone far to induce a profession of Christianity on the part of the Sikh troops, if not of the bulk of the Sikh race, and that the encouragement was withheld. The only idea of the Sikhs was that the Cross was in the ascendant; but the same idea had often before been the only one in cases where whole nations had been brought under the influence of at least Christian teaching. What might have been the result if a professedly Christian nation had been established in the Punjab? It were to little purpose to say that such a conversion would have been worthless in a religious sense, for many "conversions" at present are of no greater value to man or more reverential to the Almighty. The political motive in favour of the encouragement being given would have been the increase of strength that would have accrued to a professedly Christian government. The motives against it were probably of a mixed character. Some men would, rightly and honourably, stand on the principle that mass conversions belong to days which can never return; but there must have been others who would perceive that an army of professedly Christian Sikhs would mean an entirely new relation of rulers and ruled. That would be the low and ignoble reason for the refusal; but whatever the reason, we escaped the experiment in these times of a renewal of an old-world practice. That the East India Company (which, after all, was England) was wise in discountenancing proselytism, I take to be a clear historical fact; but there was no merit in what simply indicated that trade, and not empire, was our object in India. Mention of the higher object of doing good to the people may be set aside as not merely a fallacy, but an absurdity. No such motive contributed anything worth speaking of to the warp or woof of the policy of the East India Company.

CHAPTER XI.

CALCUTTA—ENGLISH AND NATIVE LIFE—HINDOO READINGS—HOSPITALS AND ASYLUMS—SEWAGE AND WATER WORKS—THE MINT—SURVEY DEPARTMENT—CHEENEE BAZAAR—COOLIE EMIGRATION—AN EX-KING.

It was on the low land—the swamps—of Lower Bengal that the English in India first laid deeply the foundations of Empire. Madras and Bombay were powerful factories, with a great array of mighty deeds in arms, but imperial power sprung from Fort William. The dark year 1756, the year of the Black Hole, was nearly at an end when Clive reached the Hooghly. He had not made his way from the south without losses; but already his name was one to conjure by in war; and when he advanced from Hooghly to Fort William the history of Calcutta as the capital of India began. Suraj-ud-Dowlah and a great force had retreated to Moorshedabad; the French, against whom war had been declared, held Chandernagore. Before the end of June 1757 Clive had captured Chandernagore and won Plassey. The site of the Black Hole has now to be sought for, with special information, on open ground. Fort William is its own mark, and one of the first objects that attracts the attention of a stranger in Calcutta. It has no grand elevation like Gwalior, or even like Agra or Delhi; but the low-lying ramparts, and the heavy guns, pointing at once to city and river, and commanding a great plain on the side nearest the sea, tells its story of present power and resolution.

On the river the visitor will find vessels of all nations;

ashore, in truth, a "city of palaces"—flat-topped palaces, with broad verandahs, and imposing carriage drives, and durwans (porters) at the gates, to prevent any one passing inward till sahib has received the warning of the durwan's bell. Missionary, soldier, civil officer, merchant, or what not, sahib has his durwan and his bell. If you call at six or seven o'clock in the morning you will find sahib and mem sahib (his wife) at their little breakfast (chotee hazree) —a cup of tea with a biscuit, or some "trifle"—sahib and mem sahib in comfortably light attire, enjoying the blessed cool air. Punkah-men will be behind, waving their great hand-fans; or on the verandah, pulling those larger fans which take in the width of the room. Mohammedan table servants, and Hindoo bedroom servants, and low-caste sweepers, will be busy within, while the mallies (gardeners) adorn the rooms with freshly-cut and well-selected flowers. If you call at nine you will find sahib and mem sahib at their large breakfast (their burree hazree) of mutton, fowl, fried potatoes, curry of various dishes, beer, wines—everything the reader can conceive as belonging to a very "big breakfast." Meanwhile sahib and mem sahib, to the never-ceasing wonder of their servants, have probably had poojah (prayers). Then sahib will go to his daily duties, part of which he may have done at his little breakfast, and mem sahib will look to her he-dressmaker, or her bazaar book, or the pedlars ("wallahs") who are waiting to fight her a glorious battle of barter, even to the half of a farthing—a fight which mem sahib often enjoys as a foretaste of heaven.

If you seek sahib at his office a little after mid-day, he will ask you to tiffen (which means lunch), and you may dine on meat and potatoes, with beer, salads, and so on. In the evening, while the sun is still above the horizon, you will find sahib and mem sahib driving leisurely in front of the beautiful Eden Gardens, and listening to the music of a regimental band. As the sun begins to approach the regions of night, sahib and mem sahib drive home, to the supreme event of the day—to Dinner. Then it is that you should see sahib and mem sahib—presiding over endless courses, endless bottles of champagne and beer — mem sahib in fashionable attire, sahib in his swallow-tailed coat; a scene, one regrets to think, such as the Queen never saw, and cannot well imagine.

Outside you will find the Hindoo and Mohammedan on their way to the bazaar, or to their bamboo huts, to smoke and tell stories; or to their theatres, or to hear some reading; or to fly kites, and fight them in the air. I was present at one reading of the Ramayana, provided by a public-spirited landowner for the late Bishop Milman. The reading was given a few miles from Calcutta, in a Free Library, founded and maintained by the landowner. The books were on all manner of subjects, from Newton's "Principia" to the latest novel. I asked the son of the proprietor which class of books—the religious, the historical, or the scientific—was most sought after. His eyes twinkled with real fun as he replied: "None of them—the novels." The reader of the Ramayana was a fat, and I hope it is not disrespectful to say, a rather ugly man, with a ludicrous sense of dignity; but his gesture and intonation were perfect, and charming even to one who did not know the language. He was listened to with lively interest by a great crowd of all classes of persons, admitted without any payment, and whose alternate laughter and sighs marked the stages in the story of the joys and sorrows of the great Rama. The reader or reciter, I was told, earned £1200 a year. Readings by less notable artists are a feature of everyday life.

Not far from the European residences are the native hospitals and asylums, representing human misery at its worst, and human kindness at its noblest. I visited every hospital in Calcutta. The Lock Hospital—with its long lines of open sheds, and its child-mothers of suffering infants—was inexpressibly painful to look into, yet very cheering in the relief it afforded to fearful suffering. The laws so much opposed in England with reference to misguided women are in force here, and in spite of a thousand difficulties, had, I was told, done immense good. The Native Lunatic Asylum, under the same superintendence—Dr Payne's—stands in the midst of beautifully laid-out grounds, cultured and tended by an army of lunatic gardeners. A system of irrigation, magnificent flower-beds, well-kept walks, artists in painting and sculpture, builders, and workers in cloth and jute, were among the features of this refuge for persons suffering from the most hopeless of all maladies, and, next to those of the Lock Hospital, the most distressing.

On the opposite side of the river, at Howrah, is the European (one may say, the Sailors') Hospital. On verandahs, or rooms, open to the river, I found forty-three sailors and railway men, as comfortable as sick men can be under such a sun. In the cemetery I sought out a young sailor's grave, and engaged a poor native gardener to plant some flowers upon it. I am relating the facts, because they are significant. The work was done, and when I finally left Calcutta I again saw the man, and telling him that we should never meet again, I gave him a small sum of money. "*I* look to it, sahib," he said; and he did. Two years later I found that the flowers had been as carefully trimmed and watered as if I had been there all the time. I wonder if I should have found equally honourable conduct in a like case in England.

The water works and drainage of Calcutta are among the most important achievements of any land. The engineer, Mr Clarke, found along the sides of the houses open drains and no side paths; a great difficulty as to where the sewage could be taken to, and a supreme question of all whether the Hindoos could, without breaking caste, drink water that had come through infidel pipes. He had zealous help, Native and European, and the difficulties were removed. The water works, with a system of filters, to make the Ganges water pure, were of themselves an immense undertaking. For the sewage a piece of land, a considerable distance from the city, and called the Salt Water Lake (a swamp of large extent), was taken up. The sewage, carried through close drains this long distance, was at different stages poured into vast quantities of water, and mixed therewith by machinery, till at last it appeared at the outlet at least as clear as the water of the Ganges, and devoid of smell. It was then left to harden on the lands. This, in a hot climate, was a real victory, and it became a feature of daily life. In the same way the open drains—"institutions of our forefathers," like stage-coaches—were covered in, and side paths made. Altogether it was a work of great utility, accomplished in the face of enormous difficulties.

Near to the Salt Water Lake the municipality had provided a grand dining-place for birds of prey—one class of the scavengers of India. Here the carcases of Calcutta's old horses are thrown out, amid a war-whoop which a Red Indian in his best days might have envied. I saw three or four carcases arrive, amid the mighty rejoicings of the vultures and birds of many names, which fought like paladins for their places at the feast. The carcases certainly would not remain to become putrid. What the birds left by day the jackals would appropriate by night, and there would be little but bones in the morning. What a field India affords to the naturalist! A bird of prey coolly taking possession of a pretty paroquet, carrying it to the top of a mahogany tree, and holding it in one claw while plucking it alive, is a dismal sight, rendered more dismal by the impassive face of the destroyer, and the plaintive cries of the victim. A cloud, of myriads upon myriads of white ants, rising from the ground at eventide, unwittingly to afford sport and food to a lesser but still numerous cloud of birds, ever increasing in number as the joyful announcement of the treasure-trove goes abroad, the mighty swoop of the large birds, and the finer curves of the smaller ones, are really beautiful. There is also the one comfort in this case, that a very useful work is being done, for every ant that escapes and falls wingless to the ground is an element of destruction in an Indian house. In all nature, indeed, the riches of India can only be conceived when seen. Some of those riches especially with reference to vegetation we shall see later; but no pen can depict the real fact.

If we pass to the Mint of Calcutta we may find a great historical institution, with important historical lessons. We realise the fact that the coinage of India is silver at its highest, with copper, or bronze, supplemented by cowries (shells, so many of which go for a small coin); that in this land of once fabled wealth it has been found impossible to maintain a gold currency. The mint, when I saw it, had a European head in Colonel Hyde, but next to him was a Hindoo. Nearly all the labour was done cleverly and expertly by native hands—a fact which will be partly understood when it is added that, in one day during the Bengal famine, a million copper coins were struck. Much might be said of the way in which the mint supplies the Government treasure-chests throughout immense districts; of its relation, past and present, to all the operations, military and commercial, great and small, of Anglo-Indian history. It is impossible, too, to look into any one of several rooms—for instance, the engraving room—without perceiving that the mint is educational. A number of the bright-eyed nimble-fingered boys of Bengal are there, as busy as bees, etching and drawing with a cheerfulness as of play, and an intentness as of the labour of matured workmen.

Another marvellously suggestive scene is presented in the great Survey Department, presided over by Colonel Thuillier. I use the term great here in the strict and not in any conventional sense. It is a mighty department, engaged in the scientific conquest of all India. My notes of the surveys might fill a chapter of this book, and still leave facts of great value untold. First, the department undertakes a Trigonometrical Survey of all India; secondly, a Topographical Survey on the trigonometrical basis;

thirdly, a Revenue Survey. In the first case latitude and longitude, heights above the sea, etc., are marked; in the second, the conformation of the country; in the last, villages, parishes, and boundaries. Each department requires different men and a different equipment, and the operations extend to the coldest and wettest, the hottest and driest, the lowest and highest parts of India. Where fever is rank, or life least secure because of savage populations, there the officers of the survey department—men delicately nurtured it may be, and in all cases highly educated—sit down, in isolation from all European society, to do work to which the whole world will be indebted, but which only a small part of the world recognises at its true value. One skilful officer had charge of the lithographs and photography. Two officers at the time I saw the department (divided into five parts, in as many different streets, of Calcutta) had just returned from the two columns of the Looshai expedition, lamenting as a calamity, a blank in their surveys, from the fact that the two columns never had come together. During the year there had been surveyed for the revenue more than 6000 miles in Lower Bengal, nearly 6000 in the Central Provinces, and lesser extents in the Punjab, the North Western Provinces, and Oude.

Turn from this to the view of native life presented in the "Cheenee (China) Bazaar." The bazaar is not in one sense so interesting as some in India, because not so characteristic of any special race, but it is indeed a marvel of life and industry. The moment you enter the first long narrow street you are surrounded by a race of the best and worst touters in the whole world. If you close your carriage door they politely open it and laugh defiantly in your face as they ask, "Does sahib want" this or that, in an endless string of unceasing chatter. The dignified Hindoo shopman sits at his door smoking or gossiping. The stolid Chinaman does likewise, and perhaps convinces you or mem sahib in a very dignified way that he has "only one price"—a very parade of defiant stolidity. Beyond question he is king of the bazaar that bears his name, and in which, eschewing all unnecessary talk, he goes on to comfort if not to fortune. Go where you may, indeed, John Chinaman is the same. Even in gaol he makes it worth people's while to give him light work, which he does well. On the deck of a Peninsular and Oriental steamer he heaves the lead without looking to right or left, though the prettiest of ladies and the most playful of children may be laughing, dancing, playing at his side. In the bazaar he is master or nothing—a master shoemaker generally. You are cheated in the Cheenee Bazaar at every turn. Sometimes you are vexed; yet you return; this time, however, you say, "only to see the variety of life," yet you are cheated again. Handicraft from all parts of India, Japan ware and Indian shawls made in England, books of all kinds, good and bad, in all languages, articles of which the seller can only guess the use, and often guesses ludicrously. You are recommended to buy the Bible as "a very good book, sahib," and Paine's "Age of Reason" also as a very good book, sahib. The bookseller is of the Universal Church. You may perceive also, I think, even here, that the Bengalee is the brain of India; the Parsee is hardly native to India in the sense of influencing its thoughts and views. The merchant asks his confidential clerk of this bazaar as of others, "What are the rumours to-day?" and he attaches importance to the reports.

A short drive further down the river would bring you to the West Indian coolie emigration depôts. I paid particular attention to these places for several reasons, and I think I may say I examined the subject from all points of view. Some very serious questions are involved. Are the coolies taken away to virtual slavery? Are the provisions for the voyage carelessly made? Do the people come back to India better or worse, if they come back at all? I noticed chiefly the depôts of Trinidad and Jamaica, and the former especially. The agent, Mr Mitchell, an able man, was sent from the colony to Calcutta to provide labour for

Trinidad on certain conditions, for which the Indian Government stipulates. First, the utmost care must be taken not to engage any coolie of whose freedom of will there is the slightest doubt. For this some stringent provisions have been made. Brought to Calcutta, the coolies must be lodged in comfortable quarters, provided with medicine and surgeons, food, and tanks for bathing. The ship also must be rigorously inspected. If the orders are adhered to, it is hard to see in what respect a coolie emigrant differs from an emigrant from England. If the orders are disobeyed, it can only be by running several very hazardous gauntlets, which are guarded by magistrates, doctors, and inspectors, with the very reliable security behind all, that if a man dies on the voyage the colony loses his value.

The depôts I visited were formed, in very pretty rural places, of several long lines of sheds for beds, living, and cooking. I saw a large party ready to embark, timid, restless, doubtful, half afraid to speak. I saw groups from other parties newly returned and waiting for transit to their up-country homes, different beings in every respect; many bringing home considerable wealth in money and ornaments; all possessed of some wealth. Men and women alike (for the women are protected in their earnings), they had the independent air of people who had seen the world. Many who had gone out poor had risen to be planters and store-keepers on a large scale. They had grown too into the knowledge and the possession of rights. Many, of course, had died; many more had suffered; but I thought I could see a clear gain in the proper application of the principle of coolie emigration. There is an improper application. Wherever such a principle is left in the hands of men to develop, there will be loop-holes for cruelty and oppression; and rigorous checks are needed. The first experience of the sea also must be dreadful to an inland people. But so would it be to the people who went out to New England in the "Mayflower." I may be wrong, but from all I saw, I came to the conclusion that coolie emigration, though but a subsidiary, is an important factor in the material education of India in these times.

Close to these depôts stands that great institution of India, the domain of the ex-King of Oude. When the dominions of the king were transferred to the British Government, he was granted from the revenues of his kingdom a large pension, and was allowed to make for himself a little walled town on the banks of the Hooghly. The "Resident" at his court in 1874 was Colonel Mowbray Thompson, who kindly went with me over the little "kingdom." Without much trouble, it was quite possible to see how the ex-king could spend his allowance of £10,000 a month, and an additional sum which he receives as rent from a bazaar outside, and still run into debt. He had 6000 subjects who would have fought at his orders; but only fifty, I believe, armed; a court with all the gradations of rank, as in Oude; two married wives; thirty-nine unmarried wives, called Mahuls—bearers of children—and a hundred others, called Begums, who were presumed, it was said, not to bear children. These, however, are of the mysteries of the ex-king's court. He had living a family of thirty-one sons and twenty-five daughters. He had three or four palaces, in which he spent his days and nights alternately, or at choice; and amid and around all was a menagerie said to be among the finest in the world. The reader may judge. There were 20,000 birds, beasts, and snakes—some in cages, some walking, some flying—in all manner of creeks and crevices and leafy bowers, around a tank or lake 300 feet long by 240 wide, and alive with every kind of fish that money could procure or art tempt to live on the banks of the Hooghly; 18,000 choice pigeons (the king's especial favourites, or dividing that honour with the snakes); pelicans and ostriches; swans, geese, and birds of many names, intermingled with dromedaries, ibis, sheep, and goats of a vast number of breeds. All these, amid the fine foliage and highly-cultivated grounds, formed a remarkable and beautiful scene.

Then there were the snakes, the ordinary kinds possessing to themselves a mountain, in shape like a dome, about thirty feet high, and perforated from top to bottom with holes, the snake retreats; the extraordinary ones—the cobras—kept safely indoors, to be produced when required. The possessors of the mountain, fed with frogs and other delicacies, prowled about, curled themselves up, basked in the sun, or retreated into the shade at will, subject only, like their master, to the law that they must keep within certain bounds, in their case represented by a small trench of water. The cobras, brought out and handled by a short grim man (hereditary to snakes), could hardly, perhaps, be matched for size and the appearance of deadly power. The servants gathered eagerly around to see the grim man wait his turn, and then seize upon cobra after cobra, as in fierce play. This is one of the king's great amusements. Some years ago his Majesty had a sore and touching trial. Several thousands of snakes on their way to his little kingdom were seized as dangerous by order of the British Government. Then the ex-king paints, writes songs which are sung by nautch-girls all over India; has dancing-girls and musicians for each passing day; and, when the doors of his kingdom are closed at night, is beyond all dispute a monarch. His grounds employed three hundred gardeners. His menagerie cost for food £500 a month. What his ladies—wives, mahuls, begums, and others—cost, it would be highly improper even to surmise. I have ventured to tell this story as illustrative of a phase of Anglo-Indian and Indian history, with which subsequent chapters will be concerned.

A drive back along the river's bank, past Fort William, would bring us to the shops and hotels around Government House. A Calcutta hotel and a Calcutta lodging-house are pretty much alike, so far as sleeping-rooms are concerned; the rooms, like cells, ranged on both sides of long corridors, in the case of the hotel, and of shorter ones in that of the lodging-house. One notable Calcutta hotel, however, is a perfect compendium of everything to eat, drink, wear, read, or otherwise enjoy. The "table" is supplied from the Company's own farm; below stairs, in rooms from the main shop or store, are iced drinks and lunches ready all the day through. Here Englishmen meet with friends from all parts of India; the fresh arrival, the homeward-bound man, the hale and hearty, and the weak and infirm. For an hour or so before breakfast the corridors, the news-room, and the billiard-room are crowded. Breakfast and dinner are laid out on a grand scale. Indeed, if a man is well, and can laugh and talk, and brook a fair share of rubbish in conversation, and has time to throw away, he may enjoy an Indian hotel. If he is sick, and at the same time is bound to work, he will be likely to pray God to take away all the attractions of table and amusements, and give him, in their place, a humble cottage and simple fare, and the kind hearts of the untravelled simple people at home. To a person broken down in health, the sights and sounds of an Indian hotel are inexpressibly melancholy. In this, however, human life is much the same in all lands.

Of the burning ghât, where perhaps a dozen bodies, of old and young, may be seen at one time slowly consuming on the funeral pyre, a ghastly story might be told. To the life and trade on the river I shall refer later. Of the cordial feeling, the earnest work, the oftentimes curious drift of opinion (soured perhaps by disappointment, or sweetened by success), one might write at great length. The Government Offices even might convey a story not without significance. Much, however, that these names may indicate, we shall see in another form.

CHAPTER XII.

THE GOVERNOR GENERAL'S COUNCIL—FINANCE AND LAW REFORM.

The Imperial Council of India, when in Calcutta, sits at Government House, with a drawing-room for Council Chamber, and dead statesmen—Marquis Wellesley, Eyre Coote, and others—looking down upon the councillors from the silent canvas. When I saw Lord Mayo in 1870 he sat at the middle of a long table, with men like Lord Napier of Magdala, Major General Norman, Sir James Stephen (not yet Sir James), Sir Richard Temple, and Sir John Strachey, around him—military and legal members; Foreign Secretary, Lieutenant Governor of Bengal, commercial members, members for the provinces, and others.

The "sitting of the Council" was correctly designated. Sir Richard Temple, with a whole community to confront on the income tax, and Mr Stephen, with new principles of law to expound, were bound to speak sitting. It was not always so. People remembered and told of a time when men rose to their feet, and raised their hands, as Fox raised his to denounce Pitt, and pointed their fingers, as Pitt pointed his in reply. The Council, it is said, was fast becoming "popular," when a heaven-born genius suggested the idea of sitting, and embodied the idea in what became known as "a bill to extinguish Sir Barnes Peacock." From that time all was decorum. In the first Council held in Calcutta in the cold season of 1870, the members met silently, as in a meeting of Quakers, looking at each other and at the Viceroy, while the punkahs moved solemnly overhead, and a few birds, flitting backward and forward, bore witness, in that dull solemn room, for life and freedom.

About two hundred persons were present when Sir Richard Temple's "Exposition," as it was called, of Finance was read; and among them was Mr Seward, then on his way through India—a bright-eyed white-haired genial old man, still suffering from the felon blow inflicted on him when President Lincoln was murdered. He had in his day listened to Mr Sumner and Mr Wendell Phillips in America. He had now the privilege of listening to Sir Richard Temple in India.

The main feature of the Budget was what was called the Decentralisation of Finance. That is, the Imperial Government had determined, under certain restrictions, to hand over to the Provincial Governments duties represented by the terms gaols, registration, police, education, medical services, printing, roads, miscellaneous public improvements, and civil buildings; and to make to each government an assignment of money for the purpose. The local governments were also to find for themselves the best modes of taxation suited to each particular province. The idea of separating the local and general accounts was an old one, which Colonel Chesney had enunciated, among many more masterly thoughts which have not been associated with his name. To Lord Mayo simply belongs the honour of giving the idea practical effect, and to Sir Richard Temple must in common fairness be ascribed many of the carefully arranged details. The Governor General stated the policy in these terms:

"The local governments are deeply interested in the welfare of the people confided to their care; and, not knowing the requirements of other parts of the country or of the empire as a whole, they are liable, in their anxiety for administrative progress, to allow too little weight to fiscal considerations. On the other hand, the Supreme Government, as responsible for the general financial safety, is obliged to reject many demands in themselves deserving of encouragement, and is not always able to distribute satisfactorily the resources actually available."

This statement embodies the gist of the scheme, and of the grounds on which it rested. The total amount set apart for the Provincial Governments was £4,688,711, or about £330,800 less than the expenditure for the same purposes in some previous years, on the data of which the assignments were made to Oude, the Central Provinces, Burma, Bengal, the North Western Provinces, the Punjab, Madras, and Bombay. I omit the figures as not likely to have any definite meaning to the general reader. The principle involved that the government of each province was better able to adjust its own taxes and expenditure than the Imperial Government was to make that adjustment, requires no interpreter. Of the army Major General Norman, after referring to certain reductions and some unexpected charges, said: "I am decidedly of opinion that we have now reduced our European force to the very lowest safe strength." Lord Napier of Magdala had previously made a similar statement, with some additional serious and pregnant words.

For the principle of the income tax Sir Richard Temple fought hard, and defied his critics of all orders and names. They had, he said, written and spoken to a great if not an unwarrantable extent, but all that they had advanced was defeated by one fact. The Government had sent out a circular to the Local Governments, requesting them to return lists of all known cases of oppression under the income tax, and—would the Council believe it?—the only affirmative answer was from the Government of Bengal, and with that only thirteen cases had been returned. Lord Mayo turned curiously in his chair and laughed—a low merry laugh, almost, it now seems, like that of a boy at play—while his finance minister was, in this way, defending the policy of a tax the doom of which was fixed. In the end the tax was reduced from $3\frac{1}{8}$ to 1 per cent., and the income on which it was levied was raised in amount. In that form it was passed for one year "for investigation." There was no doubt, however, that Lord Mayo intended to entirely blot the tax out, as it was blotted out by Lord Northbrook. Long before the end of the year well authenticated instances of terrible oppression by income tax collectors were made public. Mr Inglis, senior member of the Board of Revenue, North Western Provinces, said:

> "It might be true that only a certain number of persons paid the tax, but a large number more were subjected to the most vexatious oppression, inquisition, and extortion, . . . and many had to pay to keep their names out of the lists." And again: "I believe it is no exaggeration to say that for every man who pays income tax to the Government, twenty pay to get off, . . . that is, that the natives of India paid last year upwards of two millions sterling as income tax to the Government, and two millions more as bribes. Everywhere through the country the people are being demoralised by the tax, everywhere the trading classes are beginning to keep two sets of books, one showing the real transactions, the other containing a carefully garbled account to be shown to the income tax assessors."

Sir Richard Temple and the gentlemen of his department were startled. The thirteen cases of oppression under the income tax were held up by the newspapers to public reprobation and derision. The Government of the Provinces was then appealed to against Mr Inglis; but Sir William Muir's reply was a calm confirmation rather than a disavowal, and his opinion was also supported by a host of instances, some of which, by the strength of the language in which they were couched, went further even than the statements of Mr Inglis. The question had been removed altogether from the domain of argument to that of examples, and the examples abounded. Poor men, it was shown, had been compelled to walk many miles to appeal against an unjust rendering of their income, and then had found their efforts thwarted by some man whom they had refused to bribe. Facts upon facts, clear, irresistible, damning to the income tax policy, were made public. To Sir Richard Temple's honour, it must be said, however (and I write here from knowledge), that though he fought bitterly for his policy, and accepted all the opprobrium, which of right he only ought to have shared, when the decision had been come to he cheerfully accepted the inevitable, and did not carry the recollection of his personal opponents (as opponents) a step further.

Lord Mayo had then, as he said, put an end to deficits. He had husbanded his resources like a miser. His oversight of public works never had ceased; and now, when he had looked for a deficit, he had in 1869-70 (Sir Richard Temple admitted, however, from a series of accidents) a surplus of £180,600, and in 1870-71 an estimated surplus of £1,569,315. This was a triumph, but with a drawback. The increase was chiefly in opium revenue, which had been estimated at not quite seven millions sterling, and had produced close upon eight. Instead of £97, 10s. per chest, as estimated, the price, owing chiefly to a failure of the crop in China, had been £112, 3s. per chest; besides which there had been 38,740 chests of Malwa opium, instead of only 33,600 as estimated. Surplus or deficit therefore depended on opium, which might any year fail. In military expenditure there had been slight reductions owing to exceptional causes, but with the ominous words of Lord Napier and Sir Henry Norman on record, no one would talk of permanent reductions in the army. The main issue, however, was in the fact, that a failure of opium might overturn everything. What remained? Customs, Excise —everything in fact known as taxation—seemed marked as inelastic. That they are so I do not believe. I feel assured that men like Sir Mahdava Rao, whose great deeds in Travancore I shall show hereafter, and Sir Dinkur Rao, to whose masterly administration reference has already been made, could instruct us how, at the same time, to make taxes lighter and revenue greater. We refuse the services of such men. And at present the revenue is essentially a fixed quantity.

Taking one year with another, at this date the revenue may be stated at, say £50,000,000, and the expenditure at a little less. The great items in the receipts are Land Revenue (from twenty to twenty-one millions sterling), Opium (seven millions), and Salt (close upon six millions). Excise, Customs, Stamps, Post Office, etc., represent smaller but important sums, ranging downward from about three millions in the case of the customs. On the other side there is interest on debt (say five millions), law and justice and police (together say from five to six millions), and finally (omitting other amounts, including a large sum for public works) the army, £16,000,000; an item which, as we have seen, the commander-in-chief and the military member of Council decided must be accepted without question, unless some one could at less cost maintain the same efficient army.

One of the special facts of the Budget was the loss on exchange and the position in the money-market of the India Bills. The Secretary of State had drawn on India for £9,000,000, on which £600,000 had been lost by exchange; about a half more than the estimate, the rupee selling at only 1s. 10½d. instead of 1s. 11½d. as expected; and at last the bills having become unsaleable, the specie itself had been shipped to England, at a loss on the shipment of £620,000, amounting to as much as twopence on the rupee; the total shipment was reduced to £571,812. In all, India does not pay less yearly to England in various ways than fifteen or sixteen millions sterling for home charges. The cash balances of the Indian Government—that is, the amounts in the various treasure chests in Calcutta and the Provinces as working capital, "cash on hand"—was stated at £16,000,000.

Reading the story of these Budgets calmly and dispassionately, is it possible to doubt, not merely that the finance of India is not cheering, for on that all are agreed, but that its evils rest on known if not removable causes? Sir George Campbell in the debate on the East Indian Loan Bill (30th July 1877) said:

"It was a great source of weakness and a great evil that the amount of remittances to this country from India should be continually increasing. It was said that the debt due to England from India was for value received. To some extent that was true; to some extent it was not. In time of trouble the amount of debt would become a great source of weakness. The great debt of France had become a conservative element, while the debt incurred by India to England was a great danger. He wished also to object to the system of borrowing from great capitalists. Instead of having, as formerly, loans open in the villages to all the natives, the Government now issued advertisements in the great towns for loans from great capitalists. The result of abandoning the system of open loans had been that India had to pay a higher rate of interest for the money, and that the faith of the natives in the British Government as the depository of their savings had been diminished. The total Rupee Debt was some £71,000,000, of which the natives held 25 per cent. only, while 75 per cent. was held by Europeans. But taking the whole debt of India, including the English and the guaranteed railway debt, the natives did not hold more than one-tenth in all."

A volume might be written on the subject of Indian finance without perhaps conveying the full meaning of these few words. I question, however, whether India has anything like the value for her outlay that even Sir George Campbell would admit. I do not of course refer to money investments, but to those of service. Peace is maintained, it is true, and the country governed. India also escapes some important charges, as for instance for a fleet. But it is doubtful whether those charges would not be for her benefit. Her money is to a large extent spent in England. Not merely every retiring pension, but a part of almost every salary during active service, as well as during furlough, is sent out of India. The life-blood of commerce vanishes like a dream. The English officer—chief and centre of a district—never intends to become a district landowner. He cultivates no acres, provides employment for no tenantry or labourers. He in fact rather cramps the energy, by dwarfing the position, of resident landowners. When he leaves India his connection with it is generally one of money paid in the one case and received in the other. If we intend to retain this great empire, the difficulties of its finance must be dealt with at the roots. We must assist

India to become rich in commerce, in resident enterprising men. To put an end to deficits was something. To separate the local and general accounts was something more. But while the soundness of the revenue rests on the crop of a baneful drug, the Government of India are merely living from hand to mouth, and in spite of surpluses can have no healthy finance.[1]

The other subject at the head of this chapter is in more than one sense vaster, as it certainly is more difficult to deal with in a brief space, than even that of finance. In 1870 the labours of four eminent men, assisted by a man less known, but who has since become their successor, was fast assuming an aspect which seemed to indicate that the "reform, consolidation, and codification" of the law of India had reached a great, if not a final, stage. This work which Sir Barnes Peacock had begun, Sir Henry Maine had continued from an independent stand-ground, and Sir James Stephen was now dealing with in a new way, and on a principle as essentially his own. For the true parentage of Indian law reform we should have to go back to one whose genius infused health into whatever he touched—to Lord Macaulay. How he chafed and frowned when brought face to face with the absurdities of Indian law, will be told for ages. He attracted to the subject the attention of Englishmen skilled in the law. He made the subject popular and intelligible. Yet when he left India the subject slept for more than twenty years, till it was revived after the Mutiny by Sir Barnes Peacock.

Putting aside, however, as of necessity, the work of Lord Macaulay and Sir Barnes Peacock, I shall ask the reader to notice some features of the labour of Sir Henry Maine, as a necessary introduction to what I personally knew of that of Sir James Stephen. Sir Henry, then Mr Maine, began his work of law reform in 1862, and he did not leave it till 1869. Seven long trying years. Among the measures framed, and in most cases carried, were bills to deal with—

[1] Appendix V.

"Works of Public Utility by Private Companies, Articles of War (native), Breaches of Trust, a number of bills for the Control of High Courts in the Presidency and other Towns, Municipal Assessment, the Law of Divorce, Treaties, Imprisonment of Convicts, Civil Justice in various parts, Stamp Duties, Oude Claims, Bank Receipts, bill relating to Foreigners, Coolie Emigration, French Bank Bill, Tolls and Port Dues, Customs, a Whipping Bill (a measure warmly opposed by Sir Charles Trevelyan and others), Official Trustees, Military Cantonments, Municipal Bills, Small Cause Courts, Magistrates' Courts, Registration of Assurances, Re-marriage of Native Converts, Oaths of Justice, etc., Akbari Acts, Civil Procedure, Criminal Jurisdiction, Civil Code, Ceded Lands, etc., Government Forests, Administration of Estates, the Succession and Inheritance of Parsees, Partnership, Indian Companies, Pleaders' Bill, Summary Proceedings on Bills of Exchange, Recorders' Bill, on the Manufacture and Sale of Arms, Assam Tea Company, Execution of Process, Religious Endowments, Mortgagees' and Trustees' Property, Removal of Prisoners, Horse-racing, Public Gambling, Escaped Convicts, Presidency Gaols, Murderous Outrages, Madras Salt, Oude Rent, European Vagrancy, Contagious Diseases, Principal Sadr Amins and Munsifs, Oude Talookdars, Native Marriages not Christian, Punjab Tenancy, Lock Hospitals, and others."

This bare list of measures seems necessary to convey even an approximately correct view of the process of Indian law reform. Some of the measures here referred to are of the nature of mere routine. Some involved immense labour, patience, and resolution. The Native Marriage Bill was a measure which set not merely all Native India aflame, but also aroused the missionaries to extraordinary exertions, still spoken of as things of yesterday in Calcutta. Two attempts to settle the question had failed. The issue was simply whether a man or woman converted to Christianity, and in consequence deserted by husband or wife, should be allowed to re-marry. It seemed a simple issue, but in fact while the missionaries differed and argued with respect to it, the Hindoos and Mohammedans were roused to the very depths of their communities in opposition to what, in fact, was an attempt to prevent them from making a change of faith a crime. In 1865 Mr Maine defined the bill as "an interposition of secular power on purely moral grounds" as to marriage, leaving the clergy or ministers to re-marry native converts or otherwise according to their views and the views of their churches. In 1866 Mr Maine re-argued the whole question in a remarkably fine speech, and from every imaginable point of view, of history and existing fact of race and creed. The bill, somewhat altered, was then passed.

The Law of Divorce, the Native (not Christian) Marriage Bill, the Oude Claims, referred to in another chapter, and several other subjects, were marked by equal difficulty. The variety of these measures indicates that the work of Indian legal reform had advanced another great stage, and that distinct enactments were giving place to a complete reconstruction of the law. It must not be understood that Native India looked upon these efforts with apathy, or without alarm. In truth, every step (taken it must be remembered without the test of a Parliamentary opposition) was viewed with jealousy and at times with terror.

Mr Stephen defined his aim as one—(1.) of consolidation; (2.) of codification; (3.) of new acts; and in the end it was seen that he had to the extent shown in this table, abridged and simplified the law:

Number and Subject of Act.	*Acts and Regulations thereby Repealed.*	*Number and Subject of Act.*	*Acts and Regulations thereby Repealed.*
23 of 1870 Coinage repealed,	6	10 of 1871 Excise,	5
26 ,, Prisons,	6	13 ,, Customs,	7
1 of 1871 Cattle Trespass,	3	23 ,, Pensions	15
3 ,, Paper Currency,	5	26 ,, Land Improvement,	10
4 ,, Coroners,	4	29 ,, Repeal of Obsolete Regulations,	53
5 ,, Prisoners,	7	32 ,, Oude Courts Act,	10
6 ,, Bengal Civil Courts	13		
7 ,, Emigration,	5		
8 ,, Registration,	4	15 Acts replaced,	153

A Repealing Act also abrogated the whole or parts of 17 acts and 188 regulations. The Punjab Land Revenue Bill and the Punjab Laws Bill reduced a mass of regulations, rules, orders, and unascertained laws, scattered over many volumes, to two acts of moderate dimensions. Mr Stephen also introduced a "Land Revenue, North Western Provinces,

Bill"—consolidating forty-one acts and regulations; the Local Extent Bill—consolidating into sixteen sections, seventy acts and regulations; the Mortgage Procedure Bill, and the Christian Marriage Bill. When these were passed it was said that not more than thirty or forty regulations would remain unrepealed, and in each case the law on any particular subject would be contained in a single act.

It may have occurred to the reader as curious, that the Christian and Native Marriage Bills never seem to have an end; and, indeed, they have not—so far in Indian history. Unforeseen difficulties have arisen from time to time, and re-opened all the old sores. In the Brahmo Marriage Bill, for instance, it was found that by an exceptional marriage ceremony for the Brahmists, Mr Stephen had given the name solely to the younger body, who alone claimed the bill, and by inference excluded, as not Brahmist, the elder body who were content with the Hindoo marriage ceremonial. Of course the bill was at once amended. Codification Mr Stephen, in other words, described as the reduction to express written rules of principles of law which it had previously been necessary to infer from illustrations by decided cases; in short, the reduction of text books to the form of statutes. There were passed by Mr Stephen—the New Limitation Act, founded on the existing law, but so drawn up as to dispose of perhaps 1200 or 1500 judicial decisions. The Evidence Act, of which Mr Stephen said, "I assert that every principle applicable to the circumstances of British India which is contained in the 1598 royal 8vo pages of 'Taylor on Evidence,' is contained in the 167 sections of this bill." The Indian Contract Act, which was originally drawn by the Indian Law Commissioners, but was a good deal remodelled by Mr Stephen. This Act contained 267 sections, which Mr Stephen did not hesitate to say were the equivalent of many cumbrous volumes of decided cases. The Code of Criminal Procedure which re-enacted the Code, but rearranged it in such a manner as to be intelligible, and cleared up innumerable doubts as to the meaning of the old Code. It also contained several substantial improvements; and, in particular, put on a proper footing the "European British Subject" question, defined the duty of troops in suppressing riots, and became a Criminal Courts Act for the whole of India. In dealing with the penal law, Mr Stephen caused great excitement by this clause, which, however, was carried: "Whoever by words, either spoken or intended to be read, or by signs, or by visible representation or otherwise, attempts to excite feelings of disaffection to the Government, established by law in British India, shall be punished with transportation for life, or for any term, to which fine may be added; or with imprisonment for a term which may extend to three years, to which fine may be added."

There can hardly be two opinions as to this clause conferring on Government all but despotic power; but Native India has the safeguard that, in times of peace, the clause could not be put in force for anything short of treason, and that in time of danger the power would be put in operation, with or without any such clause. The unpleasant words were intended to meet some existing facts, which were not easily met by the existing law, but which, all the same, were met in reality, as, for instance, in the case of the Wahabees.

The concluding part of Mr Stephen's work, the enactment of measures more or less of a political character, included—An Act to Amend the Penal Code by providing punishment for Political Offenders; the Hindoo Wills Act; the Criminal Tribes Act, which put under the ban of the law tribes which heretofore had set the law at defiance; the Native Marriage Act, the Oaths Act, Acts for Local Cesses, Income Tax, Land Acquisition, and others.

It would be both invidious and unjust to compare in other than general terms the work of Sir Henry Maine with that of Sir James Stephen. Each perhaps did that for which he was best fitted. The latter would never, I think, have plodded through so many weary years, opening up and determining such a vast variety of subjects; the former, I think, would not have applied the same powerful magnet to bring the whole into one system. The gift by which the latter was accomplished was peculiar and masterly; but that too was a great gift which prepared the way. In neither case was the work claimed as perfect. Sir James Stephen retouched some of Sir Henry Maine's work, as Sir Henry Maine retouched some of Sir Barnes Peacock's, and as Mr Stokes may have to retouch some of Sir James Stephen's. Mr Hobhouse, the late legal member, represents an interregnum in the massive work, which is really a concatenation of many ideas wrought out into life, by a few master hands. Lord Macaulay, with all his genius, could do little more than throw light into darkness. Sir Barnes Peacock broke the ground, which he had not time to utilise, and which Sir Henry Maine did vastly utilise. Then there came a fresh mind, with loyal support from another fresh mind (the Governor General's), and the Law of India was brought into the shape in which it will probably remain long, subject only to the necessary changes indicated by changing times. I never gathered from Sir James Stephen's speeches that he claimed more than this for his labour in India. He found a strange old building, of every possible order of architecture, unsuited to modern times. He also, however, found new beams, rafters, windows, and stones—some in their places, some on the ground—material for a general "restoration." He took up with a firm hand the work of former architects, and he remained in India till he saw the scaffolding taken down, and the old building transformed. I think this, as far as it goes, is the simple truth as to this reform of India Law.

CHAPTER XIII.

VICE-REGAL CEREMONIAL—THE STAR OF INDIA—FOUR LIEUTENANT GOVERNORS OF BENGAL.

On an afternoon in February 1871, three representative men were invested by Lord Mayo with the Star of India; the Maharajah of Puttiala, a young man, the heir to a long line of chiefs, in later days distinguished by great loyalty and services to England; Prince Gholam Mahomed, an aged man, and very infirm, the last of the race of Hyder Ali, and the son of Tippoo-Sultan, one of our most redoubtable enemies; and Sir William Grey, the retiring Lieutenant Governor of Bengal, spoken of on all hands as one of the last of the old Bengal civilians. It was a curious scene to any one who strove, ever so little, to connect the past with the present time.

The floor of the united throne room and marble hall of Government House is in the form of the letter T, with the entrance door at the foot of the letter, and the throne at where the two arms branch off to right and left. From the door to the throne there are two lines of fine pillars, and along the avenue formed by them, and also between two laughing, talking lines of ladies and gentlemen behind and between the pillars, the honoured guest of any particular day at this palace of the Governor General of India, has to walk (not run) a gauntlet more terrible to some men than leading a forlorn hope. Those critical eyes of ladies, those freeborn tongues, which no prince, power, or potentate, by the mere dignity of his presence, ever yet succeeded in reducing to silence! The central figure of the day was the young Maharajah, who was to be made Knight Grand

Commander of the Star of India. Prince Gholam Mahomed and Sir William Grey, who were to become Knights Commanders, merely entered quietly and without display. The Maharajah of Puttiala, gorgeously attired, was conducted with great ceremony to the dais, on which sat the Grand Master, the Viceroy. The Maharajah of Vizianagram, tall, spirited, affable, and spangled with jewels, sat, or rather stood, among the distinguished personages of the order, conversing gaily with English ladies, and asking old acquaintances to introduce him to persons whom he wished to know—the very picture of genial good-nature. Near to him was the Maharajah of Jeypore (referred to in the chapter on "Lord Mayo"), short of stature, pale, grave, thoughtful, and evidently anxious to be as little seen as possible—a fine chief, whose Rajpoot blood is his least claim to the honour of Englishmen, and whose schools, and watchfulness over his people (ruling them, it is said, like a shepherd), and good fiscal management, the Indian Government has delighted to honour.

Then there was that aged man, also bedecked with jewels, the last of the race of Tippoo, tottering at every step as if a breath would blow him over; representing in his own person, not merely a mighty race, but very nearly the entire history of England in India. Known for a whole generation as the friend of education, the friend indeed of the friendless of whatever name, honoured by the Queen of England, and foremost in all good work of peace, Gholam Mahomed had memories of very different and very critical days. Seventy-two years previously, to the very day (February 27th) his father Tippoo had been defeated at the battle of Malavelly, which threw open the way to Seringapatam. A little later the warrior chief, safe, as he thought, in his impregnable fortress, was sitting down quietly to his mid-day meal, when the dread news came that the English were upon him, putting an end to mid-day and all other meals for ever. General Baird, long a prisoner in Seringapatam, led the forlorn hope. Tippoo died bravely, and was buried next day with military honours, and in the midst of a grand thunderstorm, the peals of which blended with the roar of the English guns over his grave. The old family of Mysore was restored to part of the territories wrested from it, and the family of Tippoo were pensioned at Vellore, Prince Gholam then a very little child. What traps and pitfalls he afterwards escaped, what intrigues he discountenanced, and what a peaceful life he led, have often been spoken of with wonder. He died a little later.

Of the Maharajah (also since dead) there is little of a personal nature to tell, save that he was eighteen years of age, the husband of two wives, and the father of a boy then three years old. He was, however, the son of that Narindar Singh, who, in the time of the Mutiny had been one of the best friends of the English, as his father in a like critical time had been before him. The story is as interesting as a novel. How Karem Singh gallantly stood by us during the Sikh war of 1845, and died before his great services could be acknowledged. How his son Narindar succeeded at once to his power and policy, and lived to believe, rightly or wrongly, that our gratitude had vanished with our danger. How he then retired, sullenly, if not discontentedly, to his dominions. How the Mutiny came, and all India looked with suspicion on Narindar Singh. How he replied to the suspicion by splendid services, heading his troops, guarding several important stations, lending the Government his money, providing carriage, keeping open the vital artery of the Grand Trunk road. How rewards were then gratefully bestowed upon him, with a full sense of what our debt really was; and finally, how, a member of the Imperial Council, with the Star of India on his breast, and the thanks of England conveyed by Lord Canning in public durbar, among his treasures, he died in 1862, in the forty-sixth year of his age and seventeenth of his reign. The education of the son of the dead Maharajah was considered a special charge of the Indian Government. He was an ever-welcome guest at Simla. He had place at the Umballa durbar. He exchanged visits with the Duke of Edinburgh at Lahore. And now he received the highest degree of the order of the Star of India. The ceremony therefore was no mere pageant. The young Maharajah, heir to a line at once so noble and so friendly to England, beginning life; Gholam Mahomed, closing a century of history; and English Sir William Grey, closing a long thirty years of Indian service, formed a fine tableau. Lord Mayo's last durbar was in January 1872, for the reception of the young King of Siam, an extraordinarily self-possessed young gentleman.

The position of the Lieutenant Governor of Bengal is an exceptional one in Indian governorship. Down to the time of Lord Dalhousie the Governor General was also Governor of Bengal. The first Lieutenant Governor was Sir Frederick Halliday; the second was Sir John P. Grant; the third, Sir Cecil Beadon; the fourth, Sir William Grey. It is an office which requires greater tact and decision than any other in the country, if the Lieutenant Governor would at once avoid obstruction and preserve his independence. In his own Council he is supreme; in the Imperial Council he is only a member. In Calcutta, where his power is indisputable (unless the Governor General exercises a veto, as Lord Northbrook sternly did), he is still only the little Lord Sahib. The Governor General is the greater Lord Sahib; and Government House, Calcutta, though not to be compared for comfort and beauty of situation with the Lieutenant Governor's house at Belvedere, Alipore, is the centre of greatness in ruling power. The duties of Lieutenant Governor, therefore, require self-assertion when necessary, and tact and courtesy always.

In contrasting three rulers of the North Western Provinces and the Punjab, I did so, as then stated, with a view to the greater contrast of Sir William Grey, Sir George Campbell, Sir Richard Temple, and Mr Eden. When Sir William Grey left Calcutta, the whole educated native population deplored the loss. Not perhaps with enthusiasm, for he was not a man to evoke enthusiasm, but I believe with sincerity. His gentleness and forbearance, his considerateness, his justice, and his conscientiousness, seemed to have found a way to the heart of the people. He was not a broad man, people said, not broader than an English Whig, but in his own groove he was reliable where only justice, or mercy in need, was sought for. I gathered that he had not been a strong, though he had been a careful administrator; that he was a dangerous disputant, with a keen eye for crevices in the armour of his opponents, and that his minutes—the delight of his heart—while pitiless in logic, in insisting that one and one and one should make three, were often tempered by an afterthought which smoothed much of the sternness away. That is, he was a Bengal Whig of the better kind, with a view of administration resting on a tolerance of opinions, and even prejudices, and a great kindness to Native India; and Native India has preserved his portrait, as that of a friend.

His successor was Sir George Campbell, who arrived in Bengal with a high character for administrative ability. He had done excellent service in Oude, the Punjab, the Central Provinces, and elsewhere; had been the indefatigable president of a committee of inquiry into the Orissa famine; had written a book highly spoken of on the question of Irish land, and had striven, though unsuccessfully, to find a seat in Parliament. His greatest laurels, however, had been won as President of the Famine Committee, and he was destined to be confronted by a famine as threatening as that which Sir Cecil Beadon failed to meet till too late. In the end, after a fierce and laborious term of office, he left India with very little popular goodwill, and very little of the goodwill of the English in Bengal; although in losing him the people of India lost a man more capable of serving them, if they and he could have found a common ground, than, save in a very few instances, any man they had known in all the century of English rule. His views were clear, but his temper was uncompromising. He seemed to allow nothing either for native habits of thought, or for the weakness of his own officials, and he speedily acquired the character of an abrupt uncourteous man. His whole term of office was characterised by contention, not in the sense of wrangling, but of disputation. In the Imperial Council, where his sound views ought to have had, and indeed had, weight, his contentious tone and persistence did much to destroy the effect that his perception of facts created.

He developed a system of education for the very poor, a really honest public-spirited project; but he created and promulgated it without consulting the feelings of the landlords, whose support he nevertheless demanded. With ever so little real conciliation he could have won them to a man. In the case also of the Pubna riots and the Santal outbreak, referred to in an earlier chapter, his course, just in fact, was made by the strength and nature of his language to assume a form of partisanship, honourable perhaps in an individual, but dangerous in a ruler. He was no partisan, but he forgot that when the sun and the north wind contended which should first cause a man to doff his coat, the sun was victor. Other and far lesser men than Sir George Campbell had caused the landlords to doff their coats. The reply to Sir George was an extra row of buttons. In allowing so little for existing facts he set at nought, not merely Indian, but also English history, and he failed.

In striving to give effect to his views of popular education (to utilise, by small grants, the old "Guru patshala" schools), his laudable aim was further marred by an extreme condemnation of the provision by the State for high-class education. If rich men wished their sons to be educated, let them (he said in other words) pay for the education; which in one sense was right, although rich men did not of themselves provide Oxford and Cambridge, and this was a point which the Hindoos did not lose. But they had also the much stronger point, admitted by the Duke of Argyll (despatch, May 1870), "that those among whom our English system of education has struck deepest root, though generally of the literary and higher castes, can by no means be described as of the wealthier classes of society." The public services are now presumed to be open to all, Native and English alike, and to depreciate, as Sir George Campbell did, in different ways, this high-class education was to place Native India out of the race of competition. To say that such was his aim would be absurd; but such was the drift of his language and of his action, and in this sense he was understood. The tests of the competition are not merely English, but high-class English, and in even that young India has, in spite of all tests, excelled.

Then there came a fine opportunity for Sir George Campbell to express his views on the whole question of prisons. An experienced inspector general of the prisons of Bengal, Dr Mouat, had just retired from the service. He had spent a lifetime in the work, and had developed a prison system, which will be referred to later, so effective that it had received many encomiums. The death of the governor of Alipore gaol, an able medical man, led to Sir George resolving to have no more doctors as governors, and to determining that the prison system should, even if less remunerative, be made more punitive. In reality, on the strength of what could only in comparison be mere general knowledge, he condemned the carefully matured system of a man who, whatever his views might be worth on other subjects, had made this one subject his own in principle and detail.

To the famine policy of Sir George Campbell reference is made in another chapter, and I believe that everything goes to show that his view was the right one. In fact, the King of Burma has already raised the price of grain in consequence of the Madras famine. The foregoing shows but a very few of the contentions of Sir George

Campbell; some with officers, some with landlords, some with the Governor General. But Bengal, at all events, will by-and-by learn to forgive the mannerism and isolated temperament (more than temper), for the value of his aims and of many of his acts. As an opponent he was an open opponent; as a friend I should say he could not be a false friend. Indefatigable in work, and loyal to good workers, his failing was to expect too much from men who, though perhaps worthy and good men, were quite incapable of his own sustained efforts. That he could be merciful and kind some facts which I could mention would very amply prove. That he was more than a mere executive officer every one knows who knows India. That his governorship represented a virtual revolution, succeeding that of Sir William Grey, I think the reader will perceive. It was a change from desk management to root-and-branch administration, resting on fixed and matured views as to political principles underlying action.

Sir Richard Temple succeeded to the lieutenant governorship, with the cordial goodwill of Lord Northbrook, whose, rather than Sir George Campbell's, famine officer, or dictator, he had been. He was in robust health when he took up the duties which his predecessor in ill health had let fall. His career as an officer had been one of marked success; in particular, as Chief Commissioner of the Central Provinces, he had shown qualities scarcely expected in him, for healing the wounds of war by developing and fostering arts of peace. That he had a powerful pen, and an extraordinary amount of physical endurance, were spoken of as facts known to every one; and he had a knowledge which Sir George Campbell did not possess, of what is meant by the phrase "live and let live," together with a faculty of infusing a cheerful spirit into other men, while carrying out his own ideas in cases of dispute. The Viceroy and Sir George Campbell had appeared to clash from the first. The Viceroy and Sir Richard Temple agreed from the first, and agreed to the end. To the famine work I shall refer as a whole. In the relation of Sir Richard Temple to his officers and to Native India, there cannot be a doubt that the change from Sir George Campbell was welcomed generally. The new lieutenant governor did try to please. A noble project, worthy of further reference, to create a Native Science Association had for some years hung on the verge of success. Sir Richard Temple pushed it over the verge and it succeeded, or at all events lived. Even his financial speeches, opposed as they justly were in much, exhibited a wonderfully facile power in the mastery and arrangement of details. That he soon forgot the opposition to him is perhaps a proof that he cared merely for performing well the duties of the passing hour, whereas Sir George Campbell would have proceeded on some hard and fast line of principle which years would not have obliterated. When Sir Richard left Bengal for Bombay the native press was, as far as I saw, all but unanimous in asserting that he had meant to rule justly and well. His great qualifications were, good administrative ability, cheerful spirits, an interest in other people, and a valuable power of forgetting. He could be a veritable lieutenant governor without state, and could maintain his dignity without perpetually insisting upon it in his intercourse with men of any rank. Sir George Campbell, in the important speech referred to in the chapter on law reform and finance, quoted from one of his own statements (1874) a proof that he had not advocated the heavy famine expenditure which his successor entailed on the Government; that he drew a line between what Government could and could not do. Probably the House of Commons saw that this was not fair. Sir George, having stated his view without repeating it, had no further responsibility. If events confirmed it, he was right. If events overturned it, the fault might have been in the unforeseen. To establish such a view, as a test of foresight, or as a justification of a policy, the view should not merely have been stated in advance, but re-stated during the progress of events. Chiefly, however, it will be observed that again, by a change of lieutenant governor, the affairs of this great province were completely disturbed, and in a social sense were revolutionised. From Sir George Campbell to Sir Richard Temple was like a stride from one to another of two opposite poles.

Sir Richard Temple has been succeeded by Mr Ashley Eden; and again there is a great change. Mr Eden's public career has not been unquestioned, and there was a time when he was bitterly denounced. I have, however, fixed upon three facts, which I think will counterbalance much criticism. First, that if Bengal had had a lieutenant governor to choose he probably would have been its choice. Secondly, that his administration in Burma was characterised not merely by ability, but by a return to the noble educational policy of Sir Arthur Phayre, which Major General Fytche had abandoned. Thirdly, that before the indigo commission in 1860 Mr Eden gave evidence, which for firmness and decision could hardly have been surpassed. He was at the time magistrate at Cuttack. The indigo disturbances were in question, and the Cuttack magistrate in direct and forcible terms fixed much of the responsibility upon at least some of the planters and their policy. These facts I have taken from a report of his evidence, filling thirty-seven large and closely-printed pages, which were published in a separate form by a Native Association. He was questioned and cross-questioned, but his evidence was not shaken.

The feeling of that time may be judged from the fact that a respected missionary (of the Church Missionary Society), the Rev. James Long, a devoted friend of the poor tenants, was tried, fined, and imprisoned, for translating a spirited little native drama, "Nil Durpan" ("The Mirror of Indigo"), now acted in all parts of India. Of the native writer of the drama, a genial, cheerful man, to whom bitterness was unknown, the reader will perhaps be pleased to learn a little more later. He wrote his drama in good faith for a public purpose, and he was present in court when Mr Long was tried, and ready to exchange places with him if that had been possible. The Bishop of Calcutta resolutely supported Mr Long (one of the last men in India to excite ill feeling among the people); but the bitterness of the time prevailed. The fine was paid at once by a native gentleman, but Mr Long was imprisoned. It was at this time that Mr Eden gave his evidence. Of its accuracy I can say nothing, but it has an accurate appearance; and from that day to this Native India has stood, through good report and evil report, by the outspoken witness.

In Burma Sir Arthur Phayre had found the whole country covered with a network of Buddhist monastic schools, and there was scarcely a Burmese child who could not "read, write, and count;" but much of the education was absurd. He conceived the idea of utilising the monasteries, by sending to them teachers of a more advanced education. No Burmese phoongyee (priest) can receive money "on any pretence whatever." The priest sits down in the village and teaches the children, the parents supplying him with his daily food. In defending his policy, Sir Arthur Phayre said: "We are asked, why not set to work independently of the Buddhist monasteries? My reply is, because the main object is to establish a vernacular school in each village and hamlet. It would be comparatively easy for Government to do this in towns; but most difficult to accomplish it in the remote country places. But there is found in each small hamlet a monastery supported by the people, and the building maintained by them. These institutions are regarded with reverence and affection, and are felt by them to be the national schools."

To utilise these was the enlightened aim of Sir Arthur Phayre. Major General Fytche reversed the policy. Mr Eden returned to it; two more very clear indications of how the social life of a province may be turned topsy-turvy by these ever-recurring changes of administration. The character of Major General Fytche renders it almost unnecessary for me to say that I am not impugning his motives. It was simply a matter of opinion; but I think he was greatly in the wrong. As lieutenant governor, Mr Eden is yet untried, but if he fail it certainly will not be from any want of fair play on the part of Native Bengal. As a statesman, Sir George Campbell stands foremost among the four lieutenant governors, and it is unpleasant to add that he was the least popular of the four. Perhaps he was too earnest, and saw too far into the future, for ordinary men. Perhaps he fell back too completely on "first principles," and disregarded existing facts. Assuredly he allowed too little for human weakness, for habits interwoven with life, and assuredly, also, he had a habit (markedly shown in England in the case of ex-Colonel Baker) of not allowing a question once raised to go to rest again. That he went to India with a noble purpose, and to some extent gave that purpose a noble life, will not be disputed in history.

CHAPTER XIV.

THE FAITHS OF INDIA: HINDOOISM AND BRAHMOISM—THE MOHAMMEDANS—A NAUTCH.

IN September 1872 the walls of Calcutta were placarded with an advertisement of a lecture, to be given by the minister of the elder body of the Brahmists (termed the "Adi Somaj"—Adi Church), on "the superiority of Hindooism to all other religions." Reference has been made in an earlier chapter to one essential and vital difference between the two Brahmist Churches, both professing to follow the great first Brahmist, Rajah Ram Mohun Roy. The younger body, the Church of Baboo Keshub Chunder Sen, may be said to be very nearly akin to Unitarian Christianity. The elder believe that Hindooism, although overgrown with excrescences, has for its germ and origin the worship and unity of the one true God, and that a return to the teaching of the Vedas would be a return to a pure though a poetical deism. I had at this time been in India about two years, and had sent home what I must term strictly and rigorously accurate, though not unquestioned, pictures of what may be seen at the festivals of Doorga and Juggernauth; and I had also in those two years formed an impression that Englishmen do not rightly comprehend the faiths, or the men influenced by the faiths, of India. This advertisement, however, was a startling one. Did the minister of the Adi Somaj (a scholar and a gentleman I afterwards found) actually mean to assert, in the face of the missionary and educated English of Calcutta, that Hindooism is superior to Christianity? I found he did; and before the controversy which his lecture caused had ended,

I had come to the conclusion that the Hindoos may, in God's good providence, and without an absolute adherence to Christian channels of faith or form, find their way backward to the key to all truth, the oneness of the Most High God. I did not think, and do not now think, of defending Hindooism. I did, and do, desire to show somewhat of the character of many Hindoo scholars and thinkers who still claim to be actuated and guided by Hindooism.

Since that time I have endeavoured in different ways to draw attention to the literature of these two Brahmist bodies—a literature so marvellously devotional, and so embued with a spirit of love to God and men, that one might seek far for a parallel to it, save in the most devotional works of the old Catholic divines. I find such passages as these: "Is not progress to be perceived in the sacred writings of the Christians also? Was it not a great transition from the Elohim of Moses to the God of the New Testament? A change passes over the Jewish religion from fear to love, from power to wisdom, from the justice of God to the mercy of God, from the nation to the individual, from this world to another, from the visitation of the sins of the father upon the children, to every 'soul shall bear its own iniquity;' from the fire, the earthquake, and the storm to the 'still small voice.' . . . Let us be pure and holy in our lives. Let us make sacrifices for our religion. . . . Lord God, our Father, our Saviour, our Redeemer! to Thee we look up for succour, for we are weak. Always grant the light of Thy countenance, for that light alone is our only consolation amid the darkness and dangers of our situation. Forsake us not, but infuse patience, firmness, and fortitude into our souls, so that we may stand as witnesses of Thy glory to generations to come."

In the same spirit a writer of the same body claims for Brahmoism the words of Abou Ben Adhem's Dream—"Write me as one who loves his fellow-men." This literature is ever growing, and its spirit pertains to both the Brahmo bodies. Each has its pamphlets, its newspaper, its societies for moral and social, as well as religious, progress. Both alike disown Christianity, save as one of the good systems of religion which "the education of the world" has produced from age to age.

The minister of the Adi Somaj undertook to prove, in the face of the younger Brahmo body, as well as of Christian missionaries:

"That Hindooism is superior to all other religions, because it owes its name to no man; because it acknowledges no mediator between God and man; because the Hindoo worships God as the soul of the soul, and can worship in every act of life—in business, in pleasure, and in social intercourse; because while other scriptures inculcate worship for the rewards it may bring, or the punishment it may avert, the Hindoo is taught to worship God and practise virtue, for the love of God and of virtue alone; because, being unsectarian, and believing in the good of all religions, Hindooism is non-proselytising and tolerant, as it also is devotional to an entire abstraction of the mind from time and sense, and possesses an antiquity which carries it back to the fountainhead of all thought."

These are some of the points which the lecturer endeavoured to illustrate from history, and by well-put references to existing facts.

His position was disputed by a genial and accomplished missionary, the Rev. Dr Murray Mitchell, and by several members of the younger Brahmo body. Dr Mitchell claimed to include the Tantras among the sacred books of the Hindoos, and adduced from them immoral passages, which the minister of the Adi Somaj, Baboo Rajnarain Bose, promptly disowned. "I am not," he said, "a Tantrist, and therefore decline to enter into a discussion on the merits and demerits of any of the Tantras. The position which I took up in my lecture on the superiority of Hindooism was this, that even the lowest Shastras, the Tantras, not to mention the Vedas, the Upanishads, the Smritis, and the Puranas, contain monotheistic sentiments of the most exalted description." The younger Brahmo body maintained that the Church represented by Baboo Rajnarain Bose had drifted from the teachings of Rajah Ram

Mohun Roy, and of his successor, Debender Nath Tagore, neither of whom confined his search for truth to any one system, and the latter of whom claimed all great and good men as teachers, all "náture as revelation," and "pure reason as minister." Baboo Jotentro Nath Tagore (a notable Calcutta zemindar, kinsman and successor of Rajah Ram Mohun Roy's distinguished disciple, Dwarkanath Tagore) maintained that Hindooism is an illimitable fount of truth, and in confirmation of this view produced many beautiful passages from the Shasters.

This controversy produced little effect in India, so far as making known the tenets of the two Brahmist Churches was concerned; but it was valuable to me, and it may be so to the reader in two ways. First, it shows that while the Church of Baboo Keshub Chunder Sen is drifting further from Hindooism, the older body is coming nearer to Hindooism, while, at the same time, endeavouring to raise it from an idolatry to a philosophy and a monotheistic faith. Secondly, that the younger body in drifting from Hindooism is not drifting any the nearer to Christianity. The forms of worship of both Churches are thoroughly, and at festive times markedly, Hindoo in the apparent intensity of the devotion, and in the appeals to the senses by music and flowers. An "Inquirer from the outside" during this controversy having asked some questions indicating his view of the greater simplicity, solemnity, devotion, charity, and purity of the Gospel of Christ, the *National* (Adi Somaj) *Paper* replied with some fine instances of Hindoo charity, of honour paid to parents, and much besides; facts which may be freely admitted, while, at the same time, a glimpse into these ancient writings, as into the Koran, is sufficient to show what a marked contrast they present to the New Testament. I cannot see whither the spirit of inquiry now abroad in India is tending, but I venture to ask the reader to view it in a generous and kindly spirit.

It is now little more than a century since Ram Mohun

Roy (created Rajah by the King of Delhi) was born, of a high caste and powerful family in Burdwan. Instructed in all the learning of his caste, he nevertheless began to doubt, as Sákya Muni ages before had doubted. He studied, travelled, sought communion with men of intelligence wherever he could find them. Finally he began to teach, and in one tract "Against the Idolatry of all Religions," made himself a host of enemies and opponents, including many missionaries. He certainly held that the Vedas, so far from inculcating idolatry, established the worship of the one God. He selected portions of the words of Christ, and wrote of them with enthusiasm. His purity never was disputed. He died in Bristol in 1833; and a little later his disciple and friend, Dwarkanath Tagore, marked by a monument the grave of one of the true teachers of men. After some years the mantle of the great leader fell upon Debender Nath Tagore. About twenty years later still suspicions began to creep into the body, chiefly through the appeals of Keshub Chunder Sen, that the Vedas were not sure ground. In 1866 the Progressive Somaj became an independent Church.

A suggestive picture of Baboo Keshub in his early struggles was given some years ago by one of his friends, an American Unitarian minister, Mr Dall. "I remember," he said, "how simply Keshub rose one evening in the British India Society, and proposed 'that this society cultivate habits of prayer.' The presiding padree (Christian minister) reminded him that he had no God to whom to pray." The Unitarian assured him he had a God, and a God who never turned away from earnest prayer. The visit of Keshub to England, and his eloquent representation of the feeling and wrongs of his countrymen, are still in the public mind. Let me say that the Brahmists have disowned caste, risen altogether above idolatry, and partly above the seclusion of woman; that they are ardent friends of education and temperance, and of the re-marriage of widows; that, in short, they represent new-born impulses of light and freedom. Their relation to missions will be partly shown in the next chapter.

We turn now to Hindooism as a creed. The Juggernauth Car (at Mahish, near Calcutta) is as large as a mountain cottage, and elaborately carved. Except at the festival times, it stands in the village and is covered, but not sacred. At a stated time the god is presumed to enter the car; and the people in thousands draw him with long ropes, and amid wild shouts of rejoicing that may be heard for miles, for a considerable distance along the road. It is at this time that the deaths, by accident or self-immolation, occur. There were several deaths during the time I knew India, but in all cases proved accidents. The festival lasts about three weeks, and I made a point of seeing it under all aspects by day and night. I described it as not unlike an English fair, only without "drink." Men, women, and children came in multitudes from all the country round, bringing their offerings of flowers for the god, and a few copper coins (a penny, or less perhaps, in value) for the priests. By day they formed a sea of human faces; by night they slept in thousands by the road-side. Merry-go-rounds, Aunt Sallys, kite-flying, marble playing, and other like diversions, prevailed. I neither heard an angry word nor saw an angry look among all those innumerable crowds. A young priest of the car I knew well—a poor man earning only a few rupees a month, yet managing (gratuitously) in his evening hours two schools, for boys and girls, and open to any inspector. Some said, "The picture you give is a defence of Juggernauth." I replied, "It is a simple picture; a statement of fact;" and when the time again came, I repeated the picture. I was told that at Orissa the festival was bad. I only saw that at Mahish. In 1874 a wheel of the car was broken, and the festival was forbidden ostensibly as dangerous, though the engineer of the Hooghly Bridge vouched for the repairs. Sir Richard Temple was appealed to in vain. This year, I am glad to say, the veto has been withdrawn by Mr Eden, and I think to the credit of his common sense and good feeling.

The other great ceremonial of Bengal which I was able to observe, was the festival of the goddess Doorga, which (as a holiday) continues a fortnight, about the end of the rains, in autumn. During the festival proper, every kind of work is laid aside; even English enterprise for the time ceases. Doorga is an incarnation of Kali, the destroyer, who is worshipped with a fierce ceremonial, but as Doorga the goddess is the centre of a genial festival. The image, often made at great cost, is set up in many houses, and at the appointed time the goddess is implored, in her mighty power, to divide herself, and inhabit the images which people come in from all the neighbourhood to worship. Each shrine is then sacred, while dramas, and nautches, and music, and all manner of festivity, prevail throughout the house. It seemed to me like a feast of flowers, so universal were flowers both as offerings and adornments. When the goddess again departs from the image, the sacredness departs, and the deserted tenement, tossed about as a thing of play, is finally thrown into the Ganges. In reality it is an assertion that the image while inhabited by the goddess is dual, and that the image, deserted by the goddess, is but a dead thing.

I asked a young Hindoo, distinguished at the Calcutta University, and the son of a Hindoo scholar, a very poor man, to give me in writing his and his father's idea of their faith. He told me in simple and graceful language the history (from the Hindoo point of view) of the Vedas (say, from fifteen to thirteen centuries older than our era); and insisted much upon their cardinal doctrine that there is but one Supreme Spirit, the Lord and Creator of the Universe. "The three manifestations of the Deity—Brahma, the creating principle; Vishnu, the preserving principle; and Siva, the destroyer—are merely mentioned in the Vedas." The Institutes of Menu (perhaps five centuries later) developed from the Vedas an elaborate system of religion, governing caste, social observance, labour, everything known in Hindoo life, and so minutely entering into that life that nothing escapes it from long before the child's birth to old age. Ceremonies are observed with reference to the unborn babe; great ceremonies when the boy Brahmin receives his sacred thread, learns the most sacred verse of the Vedas, and so becomes one of the "twice-born." As ages passed, the faith of the Vedas was still further supplanted by the Puranas, which gradually increased the gods and goddesses, till now they are innumerable. Everything in nature, every flower and tree, sea and land, sun and moon, peace and war, wealth and poverty, joy and grief, love and hate, disease and death, has its god. Kama, god of love, Lakshmi, wife of Vishnu and goddess of fortune or abundance, and Ganesha, the remover of difficulties, are very favourite deities. Here, then, from the time of the Puranas, the principle of monotheism was gradually effaced, and the faith in some particular god began to take the place of good works. Teachers rose from time to time, and, as we have seen, continue to rise, to attempt the restoration of the old faiths; but the spirit of the faith in power has had a charmed life, and returns again and again victorious. Siva the destroyer is represented as wandering about in dismal places, surrounded by ghosts and goblins; Doorga or Kali is his wife. My friend wrote:

> "Human sacrifices were formerly offered to Kali, and she was supposed to delight in carnage on her altars. On such occasions one of the sects of the worshippers of Kali meet in parties of both sexes to feast on flesh and spirituous liquors, and to indulge in the grossest debauchery. Very few of the followers of Kali join this sect; the mass of the people are hardly aware of its existence, and it is looked on with horror and contempt by all orthodox Hindoos."

The incarnations of Vishnu have been nine; he became a fish to recover the Vedas; a boar, to raise the world sunk under the waters; a tortoise; a man, to avenge injustice on a tyrant; a Brahmin dwarf, to outwit a king who had defied the gods; a Brahmin hero, who extirpated the Khatrya race; the great Rama, and Balaram and Krishna. The tenth incarnation is yet to come. Rama is the hero of Valmiki's great poem, the national epic of India, the "Ramayana." The hero was, the story tells us, King of Oude, and his whole life one of self-denial and piety. He was banished by his father; his beautiful queen, Sita, was stolen from him by the giant Ravuna, and borne away to Ceylon, from whence Rama recovered her by the help of an army of monkeys. Sita, chaste, beautiful, lotus-eyed, is the type-woman of India.[1] Krishna is the merry god, whose festival is a pastoral, not very restrained or delicate. Doorga has two festivals. Of the greater, already referred to, my friend wrote:

> "This pooja is continued for three days. People are liberally fed with rice and sweetmeats, and in families which are not Vaishnuv flesh of goats is even allowed for guests. This is the occasion of a Hindoo's greatest rejoicings. The members of a family, both male and female, wherever scattered, meet together. The children have new clothes and shoes, and even grown-up men and women are not at all behind them in matters of dress. All seem merry, and the Doorgapooja holidays are the merriest days in a Hindoo's life. On the fourth day the goddess is thrown into the river, and we return home from the river-side dispirited, though in our gayest dresses. We feel as if something great has passed away. Especially this is the case in families where the goddess was worshipped. They feel a gloomy vacuity. Still it is a melancholy pleasure. The evening is spent in paying our respects to our superiors, parents, uncles, elder brothers, and cousins. Our neighbours also get a share of those respects. The business is rendered very agreeable by the liberal allowance of sweetmeats dealt out in all the families."

I have aimed here to place before the reader in very brief terms an intelligent Hindoo's view of his own faith. It will be seen that he does not view that faith in quite so dismal a light as it is viewed by many Englishmen. A work on "The Land of the Tamulians," translated from the German of the Rev. E. R. Baierlein, by Mr Gribble of

[1] "The Ramayana in English Verse." Ralph T. H. Griffith, Benares.

the Madras Civil Service, presents an exceedingly fine view of the Hindoo faith. "The Rig Veda," the author says, "sung perhaps before the time of Moses," seems as if "composed by men newly awake and gazing in wonder on the things around them without being perfectly masters of their senses." The second period, he continues, the collection of the Vedas by Vyasa, was the real origin of the Vedas as theology. The third period took all the true essence of the Vedas away. It is curious to observe in the deification of nature, or the vital soul of nature, many views not unlike some held by M. Auguste Comte, who has now many, and some ardent, disciples among the educated Hindoos.

A person—"An Inquirer"—chanced some years ago to say that, while these questions were brewing, as it were like yeast, throughout India, the chief aim of the Christian ought to be practical charity, after the example of the Great Teacher who went about doing good. He continued:

"India needs a great spirit of toleration to efface the footprints of conquerors who fastened upon the people new creeds. The Hindoo people have been under the impression that one of the conditions of English as of other rule, was an ultimate destruction of all the national customs as well as the national faith. The East India Company strove to erase this feeling, and strove in a way that laid it open to the charge of not caring whether the people were degraded or not, so long as the Company's balance-sheets were right. A Christian missionary who went to India in that spirit would be an evil; would have no right there at all. But he who possesses a spirit of toleration, who can bear and forbear, who can admit what he finds of truth and beauty in the old landmarks of the land, and at the same time hold up a truer and more beautiful faith—the faith that never yet divided men into castes—could scarcely fail to be a benefactor to India."

To this view so expressed there was no end of responses, and I know that the writer of the words would abide by them in the hour of death as by a true faith. Viewing Hindooism in its relation to classical mythology, it is not difficult to perceive a similarity and a contrast. The points of resemblance are many; but while the Hindoo faith is so essentially fanciful, even when it runs in every vein of the national life, the Greek faith was as essentially practical, without being suffered to so essentially enter into the life-blood. Hercules, to fall back on a well-known similitude, is like a hero in the dream of Bunyan; Rama is like a creation of the dream of Shelley. Hercules is as real as the heroes of Plutarch; Rama is essentially of dreamland. In Homer the council of gods is even more distinct than a Roman senate. In Valmiki the decisions of the gods are arrived at in the clouds. The Hindoo idealised abstraction; the Greek labour. The Hindoo had an army of monkeys for Rama. Hercules, the incarnation of individual might and manhood, had his club. Neither mythology affected to give any clear glimpses into the life after death. The Hindoo at his highest reached to far the more subtle and profound truths, but the Greek attained that practical freedom amid which less subtle truths could be carried out to more certain results. The Hindoo never yet saw that "God made of one blood all the nations of men;" that "in the image of God created He man." The Greek heathen had arrived proximately at that deep truth even before Christianity. Caste had its value in old times, and has its glory still. That it will rise above itself is certain. That it will become lost in Christianity is what I cannot yet see.

To Mohammedan views and difficulties several references have been made. In number the Mohammedans have generally been counted at only about one-fifth of that of the Hindoos, taking India through, and in the Madras Presidency they are but a very small number as compared with the Hindoos. In Bengal, however, they have increased, almost imperceptibly, till the late census (1872-73) showed them to be very nearly half the Hindoo population —20,600,000 against 42,600,000. The increase of Mohammedans Sir George Campbell deemed the main fact brought out by the census, and the increase had in many cases been where least of all expected, while where it had been looked for as a certainty, the increase had been comparatively small. Dr Hunter says that, in Bengal in 1871, of 2111 State offices 1338 were held by Europeans, 681 by Hindoos, and only 91 by Mohammedans. In Madras, till lately, Mohammedan education was hardly a name. Lord Hobart, on assuming the government of that province, set himself to rectify the great wrong. He ordered schools to be at once opened for Mohammedans on their own principles of education. The director of public instruction informed him that two schools were already provided for Mohammedans in the Presidency of Madras, and that more was impracticable. Qualified teachers, even, he said, could not be had. To so low a state had these people fallen. The new Governor freely admitted the difficulty, but demanded the schools, and as an inducement to learning decided that a certain number of State offices should be reserved for Mohammedans alone. This minute, published at the end of 1872, was one of the noblest ever recorded in India. And it is pleasant to add that Lord Hobart, while sharply criticised by some Englishmen, was generously supported by the Bengal native newspapers, which suffered no race hatred to obscure their sense of an act of simple justice.

Perhaps this chapter could not conclude more fitly than with a brief description of a family festival, one of the central features of which was a nautch. I was present at this festival in 1874, at the joint-house set apart for festivals, worship, and amusements by a somewhat notable Hindoo family. When Clive, who was no linguist, once required some Persian letters translated, and hesitated to trust any Mohammedan, a young adventurous Hindoo did the work, and did it so well that he became Clive's trusted moonshee, and died the Rajah Nobho Krishna. He was a shrewd man, and while others doubted whether English rule would or would not stand, he bought property on the strength of that rule. When the Government required ground for the extension of Fort William, he sacrificed part of what is now the Maidan, and received for it what is now termed the native town of Calcutta. On his death the property was divided, and became joint family property. It was in 1874 represented by two middle-aged men, uncle and nephew—the uncle, by one of the most pronounced laws of native life, "head of the family;" the nephew, by the grace of Lord William Bentinck first, and finally of Lord Northbrook, Rajah in succession. The families have grown to almost a little village. Each branch has an imposing house, and an income; and in the centre of the property—in the centre also of native Calcutta—is a temple and theatre, dedicated to poojah (worship), and maintained by a special fund, which no branch of the family can touch. Such is the present state of the descendants of a man who fearlessly cast in his lot with Clive at the turning-point of our history in India.

At this curiously memorable place, in company with an English lady and gentleman, I saw Doorga for the last time, late one night in October 1874. We drove out at ten o'clock, a distance of three miles, from Calcutta, through streets crowded with people from end to end, lit up with glaring dismal oil lamps, distressing to horses as to human beings, and further distinguished by shouts and cries and songs and laughter as of pandemonium. At the end of the pilgrimage we found squares of buildings in one blaze of light, and at the door of one of the chief buildings were received with high courtesy and gentlemanliness by the head of the family, politely introduced to his children and grandchildren, treated to attar of roses, and presented each with a small rose bouquet. Then, in spite of advanced guards, we had to fight our way into the poojah hall. The chief hall was covered in the centre with red cloth, and filled at the sides by all ranks and orders of men and women, English and Native, the latter seated on the floor. All at once the band struck up "God save the Queen," reminding one that Her Majesty is sovereign of millions of the worshippers of Doorga, as well as of millions of the believers in Mahomet, and holds the sword of justice for the good of many races. At the end of each of the large halls—immense buildings—was a costly Doorga. There were English ladies and gentlemen; young English lads full of life and merriment; grave elderly Hindoo gentlemen, and equally grave younger ones. Beyond these was a promiscuous crowd, which no man could have numbered, and whose infinite chatterings no man could have restrained. High above all, on a kind of veiled verandah (purdah), a number of figures flitted backward and forward, apparently bent upon finding here or there the best place for seeing. These were the ladies of the large family. In the centre of the room a young girl came forward, with two lads behind her, and one on each side—she to dance, they to play and sing. The young lady advanced with measured steps, as to the "Dead March in Saul," but making up in vehemence of gesture and sharp little stamps of her foot for the restrained motion. The dances are mostly in straight lines, the lady moving her body from side to side, with her face in one direction; now throwing up her hands over her head, now entwining her fingers nervously to indicate some inexpressible emotion, now lowering her voice to almost a whisper, now raising it till it filled the hall, and throughout all, though never ungraceful, seldom giving to any motion what in an English ball-room would be termed grace. Five faces perfectly immobile, limbs and bodies which seemed boneless, feet which never appeared to rise an inch from the ground—such are the main features of an Indian nautch. English tumbling, with the inevitable English clown, followed. Meanwhile the invited company were conducted to the upper rooms, elegantly furnished, and in many instances arranged with good taste; the pictures (for a wonder) in the right places; the books, English in most cases, within reach of the comfortable ottomans; the writing-desks ready for use. From the balcony of these rooms one looked at midnight on a vast mass of human beings, in a scene lit up by those oil lamps. In the principal room we found seated on a dais a young Prince of Nepal, Sir Jung Bahadoor's nephew, spangled with jewels; and English ladies began laughingly to compute the value of his cap, which was perhaps worth a king's ransom. "How much do you think?" one lady said, wishing to be exact. The prince was a young man, with a quiet impassive countenance, a lithe active form—and the jewels! He spoke a little English, but never smiled, though laughter prevailed on every side. When spoken to he gazed for a moment through spectacles (which rather became him), and answered abstractedly. English ladies laughed and talked, but never attracted his attention or caused him to turn his eyes to right or left from the princely straight line. By his side sat by far the most remarkable looking person in the room, if not in the assembly—a short, dried-up, and to all appearance rather old man, with a feather in his cap, a silver badge a little below it, and under all an eye like a hawk's. At his girdle was the Ghoorka "Kookerei," which told a tale. He wore a closely-buttoned blue coat, almost like a French uniform. He was the aide-de-camp of the Prince of Nepal. When the prince rose to go away, the aide-de-camp followed him closely. In the carriage they sat side by side, and any one who had meant mischief to the prince would have found the attempt perilous. Such is the Hindoo nautch at the poojah time. Provided by the wealthy, it is, in part at least, freely shared by the poorest; an institution at once of festivity and faith.

CHAPTER XV.

CHRISTIAN MISSIONS: FROM A SECULAR POINT OF VIEW.

NATIVE faiths and Christian missions in India are topics so intimately intertwined that it is impossible to fairly consider the one apart from the other; and as two parts of one subject I shall ask the reader to view them. I wish, having seen a little missionary work in Egypt, that my notes could have been continued, in an ampler form, by Bombay, and so onward. But wishing also to deal chiefly with what I strove in a legitimate way to comprehend, I cannot say that either on my first visit to Bombay, or subsequently, I saw sufficient of the inner life—the everyday work—of its missions, to speak on any point with personal knowledge. It would serve no good purpose to refer to the massive missionary institutions of Bombay as mere "sights." If they are not more than that, they are as sounding brass or a tinkling cymbal.

At Benares, however, I began a series of notes on missions, ending only when I left India the second time; and I can say that as I began I ended, with no idea that missionaries are all heroes, or anything like heroes, and with no idea that missionary work is other than obedience to the command: "Go ye into all the world and preach the Gospel to every creature." In one case in Benares I think I saw the fact below the surface of missionary work. I found the Principal of the College of the London Missionary Society, the Rev. M. A. Sherring, in the midst of his everyday duties, and Mrs Sherring in the midst of her everyday duties—mother and father of a race of young men and women, who may yet have a great influence on India. Here I learned what became to me like the opening of a new life of knowledge of many subjects, which no man surely would affect to despise; and my first was one of my best views of Indian missions. A grave simple sermon—and information, to myself—pointed by memorials of Suttee and Budha, by devotees, and temples, and sacred wells, by school lessons, and by an apparently all-pervading missionary influence, were my first real pictures of those missions upon which England relies to do what England rejoices to do by substitute; for which Englishmen certainly spend money freely, sending money in, it should be remembered, not, save in exceptional cases, taking money out of India, a fact that applies to no other Anglo-Indian institution, or class of men whatever. I sought out in Benares three American members of the Society of Friends—husband and wife, and a young lady who assisted them. I found them in the densely peopled native town, learning the languages of India, eschewing European society, and devoting themselves entirely to their work; but missing, perhaps, even in that way, one great element of usefulness, for the missionaries of Benares have a method of meeting together, and helping each other to connect past and present times; to use, as the apostle used against Athens, an old literature in the service of a newer faith. The three Friends were afterwards compelled to leave Benares—I fear sick—and their generous experiment so far came to an end. Mr Sherring's position as a teacher and writer—as a great missionary—is too well known to need further mention here.

At Serampore I found the fine Baptist college of "Carey, Marshman, and Ward" under an earnest and cultivated principal; and I had the advantage of comparing my own perceptions daily, and for a long period, with the more matured views of a Baptist minister and teacher of great practical ability, the Rev. Thomas Martin. I saw my friend labouring in the midst of his native Christians in a Christian village, devised and provided by the late Mr John

Clarke Marshman, the historian, and named after him. In particular I saw him receive into the Baptist communion, by "dipping," a number of young men and women, as a farewell to the village, on the eve of his departure for England. I gathered, however, that the well-intended close village experiment had not had a marked success. I gathered too that the lives of "Carey, Marshman, and Ward"—in one sense landmark lives—had not been all smooth or free from differences, and that their work and influence, from that time to the present, had been the subject of curious controversy in Native Bengal. A pretty Lutheran church was, after the cession of Serampore by the Danes, handed over to the Bishop of Calcutta, and is now the "station church." Much of this he who runs may read in Serampore.

He would not, however, so readily read the exact truth of one other form of European religious life. He might live in Serampore for months, might learn all about the Serampore and Barrackpore churches and the Baptist chapel, and yet not know even of the existence in one of the back streets of the place of a really living church of the Jesuits. By wandering out of the common track he would find such a church, crowded to the door—with poor people too—and, what is more, with unmistakable worshippers. There is no sahibism in that church at any rate. Rich and poor, European and Native, with a large number of the mixed population, meet together there, and learn from a cultivated Jesuit priest that the outer sign of an inward faith is a virtuous daily life. This good priest, an Italian, was so singularly unacquainted with English creed bitterness, that having procured for a Protestant an introduction with a view to presentation to the Pope, he said, "And pray ask his Holiness for a blessing for me"—utterly oblivious of the fact that to some Protestants (not to this one, however) the blessing of the Pope would have sounded rather like a ban. It was, I think, altogether conceived in a spirit as beautiful as that of a child.

Of St Xavier's College much might be said. One of the priests, Father Shea, a professor or teacher, edits a scholarly and able newspaper—the *Indo-European Correspondence*—marked by great forbearance to native customs. Another, Father Lafonte, is the best scientific lecturer in Calcutta, and ready, as we shall see hereafter, to assist in all good, especially scientific work. Finally, and chiefly, Archbishop Steins labours harder than any Calcutta coolie, and not merely gives efficient headship to a host of varied Catholic institutions, but secures the affection of Native India; not encroaching on its rights of conscience, and never, of course, hiding anything of his own faith. Of the nuns a story of real and unceasing sacrifice might be told; of labour, without punkahs or ice, or any of the means whereby life is made endurable under an Indian sun; of ministrations, in a true sense, by the bedsides of the dying, and of especial kindness to the young. One of the best testimonials to their impartiality is the fact that Protestant children too are entrusted to them here and elsewhere in India, and that the gentle influence of the teachers rises above creed. I should say that the Catholics are less indebted to outside pecuniary help than any other class of missionaries in India, and hence are more thoroughly beyond the charge (often a very stupid charge) of buying proselytes. In Madras there is a case on record of a body of wild boatmen, who, having a tax remitted, went in a body and transferred it to their priest, who accepted and utilised it. I was myself gravely reproved only a few weeks ago by the *Bengalee* newspaper for having asserted that the Pope sanctioned the massacre of St Bartholomew. The feeling in favour of the Roman Catholics was not, as we have seen feeling in England, the implied approval of one extreme as a reproof to another. An anti-Popery lecture would not be received with approval, or indeed with anything but sarcasm by Native Bengal. The Catholics have the good fortune, as a Church, not to belong to the conquering race; and the peculiarity stands them in good stead.

Reference has been made in the preceding chapter to the

progress of Positivism in India. I became acquainted in 1870, chiefly by the attacks made upon him, with a gentleman who was an earnest educationalist and an earnest Comtist, Mr Samuel Lobb, who in 1874 returned to England to die. People wished to write against Mr Lobb, and, in some cases, without their names, as they would not have dared to write with their names. He was, they said, perverting the minds of the young. As a journalist I determined to go more deeply into this charge, and I found it utterly baseless. I found him a generous, unselfish man, doing all manner of good, without intruding his beliefs on any one, and least of all on his pupils. The only time I ever saw him was in a lodging-house in Calcutta, and our conversation was closed by a flow of blood to the mouth of the then fast-sinking teacher. The last I heard of him was in a chaste and restrained address in which his struggles for light and truth were beautifully pictured by Mr Congreve in London. I mention Mr Lobb as a missionary, though he would not himself have claimed the name. He pointed to the higher ideals of duty, and his life in India was not in vain.

Soon after my first arrival in India I visited three colleges in Calcutta—the Cathedral (Church of England) College, under Mr Dyson; the Established Church of Scotland College, under Dr Ogilvie; and the Free Church College (Dr Duff's), under Dr Mitchell. What I heard I took away in exact notes, and published. From Dr Mitchell's class, in many cases of fine young men, we had these among other answers:

"'Here is a stranger who wishes to know your thoughts on some social and religious topics. Tell us what you deem the tendency of thought among the young men of Calcutta.' Here was a pause. Then: 'Do you mean religiously?' 'Yes, in that or any way.' 'I think that most of the educated young men lean to the Brahmo Somaj, or to philosophical inquiry, or unbelief.' Others expressed assent. 'Why do you think so?' Second student: 'Because I see Brahmoism growing, and people prepared to make sacrifices for it.' 'You mean, then, that there is persecution?' 'Great persecution.

socially, in families.' 'Can you say how many educated young men believe in the Shastras?' Third student: 'Not one in a hundred.' Fourth: 'Not one in a thousand. The Shastras are not believed where there is English education.' 'What is your difficulty as to Christianity?' A quiet young man: 'The Trinity.' 'You do not understand it?' 'No.' 'You believe that the soul is immortal?' 'Yes.' 'Why?' 'Because of the longing for immortality that seems in human nature. I believe that God never gave such a longing to leave it at last unsatisfied.' 'And what of Christ?' A student: 'We believe Him to be the best man that ever lived.' 'But not divine?' 'No.' And so through a quiet serious conversation."

Both Dr Mitchell and Dr Ogilvie kindly invited a repetition of the test, and on a second day I took these among other notes, from the two classes:

"'What is your view of the Bible; do you think it is a revelation?' 'Only in the sense in which all good books are revelation.' 'But we require some guide of life, do we not?' 'Yes; and we have Conscience (this was frequently insisted upon), and the lives and thoughts of good men.' 'Now, as to the Brahmo Somaj; do you not think that its foundations are laid in Christianity?' 'I think that it has owed more to Christianity than to any other thing, but it has drawn from many sources.' 'Do you think that without Christianity there would have been any Brahmoism?' 'Yes; being truth it must have been known some day; but the day might have been far off but for Christianity.' 'Do you like the Bible as a reading book?' Several: 'Very much.' 'Do you like it as well as Shakespeare?' 'Better.' 'Or Milton?' 'Yes; better.' 'Or Bacon or Macaulay?' 'Yes, better than any of them.' 'Then why don't you come oftener to read it?' 'We haven't time if we are to pass the examinations.' 'What do you think the young men of Bengal incline to, as a rule, after they leave college? I ask because there is a common belief that they often fall into drinking habits, and are lost to society?' A student, shaking his head gravely: 'It is a sad truth, sir.' 'What is the cause of it?' Another young man: 'It comes from the West,' at which there was a laugh. 'Is the balance one of good or evil for English education?' A number: 'Good.' 'What do you mean by saying that intoxication comes from the West? The Englishmen you come in contact with are not drinkers.' 'No; we have two examples, one good and the other bad; unfortunately, some among us think the latter the better worth imitating.' 'Do you think that Government could do anything?' 'It could prevent the opening of drinking-places.' 'Would that be good?' Several: 'Yes;' and one:

If it could be done without infringing liberty.' 'Do any of you believe in caste?' A decided 'No.' 'Yet you practise it?' 'Yes; it is hard to break away from family and friends.'"

This, as far as it goes, is an exact photograph, and I do not know that it ever was disputed, though a question was not unreasonably raised as to whether it would not convey an incorrect impression of the tendency of missionary education. If we are not making Christians, one or two gentlemen said, it will be to very little purpose that we are making scholars. Dr Mitchell said:

"The Brahmists have inferred that the pupils are coming round to the Somaj. . . . I regret that I did not request the young men to be more exact in their phraseology. I abstained from doing so because I wished to interfere as little as possible with the entire spontaneousness both of the thought and of the expression. . . . Your conversation was with two classes—the students of the third and fourth years. Our inquiries have extended to all the classes, and I am prepared to make decided statements regarding the college as a whole. There is not, in the whole college, so far as we can discover, one registered or initiated Brahmo; not one member, strictly speaking, of either the original or progressive Somaj. There does not seem to be one student who avows himself an adherent, in any definite sense, of either Somaj. Further—and this is exceedingly important—the young men still with us who, on the occasion of your visit, described themselves as favourable to Brahmoism, assure me that they did not mean to imply that they were opposed to Christianity, and that in fact they used the term Brahmoism as synonymous with Theism. No one when asked admits himself to be a free-thinker in the sense of infidel. *Inclined to free thought* seems to have been a grandiose form of expression for *inquirers, seekers after truth.* With regard to Revelation. It is always delicate and hazardous to ask in a class of young Hindoos, whether any of them are inclined to Christianity; and I have avoided doing so. But when the question was put a few days ago—Do you regard the evidence for the truth of the Bible strong or weak? the general answer was 'Strong.' 'Very strong?' from several the answer was, 'Yes, very strong.' Are there, then, no infidels, in the sense of men opposed to Christianity, among our pupils? I do not assert that there are none. But generally, when men are infidels, it will be found that they have only recently joined us—having come from purely secular schools. We do not profess to work miracles. We cannot, in a month or two, do away with the effects of non-religious teaching. But I am prepared to prove that, as a general rule, belief in the truth of the Gospel is proportioned to the length of time that the Bible has been carefully read and faithfully explained."

The foregoing photograph must be viewed by the light of this letter of one of the most accomplished and kind-hearted of missionaries; but all the same the photograph was a thoroughly accurate one, intended neither to help nor hinder missionary work, but to present a fact. Dr Ogilvie died a little later, and then it was remembered what a brave and modest teacher he had been. His determination in stating bare truths, and braving all consequences, was particularly insisted upon. One gentleman said to me: "Very recently, at the end of a missionary conference, Dr Ogilvie renewed a discussion as to whether the Hindoo students did or did not like to be taught the Bible. 'I was speaking,' he said, 'to some of our boys about this, and I said, "So-and-so tells me that his students like the Bible lesson." "Did they tell him that?" said the young men. "Yes," I replied. "And did he believe them?" "Yes," said I. "And would you have believed us if we told you that?" "Oh, no," said I.'" This characteristic story may perhaps exhibit more than the true character of the teacher, if the reader will observe how thoroughly both he and his class entered into the humour of "And did he believe them?" and into that of the inimitable "Oh, no"—the humour of a most serious man, whose very lightest words conveyed wisdom. The value of the joke in this case to the students would perhaps be greater than that of a sermon. Of Dr Mitchell and Mrs Mitchell, I need only say that in schools, and charities of every name, among soldiers and sailors, their genial labours were notable, and some kind words from Native Bengal followed them when they left India.

In September 1872 I saw, in his literary workshop, an aged Baptist missionary, Dr Wenger, at the very point of completing a translation of the Bible into Sanscrit. He began the work in 1847, and (with much else to do at the same time) completed it in 1872—twenty-five years of labour. Three days after I had seen him he was so good as send me a copy of the last volume of his translation. The old man, little seen, and apart from his own religious community little heard of, had gradually completed one of the greatest literary works ever attempted—giving to the Brahmin, in the classical language of India (the language he delights to read), the book of the Christian's God.

In 1874 a native missionary, the Rev. Narayan Sheshadri, of the Bombay Presidency, was on his way home from England, where he had been seeking help for a Christian village system, to be open to men of all creeds, so long as their conduct was good. This was reversing Mr Marshman's idea, and the missionary claimed for it that the plan had found favour both in England and India; and that Sir Salar Jung had allowed the purchase of land for the experiment in the Nizam's dominions. The plan had also some time previously been laid before a missionary conference, and had met with approval. Of the missionary himself there was but one opinion long before the end of the voyage. At first it was thought by one or two people that he might be made to look foolish, but that was found to be an error. Then he preached, and taught the young sailors, and won his way to the kindly regard of every one by his kindly good temper. If still alive, he is, I should say, an efficient missionary.

Many persons have asked why, with such men in India, the native churches should not be independent of England. An obituary notice of Mr Marshman, who died this year, says: "He held that India never could be converted by Europeans, and that the business of missionaries was to raise up native apostles." Mr Sherring, in a tract on "The Evangelisation of India," writes: "It has been said that there are upwards of two thousand native agents of the different missionary societies in India, men who are paid regular salaries from foreign mission funds to preach to people of their own race," and he adds that there have been cases in which, when the pay ceased, the work also ceased. If this rule were recast, and native churches made to depend pecuniarily on themselves, there would, this experienced missionary thinks, be a new order of things. The relations between the European and native missionaries would be different when the latter were independent, and the people who seek the priest's office, that they may eat a piece of bread, would find other work. I heard many like expressions of the same view. When the native churches can cast away all claim to perpetual pecuniary help from England, Christianity will have some chance of standing on its merits. It will no longer be the faith of the conqueror. The opinion that the native preacher is paid for doing England's work will disappear. At present the non-proselytising Hindoo can see no motive but a political one for the vast outlay of money for missionaries. I cannot, in the limits of this chapter, argue the question. I must simply indicate the fact, which the mention of Mr Sheshadri illustrates.

Journeying through the scenes of the Bengal famine, I went from Soorey, in Beerbhoom, to the mountain home of the Santals, where, about 1100 feet above the sea, at a place which has been named "Ebenezer," two friends, a Norwegian and a Dane, have established an independent mission. The journey had to be made by palanquin. The scenery was in many parts magnificent. Crossing a rapid little river before day-dawn, we entered a labyrinth of foliage so dense and varied, that in a square yard I counted thirteen different kinds of shrubs, the branches and tendrils intertwined like a thick mat. Comfortable-looking houses, embedded in little groves, and with cows, pigs, goats, sheep, fowls, and even piles of firewood, indicated a people and a climate very different from those of Bengal. In many cases the women were spinning at their doors; in few did they run away at the sight of the palki. From tangled foliage we passed to a vast expanse of rice-fields, the "bunds" around which were the paths for the palki-men, who moved in squares, on the ledges of fields covered with water, above which the green paddy barely appeared. A distant mountain was in this part the only landmark. In about twenty-five miles we had almost every conceivable variety of scenery; at one time as of the Scotch moor; then the Yorkshire wold; then the Sussex downs, with vast herds of cattle, sheep, and goats, feeding, under the care of one or two persons, in solitude and peace.

Sixteen palki-men, some bearing, some running alongside as relays, gave the variety of a monotonous song, to the lowing of the herds, and the cries of the birds. From the time a palki is lifted till it is set down again, the songs never cease. Led by the men in front, the songs are the guide of those behind. "Keep left," "Keep right," "Keep straight," "Beware," and so on. Sometimes the leader tells that "a flower," "a marigold" (a woman), is coming. Then a song in her praise is extemporised amid general laughter. Towards nightfall we arrived at a village with all the characteristics of European civilisation. Mr Skrefsrud, the Norwegian missionary, was in England. Mr Boerrison, the Dane, was at his post, and had been of great use to the Government and the poor people during the famine, though he made the inconvenient stipulation, not safe as a future guide, that if he distributed the "relief"—the rice—he must be allowed to preach and pray with the people. About 1700 persons came in at the time I was there, and, in several different groups, attended so many different—happily short—services. Then they had their rice. Mr Boerrison was a trained engineer before he was a missionary (as also, I think, was his friend), and the famine work was well managed. Indeed the missionary was a thoroughly devoted and capable man in every way; doctor, squire, lawgiver, lawyer, as well as pastor to his people, and, above all, the director of the young, who went with him in a drove for their morning and evening walk, laughing and talking incessantly. Roads, tanks, and in one case a small lake, had been made. At a cost of six shillings the missionaries built a church which held 600 persons, and at an estimated cost of fully fourteen shillings were building what Mr Boerrison called a cathedral, to hold 1000 persons. The walls were formed of posts, with twigs intertwined between them, and the roof of like material; all, in common with the labour, a free gift. Everything seemed admirable, save the one fact that there had been a great revival and many baptisms during the famine. I would rather have heard of them at some other time, considering that Mr Boerrison held the rice.

The two friends went out at first for a society; and their "brethren" in India strove to separate them; but they demurred. Finally they cut their tow-rope of the society, and after difficulties which would read like a romance, founded the mission in Santalia. The land belonged to seven Hindoo brothers, who raised obstacles innumerable. At last on "one blessed night," by giving baksheesh to a powerful headman, a paper was signed securing to the missionaries twenty-five acres of land at a yearly rental of £4, 8s., and on a lease of a hundred years, with power of renewal. Next morning the brothers wished to "do back;" but already the missionaries were on their way to Nya Doomka, to register their paper. It was rather an odd proceeding—on the plan, perhaps, of Jacob and Laban, or Jacob and Esau—but Mr Boerrison saw only the good he and his friend intended, and sees now only the good they have undoubtedly done. Land, of course, they must have had in some way.

They planted and built; stood between the people and the money-lenders; made their church the mother of other churches, and their school the mother of other schools, over a large district of Santalia. A committee, which was formed to raise money, visited the station at a cost of from £30 to £40 a year. The missionaries dismissed the committee, surely one of the most daring steps ever taken; and now they were independent. They give no money, but lend without interest when they can. Genial and happy in themselves and their people, the missionaries of Ebenezer have certainly attained an almost unparalleled position. The district is rich in soil and in minerals. The gardens are ornamented with beautiful spar (iron, I think), and everything betokens a much greater future. The story is at least one of what may be done by individual manhood.

The American missionaries, too, have a noble history. In Bombay they have, or rather a good man of their nation has, a missionary newspaper; in Lucknow they have another. In Calcutta they have a most important Mission Home, from which ladies go out to native houses (zenanas) to teach, and one Miss Seelye, a physician, to heal the sick, charging a fee of eight shillings a visit to the rich and nothing to the poor. Close to the Home this noble lady established a children's hospital, and with the other ladies also superintended a foundling hospital, provided by the municipality. Of the difficulties and repulses of the zenana teachers many curious stories might be told.

I met one day in Calcutta a native missionary, whose work, with a large congregation, was in the Sunderbunds, where he seldom saw a European face. I met in the thickest of the famine work with a missionary free-lance, Mr Johnson (formerly, I believe, a military officer, and not "reverend"), who in very truth held his life as if nothing that he might obey God, and who rambled all India over, as he believed the Spirit of God called him. His arm had on one journey (in company with Mr Boerrison) been nipped off by a tiger. He had been apprehended riding defiantly over the frontier (I think to the Affreedes), and had only been spared as a favour. The laws of men were against him, but he read God's Law, and in a spirit like American John Brown's, obeyed that. I saw him by the side of an Englishman who had been struck down by heat in the famine district, and I know that that Englishman felt towards him with sincere gratitude. The sight of his face was in itself a security. I know not what

Church he belongs to. I only know that he is a Christian; not rich; not, I fear, a favourite among people who like staid rules, but a man, nevertheless, of heroic mould.

On my way home the second time, I met a young missionary, who convinced me that I had missed one of the great sights of Agra, in missing the Army Temperance work of the Rev. J. G. Gregson, a Baptist. Mr Gregson, while, of course, preaching, has made this his special work, and at this time could look—with joy, I am sure—on six thousand pledged teetotallers in the British army in India—a work of which his young assistant spoke, and justly, with enthusiasm. Here are some instances among many of self-denial in missions.

I saw much of two Baptist schools (the girls, about fifty, boarding in the mission grounds), under the care of the Rev. George Kerry and Mrs Kerry. The boarders were all the children of professedly Christian parents, and the condition of the school was that the whole of the pupils should hear a portion of the Bible and a prayer daily, morning and evening; nothing of a controversial kind, however, being introduced into the prayer. The teachers were in some cases Hindoo, in others Mohammedan, in others, of course, Christian. I mentioned to Mr Kerry the general reverential deportment, to which I only saw one exception. He said: "Yes, and do you know those who are not with us think they may somehow get good from the worship of 'our' God? It is only to them like a fetish, but it is that." There were six fine separate class-rooms to Mr Kerry's school. The fees were from 6d. to 2s. a month; the Baptist mission contributing £150 to the cost; the Government nothing. I ought perhaps to say (having referred to Mrs Sherring, Mrs Mitchell, and now to Mrs Kerry) that a missionary's wife earns nothing, at least by her mission work. She is expected to have mastered the words, "And they shall be one flesh," and to seek for no separate interest.

The bungalows of the girls, separated from the mission

house by a tank, perhaps sixty feet wide, are of course secured from male intrusion, ladies alone having the right to tread the private path. The plan is, that the children dress and eat as in their villages, save that cleanliness is strictly enjoined; and they manage their own affairs. Their temper in school or at play seemed imperturbable; not merry, but a little dignified (it would be a gross impropriety to lay a hand on the head of a Hindoo girl of fourteen), perfect little ladies, yet very bright and playful. Looking from the mission window I saw them in little groups, bringing water, cooking, singing, and so on. Presently a shower of rain began to fall. First they held up their faces to catch the welcome rain, then they perceptibly shivered, cowered, and at last as with one impulse ran indoors. I had seen them at their early morning worship and lessons, and heard them singing cheerily of the "Good Shepherd who knoweth His sheep," but I thought them after all prettiest at play. Mr Kerry was proud to say that in a long experience he never had beaten a boy, and of course the same applies to the girls. The work is now under other management.

I have but one more instance of those I have selected as illustrations, but it is one of the most significant. The Rev. J. Long (of the Church Missionary Society, and referred to elsewhere as the translator of "Nil Durpan") had an admirable system of fifteen village schools, with 800, in many cases Mussulman, pupils, to whom he taught the Scriptures orally with illustrations drawn from emblems and proverbs. The children committed to memory, in the vernacular entirely, some small piece—"The old old story" is an instance—and then began the use of the symbols and proverbs; by means of which also I believe Mr Long is now engaged in illustrating the whole Bible or the New Testament. In the same way he taught the ordinary branches of elementary education, giving prizes to the girls for cooking and house management. I never saw these schools, but I have heard high praise given to them;

and one proof of their efficiency is in the fact that the system is being rapidly adopted all over India. Mr Long's influence generally on Native India has been remarkable; and I think it is in a considerable measure owing to his great tolerance and wise forbearance. It was quite a common thing for him to take a holiday at the house—the English home for guests—of an accomplished Hindoo landlord, and to use that gentleman's carriage to and from church—the carriage of the worshipper of Doorga waiting for the servant of Christ; and I know that when the missionary left India, his friend, thoroughly Hindoo, pressed him to return, if possible, as his guest—that is, at the generous Hindoo's cost, from and to Charing Cross. This does not look as if missionaries with common sense were viewed with dislike in India.

Of the Church of England generally in India, I should say, and say unhesitatingly, that all State support to it ought to be peremptorily withdrawn, and, at the same time, I think that the withdrawal might in many cases be a loss to India. No faith, as a faith, ought to be supported from the taxes of India, or assuredly ought not, unless the Hindoo temple and the Mohammedan mosque were so supported. At the same time, the chaplains have often held the even balance against the missionaries. The feeling between the two bodies has not always been an amicable one, but to the chaplain, the Anglo-Indian, and, indeed, also the native communities, have owed certain characteristics not to be disregarded. No religious service in India is more solemnising than that which may be found in some of those beautiful cantonment churches which stud the land. Let the State aid, however, be withdrawn, and the chaplain placed on the same footing as the missionary, and the Church of England would have found a higher ground of usefulness.

An attempt, made at Simla, to set on foot Union Churches, was not, I think, received with general approval. There was, and I suppose is, in Edinburgh, an "Anglo-Indian

Christian Union;" and the new Church in India, though not, it was said, connected with that Union, selected from it the minister for the first of its churches at Simla, and the forms of worship were essentially Presbyterian. There was nothing in any way improper in this, but it could hardly be wondered at if English churchmen stood aloof from the proposal, or if Independents and Baptists preferred their congregational independence to union. To a limited extent the project will succeed and prove a good. I do not think that it can do so generally. The powerful individuality of Dr Duff, yet standing out like a great rock in the weary land of India, is an example in mission work. A man to whom all subjects are God's subjects, and all humanity God's property, will desire as few restrictions as possible on his efforts. Still the idea of union was pleasant to many people who yearned to see an end to Christian bickerings in a land where every difference is magnified. A man of a serious turn of mind, who goes from a discussion as to dipping or sprinkling in baptism, to where he sees Paine's "Age of Reason, price eight annas" (a shilling), may well long for some means of peace.

The outcry against "the godless education" of the State colleges is to my view both a wicked and a senseless outcry. The State colleges are England's simple duty to India, and will tend to India's well-being in a grand sense. The mission colleges, however, have duties all their own, and no one who believes in Christianity as a missionary faith would say them nay, so long as they pay for what they provide, and do not seek money from the hard-wrung taxes of India. I have heard it said that the aim ought to be the poor to whom Christ appealed, and that therefore preaching and not school teaching is the true object of the missionary. This is simply an error. The Jesuits both preach and teach, knowing that a man works better with two hands than with one; and I never saw a missionary yet who did not rejoice to win a Brahmin. I have heard it said also, by vulgar people, that the missionary in India is a man who could not "get on" in England. The truth is, that the missionary in India is often the one man in a district who is independent of all control, and who can stand for the poor in their need; and when, as sometimes occurs, he is not merely like a hero, but also is one, he has in his hands a power which the heads of armies cannot in a just cause withstand. A man like Mr Sherring, a loyal and ardent supporter of good government, is a safeguard against bad government, go where he may, and is a positive gain, not merely to the work of missions, but to English rule in India, and to the cause of the poor and helpless in far more than the district in which his work for the time more directly lies.

CHAPTER XVI.

LORD MAYO'S LAST TOUR—LORD NORTHBROOK—IRRIGATION AND TRADE.

SOME important questions were pending, but none were markedly pressing for settlement, when early in the year 1872, Lord Mayo, accompanied by Lady Mayo and a few friends and officers in charge of departments, embarked in Admiral Cockburn's flag-ship, the "Glasgow," for a tour in Burma and the Andamans. A minute and circumstantial plan provided for quite an array of doings, from the landing in Rangoon till the final departure from Port Blair. Lord Mayo's mind was at this time comparatively at ease, and the omens seemed propitious for a more than ordinarily pleasant and useful tour. He had a short time previously reviewed, with interest and indeed delight, Lord Napier's fine army at the Delhi camp, and had been heartily received on all hands. A little later he had welcomed the young King of Siam in public durbar. The Looshai expedition was progressing with the completeness that characterised all the plans of the commander-in-chief. And finally, Lord Mayo, in a personal sense, had been especially gratified by many marked expressions of feeling from Hindoos, Mohammedans, Parsees, and Jews, as well as Christians, on the recovery of the Prince of Wales.

In a little time telegrams began to arrive, telling of meetings here and there in Burma; of merchants pleading for standard measures, for extension to Burma of the Bengal Contract Law, for a Bankruptcy Act, for railway extension; of natives of Burma avowing their loyalty and stating their grievances; and, amid all, of the festivities of a vice-regal tour. Then the telegrams ceased; the Viceroy had departed for the Andamans.

Three months previously, but with no view to this tour, I had received from a gentleman, and sent to England, some very good pictures of those convict islands. The story, at the time it appeared, read like that of a different planet. It pictured a group of four greater and a number of smaller islands, cut off, in a double sense, from all human kind, in the vast solitude of the Bay of Bengal; a native population of 10,000 naked savages, needing protection from an equal population of, in some cases, much worse savages sent there by the Indian Government; a fine climate with cool sea breezes; landscapes of hill and dale covered with rich tropical vegetation to the very water's edge; varied natural productions for man and beast, including many of the fruits of Europe, naturalised with great pains; bazaars in which ticket-of-leave men and women sold, and in many cases produced, what officers and men, military and police, required; European quarters with church and mess-rooms; convict quarters, in long barracks, each for one hundred men; a picture altogether curious when given in full; not, I fear, so suggestive in this necessarily brief outline.

Port Blair was described as situated on the southern island, with a fine harbour and anchorage, and at the mouth of an inlet, with Ross Island, Chatham Island, and Viper Island, all within easy distances. On Blair and Ross Islands there were said to be about 10,000 convicts, of whom 950 were females; and Viper Island was marked as the punishment station, with chain gangs and other severe kinds of labour. Of the charms of scenery, no language was held to convey the full fact; and photographs, taken for a melancholy purpose a little later, go far to show that the word-pictures were not overdrawn. It was to these beautiful prison islands that the "Glasgow," attended by two other vessels, was bound when the telegrams from Burma to India ceased to record the doings of Lord Mayo.

On the evening of the 12th February, there were whispers through Calcutta and the neighbourhood, that some dreadful thing had happened at the Andamans. Major Burke, brother of the Viceroy, had, it was said, received astounding telegrams in cipher, and Mr Robert Burke, now Under Secretary for Foreign Affairs, and then on his way from Calcutta to Bombay for England, had been telegraphed to return. A few hours set the sad rumours at rest, with the sad reality; the Viceroy had been murdered at Port Blair. People had been prepared for anything but this. While Lord Mayo was in Calcutta, and with his strange, but rooted, and, in fact, ungovernable, dislike to being surrounded by guards or police, nothing, after Mr Norman's death, would have greatly surprised Anglo-Indians. But to be struck down amid English sailors, close to "our own element," and in sight of the admiral's flag-ship, appeared to bewilder every one, and for a time to dominate every other feeling.

The mournful facts were stated circumstantially in the official gazette, and by eye-witnesses. The vessels arrived at Port Blair at half-past nine on the morning of February 8th, and between eleven and twelve o'clock the Viceroy, accompanied by his private secretary, his personal staff, and several officers, including the superintendent of the station, landed on Ross Island, where the barracks and other buildings were visited. They then went to Viper Island, and here, as the punishment settlement, additional care was taken to keep the convicts at a distance. From Viper Island they went to Chatham Island. At five o'clock in the evening the work of the day was done, according to the programme. Lord Mayo, however, wished for a little more —wished particularly to see the sun set from Mount Harriet, behind Hope Town, Port Blair; and one more beautiful sunset was in God's mercy granted to him.

The party arrived at Hope Town at half-past five, and a body of police was moved as speedily as possible from Chatham Island, to serve as escort. The mountain was climbed and descended in playful good humour. The sun had been seen to set, and no one suspected how very nearly a human life was to the great final setting. Some ticket-of-leave men approaching with a petition were ordered to send their petition in another way. By the time the pier or jetty had been reached for the return to the "Glasgow," it was quite dark, and the way was shown by torch-light. Lord Mayo had walked about twenty yards on the pier, the superintendent turning to give some order, the officers generally, perhaps, now less careful, with English sailors so near at hand, when a man dashed forward from the shore, and knocking one or two people aside, stabbed the Viceroy twice, above the one shoulder and below the other. It was all over, and as certainly as if it had been done with a battery of guns. The assassin was seized. The Viceroy either fell or leaped into the water; no one in the darkness and confusion could say which. He simply said, according to the hearing of his private secretary, "Burne, they've hit me;" and they were the last and only words of Lord Mayo. He was carried to the launch, which was at once put off from shore, but it is not quite certain that even then he was alive. Before the "Glasgow" was reached (Lady Mayo watching therefrom the approach of the launch) he was quite dead.

The murderer, a man named Shere Ali, about twenty-nine years of age, and from the neighbourhood of the Khyber Pass, had been transported for what he had called a family feud (vendetta), and the Commissioner of Peshawur, murder. He had previously been a soldier of the Indian Government, and was remembered by some of his officers as a well-behaved man. At the Andamans his conduct had been reported "fair," and he was then a ticket-of-leave man, earning his living as a barber in Hope Town. He confessed the murder, said he did it by God's order, and that he had no accomplices. Nothing more was elicited. He was tried and executed. Such in bare terms is the story of Lord Mayo's last tour. The motive for the murder will probably never be known; there was nothing, as in the case of Mr Norman, to cause suspicion that any act of Lord Mayo had led to it, or to connect Shere Ali with any body of conspirators. There were rumours of a message having been sent to the Andamans, and of much besides; but nothing arose to show that the rumours rested on any figment of truth. The most general opinion was that the man had acted merely under a poignant sense of what he deemed his own wrongs. It was a strange end for Lord Mayo. The memory of his light-hearted earlier days came, it is said, to some minds in India, as it was destined to come to many more in England; and this scene on the jetty, and amid the shallow water, under the dark foliage of Hope Town, far south in the Bay of Bengal, was a great mystery, before which serious men, for the moment at least, bowed.

On the 16th February the "Glasgow" gave up her charge at the mouth of the Hooghly to a smaller vessel, the "Daphne." On the 17th the body was landed at a ghât some distance below Calcutta on the river, and placed on a gun-carriage, and covered with the union jack. A procession of judges, native princes, merchants, clergy, and all manner of orders of men, had been arranged, and marshalled on the line of route, from the ghât to Fort William, falling into rank, line after line, as the gun-carriage passed. The road—which lay along the great plain, the Maidan, with the river on the one hand and the palaces of fashionable Chowringhee on the other, Fort William looming darkly in front—was lined the whole length with English and Native troops, so arranged that an English regiment on the one side faced a Native regiment on the other. On the river the ships were in mourning, and the yards and rigging manned, though on no uniform rule. The plain, a mile and a half wide, and in length from Fort William almost to Alipore, the lieutenant governor's house, was like a sea of faces, quiet, impassive, undemonstrative. The minute-guns from a battery of Royal Artillery at the landing ghât, were, as it seemed, replied to from Fort William, and echoed from the "Daphne" and from a Siamese man-of-war, in never-ceasing dull leaden roar. The Viceroy's body-guard, and bodies of Bengal cavalry and Calcutta volunteers, with chaplains and others, preceded the coffin, which was followed by the Viceroy's brothers, his little boy, about seven years old, and apparently bewildered with the strange scene, and his private secretary, who had also been his friend. Then came the acting Governor General, Mr Strachey, the lieutenant governor, the commander-in-chief, the Bishop of Calcutta, Bishop Milman, Archbishop Steins, Roman Catholic, and all the varied orders of persons, including a fine body of sailors, to whom places had been assigned. As the body passed, and the people fell into line, small detachments of Bengal cavalry rode up on each side; a strong body of the same cavalry also bringing up the rear. Regimental bands timed the slow order of the procession with a funeral march. An Englishman would have been very phlegmatic if, even in the general mournfulness, he had lost sight of the significance of that grand display of calm strength, or of the facility with which the vacant high place had been filled.

Leaving the open ground, the houses in mourning gave a new direction to the thoughts; it was a change from the grandeur to the privacy of a great common feeling, which, whatever it was not, was exceedingly solemnising. The coffin was taken into the grounds of Government House, by what is known as the North West Gate, and placed at the foot of the Grand Stair, the chief mourners standing by, while the procession filed slowly out at the opposite gateway. It was Saturday evening, and very nearly dark. The huge building loomed gloomily over the body of the Viceroy and the few mourners who remained with it, while the last of the long file of people passed into the densely-crowded, and now lit-up street. The coffin was then carried into the great festive room, where, as yesterday, Lord Mayo had received the King of Siam; and there, covered with the union jack, the orders of nobility, and a few simple but more voiceful wreaths of flowers, it remained till Wednesday, when the funeral service was read by the Bishop of Calcutta, and the funeral anthems and hymns were sung by a fine choir. Then the body was borne away once more to the "Glasgow" to be conveyed to Ireland; and India saw the last of its great-hearted Viceroy.

I have said in an earlier chapter that I am not attempting to claim for Lord Mayo a place in the front rank of statesmen. If I did so I am satisfied that history would not allow the claim. But I say again that his healthy mind, in a healthy body, made his work light, and reduced great difficulties, till what might have appeared a mountain become as a mole-hill. He was essentially a loyal man—to his friends, his sovereign, and his country; and I have been told that no one had a more reverential and child-like sense of the deeper dependence upon God.

Lord Napier and Ettrick, Governor of Madras, held the vice-royalty from the end of February till the middle of May, when Lord Northbrook arrived. The re-hoisting of the flag, however, at Government House, was anything but a token that the current of official life had returned to its accustomed channels. There was a marked change. The guards were now European, and precautions hitherto undreamt of were taken to prevent the possibility of a surprise; a curious instance of what a day may bring forth in India. The first impression Lord Northbrook made on Native India was, that he would be excessively reserved. Before he left Calcutta he had convinced the people of the sincerity of his aims, and they forgave the reserve. In a speech soon after his arrival, he declared his determination to curtail expenditure, so that it might come within reasonable income, and in all changes of policy to proceed with caution, and a regard for the feelings of the people concerned. He abolished the income tax. To one of Sir George Campbell's favourite measures he opposed a veto, which was more than the veto of one measure, for it warned the lieutenant governor of what a veto might imply.

When the famine seemed imminent, the Viceroy and the lieutenant governor were at opposite poles of thought, and I think Sir George Campbell was fundamentally right. A number of persons (including, unfortunately for the position, some grain merchants) suggested the closing of the ports, so far as the export of grain was concerned. Sir George Campbell partly took this view, but with quite a different scope. He suggested, I believe, as did most persons of reasonable views in England, not that the ports should be closed, but simply that means should be taken to prevent the grain from being carried away at a time when it was needed. That is, that the grain might be purchased in Backergunge, the great rice-growing country, or elsewhere, and the carriage saved; while the purchase, if made early, might be at a comparatively low price. Lord Northbrook believed that his appearance in the market as a buyer would be to play into the hands of the rice merchants, some of whom, there was reason to suppose, had laid up large stocks of grain. He sent, therefore, as we have seen, to Burma and elsewhere, bought at a still higher rate, but left the trade free. I believe Sir George Campbell right, for these reasons: First, I do not think that, if a merchant, foreseeing a famine and venturing to act upon his perception, bought up grain to sell at a future market rate, he was doing anything immoral. The action would be in his own direct line of business, and altogether different from a body of planters buying up or leasing all the means of carriage in a famine district that they might sub-lease it to the Government at an immense profit. Secondly, if the Government had appeared in the grain market up-country, the merchants who had been storing grain in Calcutta would have lost their vantage ground, and might have been compelled to sell. Thirdly, as stated elsewhere, Lord Northbrook's purchases—privately made in Burma—could not have been so made if the famine had continued another year. As it was, strange scenes met one in the famine district; hosts of vessels going up and down the Ganges, exporting and importing grain at the same time; grain arriving to where grain in vast quantities was already stored. Several methods were suggested, by perfectly impartial men, as means whereby, without closing the ports, the good Bengal rice might have been kept in India. Lord Northbrook's refusal to leave Calcutta during the hot season, and his anxious and unremitting labour to beat down the famine and save the treasury, while at the same time he matured a scheme, or rather schemes, of irrigation, deserve higher praise than they have obtained.

To Lord Dalhousie belongs the credit of initiating our English system of utilising native methods, supplemented by newer and more scientific means of irrigation; and if Lord Dalhousie had been Emperor of all India, with power in perpetuity, we should probably not now have had so dreadful a prospect in Madras. To Lord Lawrence, however, assisted by the clear initial policy of Lord Salisbury, we owe the practical development of the idea. During the rule of Lord Lawrence, not a part of India, or any peculiarity of India, escaped notice, when the Governor General was forming his vast and beneficent plans for irrigation. Lord Mayo continued the work, but less decisively, in view of his financial difficulties. Lord Northbrook made the subject his own on sound principles, and with a tact and considerateness for native views, habits, and even prejudices, which, if his rule had continued, would have borne all before it, and made irrigation to represent one of the greatest victories of England in India.

He recognised the fact that compulsory irrigation may be a great hardship in districts which from local peculiarities never lack water; and he knew, as some men do not, that public spirit, and the sacrifice of private to public interests, must generally depend on education. He saw a vast empire in which the districts differed, at clearly marked stages, from the thin end of the wedge at Comorin to the thick end at the Himalayas, and from Burma to Bombay. To people who said in effect, "Irrigation is good, but as you do not carry coals to Newcastle, pray also forbear to bring water to where we have enough," he replied, in effect, "What you say is reasonable; show us the exact fact." He saw in India that the Ganges, the Jumna, and the Brahmapootra, had a way in the rains, not merely of turning dry courses, not marked on any maps, into navigable rivulets, but of submerging whole districts, so that over many miles of cultivated land the people paddled their canoes. To store this water was one problem. He saw in the south a vast tank system of irrigation. He saw a little higher, and indeed all along, in parts, the Madras system, formed by intercepting and damming off the waters of the Kistna and the Godavery on their way to the ocean, and spreading over the country many small channels, in the form of a life-giving fan; a system carried out also northward, from the Soane and other canals. He saw in the Punjab an excellent system of well irrigation, the wells studding the country like forest trees; in Bombay, inundation canals, which received and stored the waters in times of flood. On the data supplied by a good irrigation map and the administrative reports, a story different from any yet told might be written of Indian irrigation; of what has been done, and what must be done if England would justify her rule by her care for the true interests of the people.

One glance at an irrigation map is sufficient to show how little has been done. The bright spots are numerous, but the darkness is vast, and, under certain conditions, means death. Yet you cannot say where irrigation begins, or where it ends. A public-spirited landlord will sometimes do much good never heard of by anybody out of his immediate neighbourhood. This kind of religious benevolence is much commoner than many Englishmen imagine. Above all, it is impossible to say where the power to irrigate ends. On those streams to which I have referred as not even marked on the maps, or, in fact, existent in dry weather, you may sail for miles and miles in diverging lines, learning what an immense security nature has given India against famine and drought. But will irrigation prove remunerative, or even pay its own expenses? In some cases it will do so; in some it will not; but it may be as necessary in the one case as the other, and ought to be so viewed by statesmen. In the sense of utilising all that was good in native irrigation, and extending the system of irrigation gradually but unremittingly, no ruler India ever had would, I think, have achieved greater and more enduring results than Lord Northbrook.

One other subject Lord Northbrook, almost beyond any other Governor General, might have been expected to equally make his own, but which I think he did not. I mean the development of Indian trade and trades. The impression existed, correctly or incorrectly—and impression is much in India—that as Viceroy he cared little comparatively about restoring the old trade routes to Western China and Kashgaria; that, in fact, Lord Mayo's policy with respect to them was abandoned. To Indian trade, by river and railway, as well as outward, I should say Lord Northbrook did give much attention, but I cannot see from it much sensible result. Look, as an example, to the Ganges for what this river trade means.

In 1871 the Indian Government requested Sir George Campbell to select some point on this river at which to register the trade. He selected Sahibgunge—perhaps as good a place as he could have had for noting the long distance boats and cargoes both of the up and down trades, though no point was of the least use for those lesser distances, either up or down, which stopped short of the place of registry. In the first six months more than 18,000 boats passed Sahibgunge—boats in size from the Dacca "pulwar," from sixty to seventy-five feet long and drawing six feet of water (for sea as well as river voyages), to the flat-bottomed boat from the upper provinces. The cargoes downward were such commodities as wheat, grain, sugar, oil-seeds, hides and horns, tobacco, timber, and saltpetre. The wheat was generally shipped as low on the river as Monghyr; the sugar in the Benares part of the North Western Provinces, and tobacco in Tirhoot. The markets were found all the way down the river to Calcutta, which itself, however, had fully half of the total traffic. Up stream, rice, metal goods, and other articles of foreign production, were carried. I have myself watched all night through the boats passing in shoals, faster than one could count them, to and from Calcutta, the dismal songs of the boatmen sounding, especially in the rains, like echoes from eternity. The true fact of the Ganges may be seen more clearly in the next chapter.

Who can say what it is that governs the India trade? One year there is not an Arab dhow on the Hooghly. Next year there are thirty. Why is it? I asked a gentleman of great experience. He knew no more, he said, of the mainsprings of that trade than he knew of the man in the moon. Each officer knows his own district, and somebody is presumed to have the skill to put all the reports properly into one; but the broad general fact is little known. Indeed, we know very little even of the laws that govern the Cape and Canal routes to Europe, though we perceive that the latter certainly has not rendered the former obsolete. Merchants, who buy "on delivery," prefer the storage on sea to warehousing on land; and from various causes the Cape vessels increase in number.

Passing to European trade, what do we find in India? I made a point of seeing or learning the facts of all works from about ten miles below to about thirty above Calcutta. I found fifteen great factories, established within ten years, between Budge Budge and Chinsurah, for cotton or jute. Opposite Calcutta there were American and Scotch firms transforming Seebpoor. At Rishra, near Serampore, near the old house of Warren Hastings, is a jute mill. Where "Carey, Marshman, and Ward" made their famous Serampore paper, a fine jute mill is yearly extending its boundaries and its trade. Where rum was made of old at Goripore, for the Australian gold fields, jute is now manufactured. At Titighur, where Lord Combermere rested from his toils, there is now a cotton mill; and where Sir Lawrence Peel had his house at Budge Budge there is a factory for jute. Garden Reach, half "spoiled" by the steamboat companies and the King of Oude, is to be wholly spoiled by mills and factories. English, American, Armenian, and Jew, run the race of this new competition. I could easily refer to many more instances. Are the mills an evil to India? People who say so can have little care for the general interests of mankind. There are, Lord Shaftesbury said, when these notes were being written, in the Bombay Presidency 405,000 spindles, 4500 power looms, and 10,000 hands, turning out daily 100,000 lbs. of yarn. Lord Salisbury, on later data, stated the number of spindles at 600,000, with "at least half a million more approaching completion." Lord Shaftesbury would enforce in these mills the observance of Sunday. Lord Salisbury would not; and Lord Salisbury is right, considering the creeds of the workers; though the English mill-owner who keeps his mill working on Sunday has little claim to the sympathies of Englishmen. I saw much of the working of the jute mill at Serampore; of the willing docile workers, and the value of their work; and I sincerely trust no body of men in England, nor any interest in England, will be suffered to interpose to fetter these new impulses of trade.

The men of Manchester, however, are determined to have, at least, Manchester goods admitted free, before India advances to the manufacture of the finer goods. One speaker in the House of Commons distinctly said so in exact words, on that memorable occasion, this very year, when the members for Lancashire went in a body, Conservative and Radical alike, to demand the repeal of the 5 per cent. duty on cotton goods imported into India. *The Times* reminded Manchester, sarcastically, of this general agreement, and of the fact that when any great Indian questions concerning only the interests of India are before the House, the members for Lancashire are too often conspicuous by their absence. Sir George Campbell and Sir George Balfour represented India in the debate. Manchester was simply impetuous—for itself. I do not say that Manchester is characterised by selfishness. Its public and private spirit would give the lie to any such charge; but assuredly it is in error. It is the duty of the House of Commons to legislate for India from an Indian, not an English, stand-ground, and with a view, first of all, to the interests of India.

Some little time ago there appeared in *Mookerjee's* (Calcutta) *Magazine* a plaintive lament over the decay of Indian trades; the muslins, the shawls, the carved work —the cunning workmanship of a hundred names. It is an article that reads like a wail; and the writer (probably the editor, but I do not know) points the whole by the fact that while India is poor, and paying enormously for money on loan, England is receiving the money that might redeem the difficulties of India, and convert its poverty into wealth. Is there nothing in this? Sir George Campbell says there is, as we have seen in another chapter. English enterprise is doing much. The mines of Raneegunge (native, in the first instance) are being vastly extended; and much enterprise of other names is tending to like results.

Still India is poor; very poor; deplorably poor. Still, also, there are Englishmen who talk of "rights of conquest," and like foolish and wicked claims, which ought to be cast aside, before they cast us and our rule aside as worthless in the day of first principles. We have no rights of conquest which are not rights of justice. We won India partly by the strong arm, partly by strong sense, partly by inducing the people to believe us. I believe with Colonel Chesney,[1] that English government, in any

[1] "Indian Polity."

case, in India is a great improvement on Native government, but it is still foreign government, and if it claim to stand on rights of conquest it will go down as certainly as it ever arose; and the fall will be terrible.

I wish Lord Northbrook had given more attention to developing the resources—not State, but popular resources—of India. I wish now that Lord Lytton may see the way to do so. Lord Northbrook did a great thing, much condemned, when he tried the Guikwar of Baroda publicly; and he did more than that. He could not, the *Hindoo Patriot* said, be "considered a brilliant ruler," for "he made no war, annexed no territory, broke no pledge, committed no plunder"—keen satire surely—but "he gave the land rest." Lord Lytton may accomplish what Lord Northbrook missed. He has had the "tamasha" of "the Empress" at Delhi. He has had more. He has already conciliated the people, who saw little to praise in the tamasha; and he may do them immense good. He has power, as an English noble, which no Anglo-Indian official could have if raised to the supreme rule. Supported by a strong party at home, and with the great fact in his favour that the Conservative in England may be, and often is, the truest Liberal as regards India; with the fact also in his favour, that he stands above all Anglo-Indian cliques and special interests, I know not what Lord Lytton may not do of beneficial work before his rule passes into history. Dangers in Cabul mean much; but India must be defended within the frontiers, by India being made to rest secure, not merely in just laws, but in material prosperity. If good government does not consist so much in perfect theories as in practical results, then India, having none of the perfect theories of government to fall back upon, and actually claiming few of them, has a more than ordinary claim to the practical results which she in common with all Eastern nations does claim. She is told that she cannot have European political freedom. Her reply, not always articulate, but generally very real, is a claim to be well and justly governed, not merely as to laws between man and man—the work of jurists, but as to development of national life, and her power to live—the work of statesmen. To some of the features of this claim I shall ask the reader's attention later. In referring, however, to the past work of Lord Mayo and Lord Northbrook, and to the existing work of Lord Lytton, I know of no fact that is better worth deepening than that of the reality of Native Opinion in India. No ruler—not even Akbar, or Runjeet Singh, or Dost Mohammed—could rule without making the interests of the people a primary consideration. All great rulers have known that the condition of arbitrary power is awful responsibility, and that responsibility is exceedingly awful when the arbitrary power is wielded by a nation that has won for itself freedom. If Lord Lytton should succeed in ruling well, Lord Beaconsfield will have made another happy appointment. He made a noble one in that of Lord Mayo.

CHAPTER XVII.

THE FAMINE OF 1874 IN BENGAL.

If the proceedings in relation to the Bengal famine had formed an isolated fact in Indian history, they might have been referred to now as illustrations of that history simply, and the story might have been read for its interest. When, however, we think of the dread famines in Orissa, in the Native States of Rajpootana, and in Persia, and when we see the whole fearful facts brought once more before us by the famine of this year in Madras, there is no temptation to attempt word-pictures; and I should be ashamed if I made the attempt. In the famine in Orissa not fewer than a million of people perished—people whom, when the season turned against us, we could not reach with the food that we at last had obtained. From three to four thousand orphans were left to be provided for. The number of deaths in Rajpootana would not, it is supposed, be fewer than 1,625,000. The people fled in hosts from their homes, over the parched, stony high land, towards British territory, and dropping, score by score, and hundred by hundred, became food for the beasts of prey that followed, and for the birds of prey that hovered overhead. This, the reader will observe, is no attempt to produce a word-picture. It is the bare general outline of a picture, already drawn by many hands, but never sufficiently known to Englishmen. Of the famine in Persia we learned less, though we had enough, in reliable statements, to make the blood curdle. The author of a work which had no relation to the famine—a very graphic journal—"From the Indus to the Tigris," wrote:

"In our march from Ghayn to the Persian capital, we hardly saw any infants or very young children. They had nearly all died. We nowhere heard the sound of music nor song nor mirth in all the journey up to Mashhad. We passed through village after village, each almost concealed from view in the untrimmed foliage of its gardens, only to see repetitions of misery, melancholy, and despair. The suffering produced by this famine baffles description, and exceeds our untutored conceptions. In this single province of Khorassan the loss of population is estimated at 120,000, and over the whole kingdom cannot be less than a million and a half. . . . On our way through the city (Teheran) we saw beggars, squalid and famished, in every street, appealing pitifully to passers by for charity. The official returns for the week represent the daily mortality within the city walls at 200, almost wholly victims to starvation and typhoid fever. Thousands of families, who have hitherto kept body and soul together by the sale of their jewellery and property, down to the clothes on their back, are now reduced to a state of utter destitution. At Mila Gird we saw men desponding, bowed, and paralysed by want; women nude in their rags, with matted hair and shrivelled features, wandering restlessly like witches; naked children, with deep-sunk eyes, and an unmeaning stare as we disturbed them at their morning meal of wild seeds and unripe ears of corn."

The Bengal famine was a break, in the cause of humanity, of a long dismal line of history. It was an attempt to save the lives of the poor people of Bengal; and if I appear in this chapter to step out of my way, to lay before the reader any mere views of scenery or of life, I beg that it may be imputed to a desire to illustrate useful facts, and not to any unhealthy craving to connect the sufferings of humanity with the vanity of a writer. We made errors with respect to the Bengal famine; but the greatest error of all would be to miss the moral, either of our failures or our success, as a guide to action in these and future times.

Of the many contradictory views as to what was done, and what ought to have been, or might have been, done, it is only necessary to say that men of differently constituted minds, and occupying different stand-grounds, saw the general fact in different lights. On my first landing in Bombay, I found a number of letters awaiting me from friends, Native and European (letters conveying opinions for which I had written from England), but no two letters represented the same view. In extending my inquiries orally in Bombay, I met one gentleman, high in official life, who assured me, from "personal knowledge," that the rumoured differences of the Viceroy and Sir George Campbell were mere imagination, save in the single instance of the prohibition or non-prohibition of food exports. I met another gentleman who assured me, also on personal knowledge, that Lord Northbrook's course had been characterised almost by genius, and Sir George Campbell's by blind obstinacy. I met a third who maintained that Lord Northbrook had held out for three months against positive evidence, and either could not see the danger—which spoke little for his clearness of vision—or supposed that the occasion was not one for administrative action—which spoke little for his humanity. Views equally conflicting prevailed from the western sea-board of India to the eastern limits of Bengal; and, of course, facts even in the case of honest men were unwittingly distorted by the colour of extreme views.

Calcutta was preparing for an unusually gay season, when the cool weather came; and, upon the whole, had no faith in the existence of the famine. Operas, a new theatre, a circus, among other amusements, were in view. Boxes at the Italian opera cost from £110 to £140 for the season. Nothing was commoner than the sarcastic question, "Ah! going on a voyage of discovery to find the famine?" Lord Northbrook, meanwhile, over-weighted with anxiety, was watching from Calcutta for the signs of fresh danger, or relief. Sir George Campbell had broken down in health; Sir Richard Temple, who had gone out to the famine district a sceptic, had, on seeing for himself, avowed a startling change of opinion; had demanded increased powers, and had organised a system of relief which in the end was censured chiefly for its over-completeness.

The ports of the Ganges from whence the famine operations were directed, from Monghyr downward to Patna upward, may be said, generally, to run from west to east. On the south side the East India Railway has a station at Barr, from whence a steamboat plied, with flats of corn, to a place called Chumpta Ghât, on the opposite side of the river. From Chumpta Ghât the famous light railway had been made, at the rate of a mile a day, by Sikh Pioneers (the Muzzbee Sikhs), to Durbunga, about fifty miles distant, and about fifty more, as the crow flies, from the Terai of Nepal. Sir Richard Temple had fixed his headquarters at Monghyr; but it was difficult to say where he was, or where he was not, while danger threatened or work was possible.

At Barr I found piles of grain and fodder, and a steamer, with her steam up, and her flats alongside, but the life of action had gone. The rains had come—those tremendous rains which in a few days plough the earth into deep gullies, and give to the rivers a volume and velocity which no masonry can resist. After some hours, however, the boat started. Then the railway had gone—miles of it carried away, and the ground left as if no railway had ever been. By trolly, where a bit of the line was left, and on foot where it had gone, the journey to Durbunga was made in fifty-six hours without any stoppage, save for the transfer of the trolly from one bit of line to another. The appearance of a number of famine parties, struggling through the mud, with bullocks or ponies, was dismal.

Durbunga was like a great camp, in which a cheerful view of affairs was the exception. The Muzzbee Sikhs had been brought down for three months, and were likely to be detained from their homes for a long period—probably a year longer. They certainly were not in the liveliest of spirits, while every hour brought in fresh parties of English officers and men, from all parts of the famine district, for refuge from the rains, and to add to the stories of undue expenditure; of contracts which had thrown great sums of money into the hands of planters and others, the owners or lessees of carriage; of fodder, which one could see piled up by the way-side, rotted and spoiled. It was a time to claim an Englishman's right to grumble; but I met with no Englishman who grudged any labour or endurance that had preserved life. "We saved grain and fodder too," they said, "when we could, and mortal men could not have done more." This was somewhat different from the view in Calcutta. And what had they done? First, they had saved a vast number of lives—that is certain. Secondly, they had now a grain store for every village where danger still threatened, a store within a mile and a half of every village where the worst was presumed to be over, and a well or tank, newly dug or repaired, for every three villages. Thirdly, they had mastered a knowledge of the district, for use if the famine continued.

I met an English contractor, a grave elderly man, of high character, and with good testimonials of contract work done during the Mutiny, who had been employing, in this and neighbouring parts, from 50,000 to 70,000 persons, whose language, even, in many cases, he could not speak. He was at this time engaged in putting up ten miles of sheds, which he had bound himself under penalties to finish at the rate of seven sheds (700 feet) a day. From very early morning till late at night, he superintended the work himself, with the pleasure at times of seeing the police drive off large bodies (in one case 3000) of his trained men to do some other work. When he complained they sent him untrained substitutes, who demanded payment in advance and then ran away. A hundred like difficulties faced the aged contractor, who had dared to undertake Government contracts during the first great famine in India that England ever had set herself resolutely to conquer.

Durbunga is a large zemindaree (estate) worth about £150,000 a year clear income. The owner, the Maharajah Luch Mahasu Singh, was a minor; his coming of age was only last year, 1876; and at the time of the famine the young chief was under a private tutor at Benares. His estate, meanwhile, under Colonel Burne, who acted for the Court of Wards, had risen greatly in value, and his treasury from a debt of £700, when the Maharajah died, to a balance in hand of £500,000.

From the verandah where I wrote the prospect was beautiful. The country, though for practical purposes apparently flat as a meadow, fifty miles on the one side to the Ganges, and fifty on the other to the Terai, which guarded the territory over which Jung Bahadoor then ruled, was prettily broken up, and the green sward was of an extraordinarily bright and beautiful green. In front of the house a grove of Scotch firs enclosed an English garden and an undulating lawn. Further away, and partly embedded in cocoa-nut trees, were red-tiled houses, white bungalows, and a host of tents ever increasing in number. In the far distance, but easily discernible in the clear early morning, were the mountains of Nepal.

Few of the people in all this district understood our famine preparations. They knew, however, that Nepal was the home of the Ghoorka mountaineers, who in years gone by fought us gallantly, and who now supplied some of our best soldiers; and they knew also that Englishmen chafed not a little at Sir Jung Bahadoor's isolation of his territory. They saw the Muzzbee Sikhs constructing a railway, and English officers laying up stores of grain as for a campaign; and an English colonel, for the young Maharajah, making roads where roads never had been made before. £200,000 had been taken from the Durbunga estate for famine works; and one of the new roads had been run to the very edge of the Terai; that is, to the limit of the Durbunga estate. Everything betokened a campaign. Nobody had ever before in the whole range of tradition taken such steps to merely save life. That one lesson, therefore, had some value.

Of course we blundered. We in one case sent out a large body of men on a new principle of work, which cost

£40 in supervision and £20 in labour, and the value of which was a mere trifle. An officer concerned said, "I was heartily ashamed of it." The first day's work on that system, however, was the last. When road-making was first ordered, it cost from £3, 6s. to £4 per cubic foot, and was in the end done for 5s. the cubic foot. Men made fortunes by the sale of grain. The difficulties with the mothers among the workers were interminable. Nothing could persuade them that their children, taken away to be fed and nursed, were not intended to be kidnapped.

Sir Richard Temple was at Durbunga at this time, preparing for a second year's famine, the provision for which he would have to make in the rains, on an altogether different principle, and from a new basis of operation. When he had once made up his mind that famine was imminent, he had laid down a plan from which he had only departed in details. Contracts were entered into with the planters for carriage. Ponies, mules, and bullocks were bought up. Different companies were engaged to supply carriage and to conduct supplies in so many different directions radiating from the basis of operations; and when any lines failed, Sir Richard Temple at once replaced them by other lines radiating from other places.

The Government conveyance from the 15th February to the 15th June, had amounted to 2,300,000 bags of grain, and a proportionate amount of fodder; or, roundly stated, an amount of grain which laid down in bags would have covered twelve and a half miles in length, a mile and three-quarters in width, and twelve feet in height. The contract service was for 40,000 contract bullock carts (with 4000 Government carts in reserve), 11,000 ponies and mules, 1500 camels, and 3000 pack bullocks. The remnants of the ponies were tethered to trees, in what was called a hospital, and I found Sir Richard Temple at five o'clock one morning inspecting them, and in mercy pronouncing the death-warrant of a large number. From six to seven hundred were mere skin and bone, and with backs frightfully lacerated, owing to hard work, bad driving, and want of food.

I went from the hospital to the quarters of the Muzzbee Sikhs. This fine regiment was one of those that joined us during the Mutiny, and did such splendid service. Many of their countrymen term them of low caste, while the men themselves maintain that they are of the highest caste of the Sikh race; but they have no caste restrictions as to meats and drinks. Their commanding officer, Colonel Williams, commended at once their courage and their honesty. He had, he said, sent them out freely day by day, with money for road-making and other work, and they had, he believed, answered for their trust faithfully. They were armed with the Enfield rifle, carrying their pioneer tools at their backs, and in a very few minutes could put the regiment (officers' horses excepted) under cover on the approach of an enemy, after which they would meet him with rifle and bayonet. A finer regiment no officer need have wished to command. It was not pleasant, after learning these facts, to speak to an old soldier who had had the honour of conveying a powder bag to the Cashmere Gate in the grand assault on Delhi, and who nevertheless remained undecorated, on the ground that the regiment at the time had not been regularly enrolled in the service. It made one almost shudder for the future of England in India. The paltry technicality was worse than an avowal that a brave man had been forgotten.

Of the work devised merely "to keep people employed," much might be said, and very much more of the stratagems, and long walks under a burning sun, by which people secured the stated amount of rice from two different centres of relief on the same day. These stories are among the jokes, sometimes grim jokes, of the famine work. I was more concerned, however, in knowing how English residents and the natives of this district had assisted the Government. Of several planters, Sir Richard Temple, and many of his officers, spoke in the highest praise. Of the leasing or buying up of carriage in advance and re-letting it to the Government, the best that any one said was that it had been done in the way of trade. I think, however, it would have been a good thing, in view of the future, to have specially rewarded those planters who had given their time and labour free.

With respect to the natives, an English gentleman handed me an exact list of works done by a banker, at a cost of £5170—a free gift. The tenants of the Durbunga estate also, at their own cost, made 124 new tanks, and restored a number. A man holding the position of chief cultivator of a village, gave, in addition to many sums of money, rice valued at £1000 to his poorer neighbours before the Government famine works were opened. The young Rajah also had cordially approved the great outlay from his estate, as poon, which is worship, or charitable work. At that time the certainty of a famine had not been generally acknowledged. The benevolent action, however, won a great victory. For a long time the officers in charge in Tirhoot had refused permission for roads to be made, on the ground that the collection of tolls, at ghâts, would be disarranged thereby. In consequence of this absurd and iniquitous rule, rice in the wet season, when the country was impassable, had been known to sell at 54 lbs. the rupee, while sixty miles distant it was selling at from 130 lbs. to 150 lbs. for the same amount. The famine dispelled this official stupidity, and now the Durbunga zemindaree has roads.

On the courteous invitation of the Lieutenant Governor, I left Durbunga with his party, which indeed was my only means of reaching the Ganges, and at the same time seeing the work. The journey began at six o'clock in the morning in a third-class carriage; a few Englishmen in the one end, and their servants in the other; the trolly-men, and some Punjabees, who had begged a passage in a truck behind. Sir Richard had met his officers and discussed their reports. He had now to decide upon a basis of operations for the rains. The train made its way slowly along a line which was now under water, till the engine was brought to a stop by a broken bridge, and a walk of some miles became indispensable. We found long strings of bullocks and carts with Government grain, each cart in charge of a number of sepoys, and each party commanded by an English officer, a most laborious undertaking, the wheels of the carts sinking deeply in the rough roadless soil. All ceremony was dispensed with by the lieutenant governor. He was an officer among officers, asking questions, making suggestions, deciding differences—on foot, and ankle deep in mud. There was much to see and inquire into on this journey. It was not, for instance, unworthy of notice that a wire, laid across country on two transverse pieces of bamboo, was the first telegraph wire ever seen on that side the Ganges.

Arriving early in the morning—a Saturday morning—at the bank of a small nulla, a rivulet partly formed by the rains, we found the tender of the lieutenant governor's yacht, and in it steamed down a distance of about seven miles through a peaceful country to the Ganges, where the yacht itself was anchored. The waters were fast rising, and in a short time the country through which we passed would be flooded, and would become the invaluable deeara land, which would long retain its moisture under the hottest sun. The first view of the Ganges, approached in this way, in the early morning, was beautiful. The river, now broad as a sea, was covered with boats and a varied human life. On the bank were hundreds of the camels, borrowed some months earlier from the North Western Provinces, and ready to be floated over the river for the return home, their usefulness ceasing with dry weather, and that of the elephant beginning. A long, dark movable line across the water we found to be a vast herd of bullocks or buffaloes on journey, their drivers swimming almost silently among them; a scene several times repeated during our run down the river.

We passed several of the Dacca "pulwars," with their varnished sides, and matchless white sails, the first of the private rice trade from the Eastern Provinces; banks crowded with bathers; villages which sent out their young and old to gaze upon, and wonder at, the crowded, busy steamer in advance, and the beautiful yacht in tow; lonely tobacco factories, in a tobacco growing country; then Monghyr itself, and the "famine residence" of the lieutenant governor. Then we anchored for the night, at the confluence of the Bor Gunduk and the Ganges.

With daybreak the tender was turned upward in the Bor Gunduk, and passed between two banks, in many parts like the finest of English parks, the green grass relieved by rich foliage and magnificent trees. A range of dark and sombre mountains loomed high in the distance; but the great house at Monghyr stood out from first to last, and amid interminable windings, the central object of all. After an hour or two on this rivulet, Mr Bernard, Sir Richard's Temple's chief assistant in the famine work, and whose exceedingly modest labour never was half acknowledged in England, and probably never will be so now, began to question the men of from fifty to sixty boats moored in one place, and of selected boats from about two hundred more which we passed, or which passed us, in a distance of about thirteen miles, to a place called Khagaria, which was to be the new basis of famine operations in case of need during the rains. The cargoes were much of the same character as those noted in the previous chapter; but the visit was like a dash into a lottery, and Khagaria was seen as it was; a rather pretty town, with good houses and shops, a well-staked river bank, and a flourishing trade in which the people said 10,000 craft were engaged. A conference of the leading people was held under a peepul tree, and I suppose they learned from Mr Bernard, who was the orator, that Khagaria was to be to a new series of operations what Chumpta Ghât had been to those of the hot months. Happily the new operations were not needed.

After a run of about seven hours, the tender again gave place to the yacht, which was turned in the direction of Monghyr.

The lieutenant governor's house, built on the site of the old Mohammedan fort, on a hill covered with verdure, is approached by a really grand avenue of grandly lofty trees, whose tops seemed lost in clouds. On every side the prospect was beautiful. In front were the Monghyr hills, which, when a gathering storm rested on them, as we had seen one rest on the previous day, were a very embodiment of gloomy grandeur. Right and left the Ganges seemed to form a circle around Monghyr. In every direction there was green undulating ground, with English and Native houses, "each in its nook of leaves," and then a pretty peaceful English church, from which, as we drove up the avenue that Sunday evening, the English bells told of the faith which had supplanted that of Mahomet in the fortress of Monghyr.

An inspection, which I did not see, of the recipients of relief gave a return of 630 women and 142 men, of whom 493 women were old, haggard, and infirm and blind, paralytic, crippled, or idiots. The rest were unable to earn a living. Of the men 26 were totally blind, and 81 cripples. A little later there was an inspection, which I did see, and to which I should not again care to see anything at all akin, unless it was for some different purpose than merely recording the facts. There were in all about 1000 persons, the males and females on opposite sides of a yard. They were mostly habitual beggars, brought in from the district by the promised relief; but this only made the scene sadder, as indicating a chronic sore. I do not indeed mention it as belonging to the famine of 1873-74, but as representing the deeper depth of the lot of the poor in India. About half the thousand people were skin and bone, and in most cases afflicted with frightful diseases, made all the more horrible by the almost nude condition of the sufferers. I do not wish to extend the picture, but simply to deepen the fact that though the famine relief had drawn the whole together a kindred whole separated exists to-day in the same places. Passing slowly up and down the lines, I did not see one really cunning face. It was not even a scene of despair. It was one of apathy as beyond hope. There was in that yard a depth of misery deeper far than the plummet of Sir Richard Temple could sound.

In the gaol of Monghyr I saw some exceedingly fine work done by the prisoners; cloths of apparently as intricate workmanship as those of Cashmere. In the bazaar I saw scores of industries, and not any great sign of distress. In the English town there was prosperity. In the waysides and hedges there was what we have seen. I wondered as I went from Monghyr if there never could be any hope of making these poor people to really live. There is this difference between their lot and that of the wretched in Europe that, in a cold climate, people afflicted as those whom I saw in Monghyr could not live a week. It is the climate alone that makes life possible. Of the fort of Monghyr I may simply add, that it encloses an area of nearly two miles; and that we have converted the palace into a gaol, and the harem into cells, and have not put them to bad uses on the whole.

A short railway ride, stopping to see relief stores and the recipients of relief, brought us again to the tender, and the tender brought us to the yacht. Next morning in the early dawn a start was made for Moorshedabad, the Ganges hourly growing higher, and now still more resembling a sea. I counted fully forty, in some cases large sea boats, in a space not greater than the united length of the steamer, its tow-rope, and the yacht. About a dozen Dacca boats were seen altogether, and they reported a fleet on the way with grain, which would probably be sold before being landed. The sides of the river, seen in the grey morning, were a deep green, with at times lofty trees, grand as English oaks, and at others long tracts of land under green paddy, interspersed again with well-built and thatched houses, and at others with scenes of vast pasture grounds and innumerable droves of cattle, some hundreds in the drove. The steamer was stopped that fish may be bought, boats hailed, villages visited. Then she glided into the Bhaguratee, probably the ancient Ganges, which becomes the Hooghly below Moorshedabad.

At about an hour or so after noon the yacht was anchored off Azimgunge, the European part of Moorshedabad, which once represented the sovereignty and power to overcome which Clive fought Plassey. We were now in the centre and heart of Bengal, and as we drew near to Azimgunge the scene was most picturesque. Native gentlemen and their retainers, in gay attire, were assembled on both banks of the river to pay their respects to the lieutenant governor. A little below there were small bodies of police, in their blue coats and red turbans; a little higher vast crowds of people; on the water the boats of Europeans hastening to the yacht; in the background temples and mosques embedded in groves of fine trees. It was a curious and pretty scene. At Moorshedabad I saw the last of the yacht; and making my way by a short railway, I visited some of the less notable stores. In one case, and I should say it was not an isolated case, the store was kept by one man, who ate and slept in his shed, and he believed, he said, that not a bag of his grain had been stolen. This short railway was a little notable, from the fact that it had been made to "pay" by the manager becoming guard, ticket clerk, and station master, and turning his van into a ticket office. His railway stations were sod huts. He had a similar line, which we shall see, from Calcutta to Port Canning.

Another series of journeys, in one direction to Purneah, and in another to Beerbhoom, enabled me to compare, on the basis of perfectly independent movements, with very different kinds of famine work, what I had seen in Tirhoot. Travelling by palanquin and by dâk (post) gharry, and gathering fresh notes from different classes of persons at every stage, I saw the operations from quite another side, though it is but fair to say that during the short time I saw Sir Richard Temple, he not merely did not in the slightest degree attempt to influence my view, but he never, as far as I know, learned directly or indirectly what my view was on any important and still less on any disputed point. When he gave me facts he gave them in a gentlemanly way, and left them. Still for a comprehension of the true fact it was necessary to be alone; and on both sides of the river I sought out, in my own way, that fact. I have said before that there were errors which no one could miss. I say, too, that Sir Richard Temple would not deny this. Grain had been sent to where it had not been needed, and to where in fact it was in the end sold. I met carts bringing grain from and carts taking grain to Purneah. I met boats on the Ganges doing exactly the same thing. I saw the river steamboats sent out from England and condemned to uselessness by the fact that they would only go with the stream. There had been some mistake, either as to power of engine, or as to Indian fuel, or something. I found people who derided the whole operations; but nearly always, if not always, people who believed that famines were "a wise provision to clear off the useless population;" a belief of which I need scarcely say more to any reasonable, not to say humane, person. I met with some harsh officers, and some who, apparently harsh in manner, were kind in fact, who had simply become soured under their many vexations and the Indian sun.

I saw also, however, an earnestness of purpose of which England will never have cause to be ashamed. From Lord Northbrook and Sir George Campbell and Sir Richard Temple to the humblest officer, there was, as it were, the one grand resolve not to let the people die. The officers in the main entered into the spirit of their chiefs, even where they did not fully approve the order given in some special case. The greatest mistake in Sir Richard Temple's work has, I think, been, since 1874, in the sharp punishment of a young officer who was supposed to be the writer of a pamphlet criticising the famine policy. If the presumed author is the gentleman I suppose, then, though I think his pamphlet an error, I am certain he has not an atom of bitterness in his nature, and that Sir Richard Temple had not a more earnest worker in the Presidency. Sir Richard or some one ought to repair the error of this punishment. In all fundamentals I am assured that the famine policy was a true policy, worthy of the men whose names it bears, and of the nation they represented. It would have been impossible for any man, of whatever gifts, to see the whole of so vast a district; and it must not be forgotten that though Sir Richard Temple had great power within limits, there were the limits of public opinion which he could not pass, and which, indeed, have since been pressed strongly against him.

Two questions remain. First, Ought England to have paid the cost of the Bengal famine? Secondly, Are the famine operations in Bengal and Behar no guide to the present and the future? There are two sides to the question of England's duty to India in such cases as that of the debt contracted for the Bengal famine. An Indian official, writing some weeks ago, asked indignantly if England, which paid four millions and a half for the Suez Canal shares, could not give as much to save life in Bengal. The reply is simple. England can, and ought, if it is necessary, and if she is able to meet such responsibilities, if established as a rule. It is more than likely, however, that if such claims were pressed by English officers, England, especially with an enlarged suffrage and her fearful amount of poverty, would be likely to ask what exact benefit she received as a nation from her connection with India, and whether she was not paying, as she might for a university, for the benefit of classes. If that inquiry ever is made by a democratic House of Commons, the chances are that the decision will not be what some Anglo-Indian writers would desire. It would be a tremendous mistake on the part of the democratic House of Commons and of England, but it probably would be made. Officers receiving an income from Indian revenue may think it right that England and not India ought to pay the bill for a famine; but what the poor in England will think, with squalor and poverty at their doors, is also a fundamental consideration.

Again, the great aim of financial legislation in India has been to enable India to pay her way legitimately from her own revenue. It is essential that she should do so. If she cannot, the expenditure ought to be reduced. Some—not all—Anglo-Indian writers, in fact, say, "Let individual Englishmen, or classes of Englishmen, draw upon India, and let England, as a nation, return the money to India in case of famines." It may be reasonable; it certainly is not wrong to receive fair remuneration for labour; but, all the same, England is much more likely to say, "Rather curtail the drawing from India." That also assuredly is the way in which, in the long run, ends will be made to meet. The argument put forward, therefore, of national responsibility, should not be pressed home too closely on England, at least by Indian officers, even in these cases of vastly solemn importance. Let England honestly pay back to India the money unfairly, if not unjustly, taken from her poverty to entertain the Sultan of Turkey and such like matters. Let her pay it even to the cost of the Madras famine; but let it be on that principle, or as a free gift from individuals, which would be highly honourable—the only two principles perceptible in this case, in either ethics or common sense, as the key-stone of English policy.

Did then the famine operations in Bengal convey no lesson with respect to the present and the future? Surely they conveyed at least this lesson, that if our professions in 1873-74 were not a mere spirit of humanity and morals, they could not end with Bengal and the year 1874. If we were bound to meet that famine, we are bound, within the range of our power as a nation, to meet every famine. We are bound to find a Viceroy who can put an end to famines, as Lord Mayo believed he had put an end to deficits. By storing water, by fostering trade, by extending railways or canals, by curtailing expenditure, some man of genius will put an end to famines. If we cannot find a man of genius, or if, having found such a man, we refuse to follow him, and give him earnest support, we shall not, by mere strength of arm and will, hold India. Sir Richard Temple is not a man of genius. He is simply a cheerful man, of great determination, with a clear eye for facts, an undoubted power of organisation, and a disposition with which other men can work, and whom no man is wounded in his self-respect by serving. Of Lord Mayo much the same statement might be made. Lord Northbrook, as Viceroy, was different; his merit was not in making hard work light, but in an essential veracity dominating what he did.[1] When, however, England can find a man of high genius—a man, as George Dawson would have said, like King Alfred, or as India would say, like Akbar, to establish her rule in justice—and England will enable him when found to act in defiance of all interests save those of humanity, she will also, in these days of steam, of mechanical ingenuity and electricity, find means to put an end to "the era of famines," save in exceptional cases beyond human foresight, and certainly as chronic sores in the social system. Native India, with whose permanent interests our transient individual interests cannot compare, knows this well; but Native India believes that, if a really great ruler were found to set special interests at defiance, the special interests would fight hard to defeat and ruin him.

[1] Appendix VI.

CHAPTER XVIII.

THE BRITISH INDIAN ASSOCIATION—THE PERMANENT LAND SETTLEMENT IN BENGAL — PRISONS AND POLICE.

In looking for some social organisation, a connecting link between the forms of English life and the enduring interests of the people of India, I have been able to find nothing more suitable to the purpose in view than the British Indian Association, whose headquarters are in Calcutta. It is essentially a landlords' association; and as such has been the butt of much sarcasm, often both unjust and stupid; while, however, it would be absurd to say that the association, on its own part, representing Indian interests, not to India but to England, has escaped error. What chiefly attracted my own attention in the Association, and attracted it in spite of the fact that, if justice were not justice, whether on the side of landlord or tenant, rich or poor, my sympathies never would have been with a landlords' association, I shall endeavour to state in this chapter.

Till this year the president of the Association was the Maharajah Romanath Tagore Bahadoor, a venerable nobleman, who died in June last, seventy-seven years of age. Created a Rajah, and honoured with the Star of India by Lord Northbrook, he was, at the Delhi ceremonial, raised to the rank of Maharajah by Lord Lytton; and the honour paid to him was accepted as a compliment by nearly the whole native community. The secretary of the association is Baboo Kristo Das Pal, editor of the *Hindoo Patriot*, member of the Bengal Council, and recently appointed by

Lord Lytton one of a committee to examine and report upon a system of educational text-books for Bengal. One of Baboo Kristo Das Pal's claims to distinction is that no man in Calcutta has been better abused; and one of the best grounds upon which his friends and enemies are justified in refusing him any sympathy or condolence in his trouble, is that the abuse seems to have fallen from him harmlessly, and often as if he knew nothing of its existence.

Of Romanath Tagore much might be written, now that his tongue is silent and his pen for ever at rest. In learning, in grace of manners, in a long course of honourable relation to commerce, and in a thousand efforts to improve the lot of the people of Bengal, his life, I have heard, was highly distinguished, and very beautiful. Like his brother Dwarkanath, and his cousin Prosuna Coomar Tagore, he was a disciple of Rajah Ram Mohun Roy, and in that way, as in others, strove to raise the tone and character of rich and poor alike, in morals, in material comfort, and in manhood. On receiving the news of his death, Lord Lytton wrote: "Both the Government and the whole native community of Bengal have lost a wise, an honest, and a trusted adviser;" and the praise was not lavish.[1]

One of the standing charges against the Association is that by its very nature it is a system of organised selfishness. If the charge is valid, it applies equally to our chambers of commerce, our landlords' and tenants' leagues, our trades' associations, and a hundred other organisations of English life. It is, as they are, intended to defend interests often assailed; and it, like them, has shown again and again that it could step out of the restric-

[1] At a remarkable meeting held a little later in Calcutta, a friend of the dead nobleman told of how nine hundred years earlier, while the Normans were conquering England, "five Brahmins came to this country from Canouj at the invitation of the ruler. On their arrival they were ennobled, and ever after maintained their nobility. They were even respected by their Mohammedan rulers. One of these five became the Rajah of Nuddea, while another, from whom the Tagores were descended, became a zemindar."

tions of partial interests into the general good. I am not saying this in ignorance of the fact that it has at times opposed great improvements, exactly as English landlords opposed railways, and English workmen broke machinery. But the reader may rest assured that this Association of Native India, while in the narrow sense of the nature of our own organisations for special interests, can also like them claim to stand somewhat higher.

I have before me a complete collection of the tracts, pamphlets, and reports of the Association since its formation in 1851. They were presented to me, as also were the tracts and pamphlets of the Brahmists, on my first leaving India; and now, five years after that time, I am attempting to make both to represent some degree of truth with reference to Indian affairs. There is scarcely a subject of Indian legislation in relation to Sir Barnes Peacock, Sir Henry Maine, and Sir James Stephen, in law, or to finance ministers, or to public works, or to anything, that is not in some way dealt with in these publications. There are pamphlets on the land, on tenant right, on revenue, on salt, on civil and criminal justice, on the representation of India in Parliament. Government despatches and minutes are republished with comment; struggling native societies assisted; the state of districts as to moral and material wants made known. The evidence at once of loyalty and of opposition to maladministration are on every hand, and are continued from year to year. One pamphlet is exhaustive of Mr Wilson's financial proposals, another of Mr Laing's, another of Sir Richard Temple's. Opinions as to the causes of epidemics are given at length, on the basis of special investigation. In 1856 a missionary memorial for inquiry into the condition of the ryots (tenants), is supported. Remarks, sometimes very pointed, are made on particular acts of officers, civil and military. The fourth report (that of 1856) has a curious interest, from the fact that it was published on the eve of the Mutiny. It is, however, like its predecessors, purely social in its character, and relates to subjects which, whatever the ruling power may be, whatever the storms and convulsions in politics or war, will continue to affect the deep sea of the human life of India. Taken in this way the reports may suggest solemn thoughts.

It will not have escaped the reader's notice that an association like this, composed of wealthy and influential men, may at times have had unpleasant relations to Englishmen. Some officers have disliked it for the power it wields, and for the resolution it has manifested. To missions some of its leading men (as, for instance, Dwarkanath Tagore) have been determinately opposed. But that such an association is other than a legitimate outcome of the relations of educated India to England, will hardly be disputed. To call public attention to questions of importance, as they arise, and thus make known the wishes of the people, is surely a service to the Government, and to all who are interested in India. There is no trace in the pamphlets of ill-feeling towards England, and assuredly no trace of disloyalty in any one of them that I have seen. In fact, in right or in wrong, the Association is an exact counterpart of associations which in England are deemed a mark and sign of public spirit and usefulness.

One of the great subjects that has appeared in the reports of the Association from year to year is that of the permanent land settlement in Bengal. In order to comprehend this unceasing controversy, it must be remembered that Indian revenue in all past times has rested, as it still rests, fundamentally on the land. Whether the State was landlord, and the nominal landowners only tenants in perpetuity, or whether the land was private property and the amount paid yearly to the State of the nature of taxation, has comparatively small bearing on the dispute.

The settlement dates from the year 1793, when Lord Cornwallis, assisted by Mr Shore, arranged the commutation, for a fixed and unalterable sum, of all charges resting on the land as the revenue of the State. For a long time this settlement was accepted by every one, English and Native of India, as including all claims of the State on the Bengal "settled" land. On the strength of this belief waste lands were reclaimed (as they had not been when the settlements were for terms of years); and on the same belief lands were transferred from the first occupants to others (from putneedar, the first possessor, to dur-putneedar), and so on, till at last, on principles common to all lands, though the original tenure remains, the property bought at the market-rate at the time of purchase, and on the tenure of a permanent settlement, may have repeatedly changed hands.

In the course of time it was discovered that the Indian Government could manage a little better with an enhanced revenue, and a question as to the meaning of the permanent settlement of Lord Cornwallis was raised. That the terms used were explicit as to the settlement including all charges, could not be disputed; but then it was said, does not this simply mean all charges as rent in the English sense, leaving the question of cesses untouched? Some of the ablest officers in the service unhesitatingly repudiated this, as a quibble unworthy of the Government and of England. The English landlords paid taxes but no rent. The Bengal landlords paid rent, which included taxes; and it was shown clearly that if any doubt had existed as to the permanent settlement covering all claims of the Government, the arrangement never could have been made. The landlords would have gained nothing whatever of the certainty which they sought, and which the Government undertook to secure to them.

Men like Mr Shore had shown at the time that a permanent settlement was a very hazardous settlement; but even that fact only strengthened the case against the new claim, since it showed that, bad or good, the first and long-accepted meaning was the correct one. That the bargain had been made in the dark as to the value of the land, did not affect the question. Yet even on that ground it was shown that the land for long periods had been unremunerative to the owners or cultivators. They had accepted risks, simply because of the certainty; and if the land had increased in value, from whatever cause, the increment they maintained, and many Englishmen maintained for them, was their own by law as well as by common sense. Then the point of the rights of the tenants as a set-off to that of the landowners was raised, and was made a prominent factor in the dispute by men who never will raise the same question at home. What it really involved we shall see. What I think we shall not see is that the permanent settlement involved only rent and not cesses; and I say this with not an atom of sympathy with any landlord in Bengal or anywhere, who refuses to accept the fair and just responsibilities of changing times.

During Lord Mayo's vice-royalty, the question fell to Sir James Stephen, who boldly asserted that cesses were not included in the settlement. The zemindars had a short time previously explained and maintained in public meeting, that when the Government of 1793 sought for a fixed in place of an uncertain revenue, they obtained a revenue so high that for a long time many of the owners of land were unable to cultivate what they had acquired, and in many cases were compelled to part with their land to persons possessing capital. All, however, it was alleged, was borne with patience because of the permanence at once of the tenure and the rent.

Mr Stephen said he had no doubt but that what Lord Cornwallis and those who acted with him sought to create was an ownership in land. Lord Cornwallis had said:

> "Although I am not only of opinion that the zemindars have the best right, but from being persuaded that nothing could be so ruinous to the public interest as that the land should be retained as the property of Government, I am also convinced that failing the claim of right of the zemindars, it would be necessary for the public good to grant a right of property in the soil to them, or to persons of other descriptions. I think it unnecessary to enter into any discussion of the ground upon which their right seems to be founded."

Mr Stephen considered three points settled:

"1. That the zemindars were the most conspicuous of the numerous persons who were interested in the land.

"2. That intricate and imperfectly understood relations existed between them and the ryots.

"3. That the right of the Government to exact a share of the produce of the land ascertained by no fixed rule, and varying from time to time in proportion to the increased yield of the land, was practically inconsistent with the existence of rights of private property, and reduced the value of such rights where they existed to a shadow.

"The great object of the permanent settlement was to put an end to this uncertain, indefinite, and fluctuating state of things, and to substitute for it a system of permanent property in which the zemindars were to be landlords on the English model, the ryots tenants, also on the English model, and in which the land revenue was to form a permanent rent charge of fixed amount to be paid to the Government by the zemindar. I need not enter into the subject of the provisions which expressly reserved to the Government the right of interfering between the zemindar and the ryot to protect the interests of the latter."

No one, Mr Stephen continued, was more impressed than he was with the importance of scrupulously maintaining the pledges of 1793. But he added:

"It is possible to construe those pledges in a manner so extravagant as to raise the question whether they were pledges which the Government of that day had any moral right to make, for legal right they could have none. If Lord Cornwallis had in direct words engaged that a certain scheme of taxation settled by him should be permanent, and that no other taxes whatever should ever be raised in the territory to which it applied, it would have been necessary to look this question in the face. I refer to it only in order to suggest to those who claim the fulfilment of the pledge given in 1793, that it is very unwise in them to put upon it a sense which might sooner or later force upon the Government the alternative of permanently arresting the improvement of Bengal, or of declaring that Lord Cornwallis had given a pledge which he had neither the legal right nor the moral power to give."

This was startling, and would, as we may see, be a little more startling if applied to England. No one knows better than Mr Stephen the right of prescription; the unassailable position of an agreement allowed to rest on what the Scotch call "use and wont." Mr Stephen continued:

"The land revenue is, in my opinion, neither rent nor taxation: it is the property of the Government just as the Crown lands in England are the property of the Queen. And the existence of a right to impose taxes for the general good upon all other property, whether derived from land or from other sources, is no more inconsistent with the proprietary right in the one case than in the other. It may be asked what good there was in the permanent settlement, what great benefit it conferred upon the landholders of Bengal, if it left their property subject to taxation? The answer is that it reduced to a certainty one particular charge on that land which had previously been of variable amount, and so freed the landholders from the uncertainty which had previously hung over them in respect of it."

This is Mr Stephen's view, which, however, was not allowed to settle the question. Baboo Degumber Mitter in public meeting denied that the settlement of 1793 was an easy one to the zemindars. While he said the land settlements in the North West, for a term of years, were on the basis of 70 per cent. of the gross rental to the State, and 30 to the zemindar, in Bengal the State had 90 per cent. and left only 10. He declared also that till the last fourteen or fifteen years the assets of the estates that contained no waste land had been very trifling, and that those which had contained waste land, in many cases "thrown in with the bargains," had required immense outlay before there had been any profit. Another native gentleman said the great Mogul (Akbar's) financier, Todur Mull, settled the land revenue at one-third of the produce of the soil, and that the Government of Lord Cornwallis effected a settlement 50 per cent. in excess of that of any Hindoo or Mohammedan monarch. "The one redeeming feature was its permanence." The following extracts from the views of distinguished Englishmen were given in a petition adopted by the meeting.

"Sir Erskine Perry said: 'The questions at issue between the Supreme Government of India and the Government of Bengal are—1st. Whether it is a breach of the engagements made by the Government at the time of the permanent settlement to subject the zemindars of Bengal to special taxation, in addition to the general taxation that may be imposed upon them in common with the rest of the community. 2d. Whether it is expedient to impose on the landholders of Bengal a special cess for education, assuming it to be just to impose a local tax on them for any special object. I object to the despatch of the Secretary of State, because even in its modified form it seems to decide, and, I believe, does decide, that there is nothing in the language or promises of the Government in 1793 to preclude the present Government from levying local taxes in Bengal for local objects. I have come reluctantly to the conclusion, after many struggles and attempts to draw fine distinctions in support of a different view, that the language and acts of Lord Cornwallis, and of the members of Government of his day, were so distinct, solemn, and unambiguous, that it would be a direct violation of British faith to impose special taxes in the manner proposed.' Sir Frederick Halliday took the same view. Mr Prinsep said: 'I have never felt so deeply grieved and disappointed at a decision given in opposition to my expressed opinions as when it was determined by a casting vote to approve and forward this despatch. To the zemindars the rate or cess, call it by what name you will, would be an "abwab" of the specific kind that the proclamation of Lord Cornwallis assured them against being ever called upon to pay.' Sir H. C. Montgomery said: 'A Government should not, in my opinion, voluntarily place itself in a position laying it open to be charged with a breach of faith. It should rather avoid any measure which would be so held in the estimation of its subjects specially interested.'" Many similarly expressed views followed.

Leaving this meeting, and going back to the time of the settlement itself, we find the exact question of permanency raised by Mr Law, collector of Shahabad, who "pointed out the desirableness or good policy of an exceptional provision for extraordinary levies for extraordinary occasions, such as war, following the English precedent in such cases." Mr Shore replied: "This qualification is, in fact, a subversion of the fundamental principle; for, the exigencies not being defined, a Government may interpret the conditions according to its own sense of them. . . . The explanation is, that temporary extraordinaries must have temporary resources, and even the land at home is liable to a general tax during war; but the land tax in England does not bear a proportion of nine-tenths to the income of the proprietor."

Nothing in language could be stronger. Passing to the Government Regulation I., 1793, we read:

"The Governor General in Council trusts that the proprietors of land, sensible of the benefits conferred upon them by the public assessment being fixed for ever, will exert themselves in the cultivation of their lands, under the certainty that they will enjoy exclusively the fruits of their own good management and industry, and that no demand will ever be made upon them, or their heirs, or successors, by the present, or any future Government, for an augmentation of the public assessment, in consequence of the improvement of their respective estates."

In a letter to the Directors it is added: "If at any future period the public exigencies should require an addition to your resources, you must look for it in the increase of the general wealth and commerce of the country, and not in the augmentation of the tax upon the land." This was most definite.

The Duke of Argyll took a curiously evasive position. "The income tax," he said, "is not an increase of the public demand levied upon the zemindars in consequence of the improvement of their estates," and "the same essential distinction may be established between the original assessment which was fixed for ever and every kind of tax, or cess, or rate, which is levied irrespective of the increased value or produce of land." Sir James Stephen took the same view, and used almost the same language.

All that can be said with respect to this is, that if the Duke of Argyll and Sir James Stephen were right in their view, the writer of the Regulation, and all who were concerned in it, knew that they were guilty of deceiving the people of Bengal as no statesmen of like character ever before had deliberately deceived any body of men in the world's history. If the Duke of Argyll said to one of his tenants, "Your rent, as established now, shall be perpetual, at the same amount, and I request you to throw all your labour and skill into the cultivation of the land, resting assured that, whatever increment may accrue therefrom shall be your own, and your rent remain the same," his tenant would understand, as the Bengal zemindars understood, that the only cause that could possibly be alleged as a plea for an enhanced rent, the increment of the value of the land, was to be for ever set aside. That is, the assessment was not to be raised on any plea whatever. There are men who boast that they never make an agreement without contriving some loophole for escape if the agreement should become untenable; but such men are not statesmen, nor gentlemen. Now Lord Cornwallis and Mr Shore were both statesmen and gentlemen, and perceiving in what light their words were being taken, it is certain that, if the impression of the zemindars had been an incorrect one, Lord Cornwallis and Mr Shore would at once, and carefully, have set it right, instead of deepening the error by language as strong as men could use. In fact, if the Government of 1793 did not mean to make a settlement including all direct charges on land, it is utterly useless relying on any language whatever. If such an agreement had been made between two individuals, the one representing the side of the statesman of 1793 would not have dared to carry it into an English law court. With respect to the Bengal lands having the same relation to the Government in India that the Crown lands have to that of England, why the one single fact that the rent, whether drawn directly by the Queen or not, is still Her Majesty's private property—that is, that the Queen is not England—the State—in relation to this land, as she is in other respects—overturns the argument. The Indian Government has the double relation unknown in England.

Moreover, although the Duke of Argyll and Sir James Stephen say that the increase in the value of the land is not the ground alleged for the virtual increase of rent by actual cesses, the gentlemen who first raised, and those who continue the discussion, do not say so. They say distinctly, "How are we to reach these rich men?" That question was the germ of the income tax. Now, considering—and I believe it is the fact—that the lands have, as a rule, only become valuable property of late years, what is the actual—leaving out of question the nominal—ground of the enhancement of rent? Why, that property is more valuable. "How are we to reach these rich men?" Why, you reach them already by a rent which was once assessed at the rate of 90 per cent. of the value. "Ah!" it is said, "but the value has increased." Then you would raise the rent because the value of the land has been enhanced? There is no escape—history will find no escape—from the plain, certain, and unmistakable fact.

If we extend Sir James Stephen's argument in another direction it will not seem less questionable. If, he says, the Bengal claims are unduly pressed, it may be necessary to deny the moral right of Lord Cornwallis—"for legal right he had none"—to make the settlement. No right to make a settlement which the Court of Directors, and, by inference, the Parliament of England, accepted? Is this great nation to proceed upon the principle that, having made a treaty by one of her officers, and allowed it to pass as a treaty for half a century, she is justified, after all the parties to the treaty are dead, in questioning the moral right, and denying the legal right, of her officer to make the compact? The argument—and I imply no disrespect to the upright motives of Sir James Stephen—could only have been used on the strength of the bayonets commanded at that time by Lord Napier of Magdala.

Sir James Stephen makes another assertion which may be more tenable, but certainly might be more awkward, taken in connection with the other parts of his argument, if pushed home in England, when he says that the zemindars were intended to be landlords on the English system, and the ryots tenants on the same system. If this be so, the argument must be allowed to cut both ways. The cases, let us say with Sir James Stephen, are alike, and the tenants in Bengal have a claim to tenant right. Then the English tenant must have the same right. That he has no exact chartered guarantee of perpetuity of tenure or the protection of his earnings, is nothing. It is quite enough that the moral right of the king who gave the grants of land to the landlord can be questioned. In fact, the arguments used in Bengal would, if applied to England, upturn the foundations of existing English society. Has the reader observed how many of the land theories of the last quarter of a century have come from men who knew India, and how likely India is to supply the examples for tearing up inconvenient compacts?

We have seen that the zemindars deny that the settlement of 1793 was a favourable one. But supposing it had been a favourable one, that the profits had come at once, and even, apart from the landlords, by some independent progress of trade—what then? The property of the Duke of Westminster and the Duke of Bedford has been increased beyond human comprehension by the progress of London, and the Earl of Derby's by that of Manchester and Liverpool. In these cases also the increment has been made altogether independent of those to whom the benefit has accrued. Yet it has not yet been proposed to the House of Commons to deny the tenure on which the land rests, on the ground that some one, in the first instance, gave the land who had no right, moral or legal, to do so, and that new times having brought new and unforeseen national needs, the tenure must be challenged. All this, however, is applied to Bengal.

"How," then, "are we to reach these rich men?" If we are in earnest, and merely require a certain reasonable thing done—do not, in fact, wish ourselves to handle the money—the question is as simple as a sum in simple proportion. "Would you," people ask, "allow the zemindars to escape their just responsibility to their tenants?" I would not allow them to escape any just, and I would not entail on them any unjust, responsibility. The law is one safeguard of the tenants; the power to refuse labour is another. The right of the tenant to a fair amount of the fruit of his labour would not involve any breach of covenants. Then,

I think, the Government would have a perfect right to say to the zemindars: "We shall not, beyond the guaranteed permanent settlement, claim to use one rupee of your money; but we shall expect you to make roads, and maintain schools yourselves, the money not coming into English hands." If they refused to do this they would be indictable as for a nuisance, or breeding fever. But I do not think they would refuse it. I believe they would accept the responsibility. Do we, apart from this, need the money? The late Mr Marshman held that India could be well governed on twenty millions a year less than it now costs. Sir George Campbell laudably tried to establish elective municipalities, which might have solved the question of how to do all that we claim to do in Bengal, without breaking a pledge which is as clear and unmistakable as the coronation oath. I do not say that the question is free from difficulties. With men whose motives are as far above suspicion as those of Sir George Campbell, Colonel Nassau Lees, Sir James Stephen, the Rev. James Long, and the Duke of Argyll, in favour of finding some means of virtually setting the settlement aside, there must have been some questionable landlordism. But so is there in England and Scotland; and so in a far weightier sense is there in Ireland. Yet we do not break compacts on such pleas in the United Kingdom.

The settlement on a permanent basis was made—first, because the Government wanted more money than they could secure on any other basis; and secondly, because the land was not improved on the periodical settlements, lest the rent should be raised. The Government have now from the land of India, generally, £21,000,000 of the £50,000,000 of revenue. It never seems to occur to some people that money taken from land or trade for mere executive government, is so much drawn from the marrow and life of industry.

If the plea of care for the tenants were real on the part of those Englishmen who generally make it, every man who wished well to India would support it, or at least try to comprehend it; but it is, in most cases clearly, and in some avowedly, used merely to show the landlords that there is behind the general question one other fulcrum from which to overturn an inconvenient settlement. Few persons in England would support that. There is indeed one substantial ground upon which the rights of the tenants ought to be insisted upon, and upon which the right even of Lord Cornwallis to make the settlement might have been disputed, if only it had been disputed in time. The true owners of the land of old were the village communities, whose contractors or agents the zemindars in the first instance were. That system we broke. We made the contractors into landlords. We effected a virtual revolution. On this ground the tenants have rights, and from this position the zemindars should not be allowed to escape, always provided the Government does not claim to itself benefit pecuniarily by what is done. In 1793 the change was convenient. In 1877 what might not have been done if we had the village communities, and had had also, as however, events show we never should have had, men who knew how to direct them aright into grooves of social progress?

From this brief statement of facts the reader may gather the true meaning of the dispute on the permanent land settlement. I am no advocate of the zemindars, as they have known. But rather than quibble with plain words, I would say with Sir James Stephen, "We disown the compact made eighty-four years ago. We shall have a new 'lotting;'" and if some shrewd man desires to apply the same law to England, to Henry II. and Henry VIII. and Charles II. and William III., why there will be nothing left for us but to admit that the application is valid. We, of all people in the world, the loudest in our talk about "vested rights," shall have shaken vested rights at home and abroad to their foundations.

From the question of land to that of prisons and police is not so long a stride as it might appear. One of the peculiarities of a native policeman is that he will not, as a rule, touch an Englishman if he can help it. First, he dreads the Englishman's prowess in pugilism, and secondly, his power to engage a counsel to turn evidence inside out in a law court. Sir James Stephen simplified much of this, however, by his reform of the criminal law. One measure to revise the law as to Pleaders and Mooktears must have almost revolutionised the practice of Indian courts. The Pleader is still, as afore, allowed to make his own terms with his client, but those terms are now subject to revision, and may be set aside by the court. This was one of the most beneficent measures of all these reforms. The lobbies and corridors of an Indian court present such a mass of cunning and intrigue as perhaps no lobbies in the whole world could surpass, and an amount of sharpened intellect which only needs physique to set European advocacy at defiance. The act of Sir James Stephen touched the intrigue in its vital parts.

That the police are often in league with thieves is well known. In Lord Elgin's time it was thought that we had arrived at a stage when the Thuggee and Dacoitee department might be abolished in British territory; but the department was still continued in native states, and a comparatively recent report (about 1871) stated that in the Nizam's dominions the chowkeedars,[1] the only police employed in some districts, being paid in kind, and often very badly, made up their wages by robbery. The dacoits were numerous and both of Hindoo and Mohammedan races. "Many of the recognised police also of the Hyderabad district were habitual robbers." The department had on its rolls at the end of 1868 no fewer than 197 "converted" Thugs, and 306 "reclaimed" dacoitee approvers. Eighty-four of the reclaimed Thugs, and 106 of the converted dacoits, had died during the previous five years. Of a gang discovered in Indore in 1865, one good man confessed to eleven murders, of which

[1] A sort of rural police.

he gave ghastly particulars, but he added that he was now touched with a sense of his wickedness and would help the cause of righteousness. The favourite plan was to entice the victims into houses and strangle them, or to appear as wayfarers on the road, and share their sweetmeats with strangers, who, of course, they either drugged or poisoned. Parents were strangled to obtain possession of their children; the hands and feet of children were cut off for the otherwise irremovable rings that Indian children wear from infancy on wrists and ankles. One young approver, a leader, who had been saved from transportation, was induced by Colonel Harvey, head of the department, to marry, and turn over a new leaf. The good-natured colonel himself attended the wedding. "But mind," he said, "if you play me false I shall follow you all through India." The approver did play false, and he was followed from Delhi to Mysore, then back by the Bombay and Madras frontiers, and recaptured. This is but a glimpse of a great romance. To touch the detective department would be to open a history out of all proportion to the limits of this work.

I visited a number of prisons, and among them, in 1870, the great gaol of Alipore near Calcutta. It was at Alipore that Sir George Campbell resolved to try his experiment as to sharper punishment; to set the "productive" system aside. What astounded people most, however, was the direct assertion of Sir George Campbell, that an abnormal death-rate must be looked for, and, indeed, was a proper deterrent from crime. The minute said:

> "His honour's impression is strong, and he thinks that most officers of experience will bear him out, that the real terror of our gaols is not (in any part of India that he knows) the gaol discipline, but that men do not like to be taken from their families. And what they much dread, or (what is more important) what the families and friends they leave behind them much feel, is the great probability that they will never come back again. With the rates of mortality we have had, and even with those we have, this probability of dying in gaol is undoubtedly a very great deterrent. If we succeeded in

making our gaols very healthy, we should be driven to make them more disagreeable in other ways; and that is just what we cannot do. The harder the work and the discipline, the greater the death-rate, is the only sanitary rule that may be taken to be pretty generally true in Indian gaols."

There are some things that it is not pleasant to even think, and there are some things a man may think, yet ought not to say. To which class Sir George Campbell's words belonged, the reader must decide. It was, moreover, such an unnecessary statement. The decision surely would have been enough without the reasons.

There were in Alipore gaol, when I saw it, 2500 persons, and with a few exceptions, of punishment, all employed in remunerative labour. There were masons erecting buildings, weavers making gunny-bag cloth of jute, a factory of jute spinners, printers, lithographers, painters, carpenters, blacksmiths, and many other classes of workmen, all engaged in task work. If they exceeded the task a small sum was carried to their credit to be paid to them on leaving gaol. An amusing story was told of a shrewd Yorkshireman who, sent out "to manage a jute mill," was faced by the reality of some hundreds of criminals not one of whom knew anything of the work. First he despaired; then he hoped a little; finally he succeeded, and had a capital jute mill. Dr Faucus, governor of the prison, told me that the men they sent out with trades hardly ever had returned; and there was an instance of a man whose time had expired begging permission to remain a little longer in gaol to more completely learn his trade. It was to my view a humane and judicious system.

Eighteen months later I visited the Presidency Gaol in Calcutta, and the governor, Dr Mackenzie, kindly showed me the wonders of the place. We saw, in the yard, "a mild Bengalee," whom flogging, short diet, and even the dreaded solitary confinement (like the cell of Guy Fawkes in the Tower of London) had failed to compel to work. "He is one of the few prisoners who ever beat me," the governor said.

A hundred or so of the prisoners were breaking stones; some were on the tread-mill, a frightful punishment under such a sun; some mat making, as punishment, on very heavy looms. At this some rioters were engaged. They had at first refused, and were taken to the tread-mill; refusing that they were flogged, put on short diet, sent to the dark cells, and were at last working at the looms.

We came to a separate cell, the inmate of which was a loose-jointed, misshapen, weakly-looking, thin-faced native man, apparently about twenty-five years of age, though he might, for anything one could judge, have been any age from eighteen to forty. That, said the governor, was one of the most daring and relentless dacoits we have ever had. In a cell a few yards distant there was a grave and venerable-looking old man who had attained the very highest grade in a different profession—that of a forger. He had been convicted in attempting to obtain money from an officer—I think the head of the police—by means of a letter purporting to be written by Mr Reilly, the well-known detective. The forgery was perfect, and no one would have disputed the letter but for one small mistake; the two initial letters of Mr Reilly's Christian name were transposed—C. J. (or something) instead of J. C. This interesting old gentleman, questioned as to the amount of work he had done, put his hands together gravely and confessed that it was far short of the task. The governor spoke sternly, and threatened short diet. Evidently the old artist was out of his vocation of slow patient work. When the same question was put to the dacoit he pleaded pitifully, "Only four bags, but I'll do forty to-morrow." Forty was the number to be sewed per day.

There were many wealthy natives among the prisoners; and I was sorry to find a number of English sailors and soldiers, for deserting regiments or ships. It was impossible to look upon them as criminals. They were kept apart from the other prisoners. Some of them were very fine fellows, who, probably, never were in prison before, nor would be again. Another class was that of the vagrants, termed "loafers." There were some very respectable-looking men among them, "turned away from the railways," they said, or "brought from Australia in charge of horses and then dismissed"—the most prolific source of "loaferism" in India.

Six young native boys were separated from the rest. They had their own yard, and each a little garden, and a division of work. One was cook, another "housemaid," and so on. They were drawn up in line and questioned, the cook first. "What are you here for?" "Murder; I struck another boy on the head, and killed him." "And you?" "Murder; I threw a child into a well." The answers were given as if they had related to common matters. We went no further in the list. An Indian prison is marvellous for its mixture of races. The Hindoo cannot eat with the Mussulman. To step inside a cook-house is to defile it even for prisoners. Yet even Brahmins, old offenders, had been known to beg for the office of "mehters" (sweepers—lowest menials), so great was their dread of the hard labour.

What were called the "non-habituals" were employed as at Alipore, and taught trades where necessary. I noticed particularly the intelligent Chinaman before referred to, busy at a lathe. I said, "*He* never gave you any trouble?" "No; he was entrapped into a robbery, caught, and convicted, and he immediately made the best of his position. He is a quiet, respectful, intelligent man." He spoke English like an Englishman. There were several Chinamen in the prison, and all of the same class. We came to a long line of men, seated on the ground, engaged in hand spinning; the fourth from one end was old Ameer Khan, the Wahabee, referred to previously. He was a tall man, I should say nearly seventy years of age, stout, with flabby cheeks, a rather fine forehead, and, as before stated, an extraordinarily furtive eye. It was, in any case, a severe punishment. On page 74 I have stated that Ameer Khan was released on the proclamation of the Queen as Empress, but I have since had reason to doubt that this was so, though proposals were made for his release.

If the prisons and police of India were judged by the prisons and police of England, the comparison would probably lead to error. Yet I think the governors of English gaols might find a few hints worthy of notice in India, and, perhaps, some facts to appal them. A Bengal report (1869-70) stated the number of prisoners at 75,751, of whom 57 males and 8 females had been executed during the year. In Madras, about 70, I found, had been sentenced to death; in Bombay and Scinde, 49; in the Punjab, 81. These executions are carried out as an ordinary affair of life, the people remarkably well conducted. The district surgeon certifies that the criminal has been executed. Then the surgeon goes home to his breakfast, or perhaps takes his wife for a morning drive. In the year referred to above, there died in the prisons of Bengal 989 males, and 40 females; in Madras, 250; in Bombay and Scinde, 193 males, and 4 females; in the North Western Provinces, 420; and in the Punjab, 419. One of the tables showed that the imprisonment of "45,319 males and 2777 females, aggregating 48,096 persons, deprived 74,590 children of their parents; that 58,896 wives were left without their husbands, who were imprisoned, and that 2489 wives were parted from their husbands for life." "What," the writer asked, "becomes of the great body of women and children deprived of their natural protectors, and what proportion of them ultimately recruit the ranks of the social evil and criminal classes?" There are some good officers in India who ask these and like questions with great earnestness of purpose.

CHAPTER XIX.

THE STORY OF OUDE AND OF THE MUTINY: SOME INDIAN CITIES REVISITED.

AT the end of 1870, fresh from the scenes of the Mutiny, I received the second volume of Sir John Kaye's "Sepoy War," and reviewed it in three numbers of the paper I edited; but with the result in my own mind, and all the stronger because of what I had so lately seen, that I was merely generalising upon a topic which had on all hands living witnesses to facts. I referred, therefore, to an officer of much experience, and he added to my articles two more on the basis of special knowledge. From this starting-point, with the help of much information from persons with whom I had intercourse, I re-read the story of the Mutiny; and twice again (in 1872 and 1874) I wandered amid the scenes which the deeds of the Mutiny have rendered memorable; the site of Wheeler's encampment, the Ghât by the river, the Sacred Well, the Residency where Lawrence fought and died and was buried, the Alumbagh where Havelock lies; the many scenes in and around Delhi and Agra, and Lucknow and Cawnpore. I had also opportunities, referred to in earlier chapters, of visiting some of the more memorable of the scenes of the campaign of Sir Hugh Rose in Central India, and then again from Patna, Moorshedabad, Benares, Allahabad, and elsewhere, of viewing the different lines of action in their relation to one great plan. It is impossible for any one passing through these scenes to miss the undoubted fact that, having won the palaces of Agra and Delhi and Lucknow, we have always been utterly at a loss to know what to do with them. As we preserve the ruins of our own abbeys, so we preserve the Marble Palaces and the Tâj and the Imambara, for show. We have no king for the palaces, as we have no abbot for the abbeys; but we have the historical faculty beneath a levelling practical faculty, and it is our delight to say: "See what things were in days of old."

I noticed also, however, how difficult it is for an Englishman in the great cities of India to fully picture to himself any period of history as he can picture that of 1857–58. Strive as one may to reach to Akbar or Nadir Shah, it is long before the mind can extend very far beyond the Sepoy Mutiny. Where Lawrence, and Neill, and Nicholson, and Hodson, and Havelock died, are the spots one visits first, and visits last. We have no great heritage in the palaces; we have an inalienable heritage in the graves. It is perhaps the failing of islanders, but at all events it is strangely real, as many Englishmen must have found.

The keys to the action of the Mutiny, and indeed to much of English history in India, are the Ganges and Jumna rivers, both sacred. On these rivers are great cities and a myriad villages, connected, as we have seen, by boats of whose number it is scarcely possible to form an estimate. The news that one boat brings from some one place, a score of boats take to as many other places, and from the bazaar of each the news spreads throughout many districts on both sides of both rivers. It is in this way that, by a power as of electricity, the native heralds of intelligence have often left the English mails far behind. We could, before the magic wire came to us with such power for peace or war, speedily span the distance between any two cities; but Native India in the same time spanned the distance between many cities and the most remote villages. The news seemed to spread as on the wind. In reality, it spread in a natural, and, when we see it, perfectly accountable way.

If we started on the Hooghly—the Ganges—and voyaged

upward from Calcutta, we should pass very near to Plassey, Moorshedabad, Monghyr, Patna, and Benares. At Allahabad the Jumna and the Ganges meet. If we continued our voyage on the latter, we should pass, on our right, Lucknow, in Oude, and on our left Cawnpore, in the North Western Provinces. In due time we would reach Meerut, from whence we might ride across country, a distance of forty miles, to Delhi. By this ride we should, moreover, have passed from the line of the Ganges to that of the Jumna. We might then again take boat, and voyaging down stream, with Central India (Gwalior, Jhansi, Indore, &c.) far away on our right, come to Agra, and so on till, passing Calpee, we again arrived at the confluence of the two rivers at Allahabad. A line struck across country would, we have seen, lead direct from Delhi to Meerut. A line similarly struck from Agra would, with some little divergence, lead to Cawnpore. On these and like lines, on road and river, the germs of the Mutiny were carried and recarried, till a thousand fires smouldered where not even the smoke from a fire was seen.

The dynasty of Oude, in the existing royal line, was not of great antiquity; but the throne of Oude, in Lucknow, the chief city, was believed to be inherited from the great Rama himself. This gave to the beautiful palaces and baghs (gardens) a still more subtle charm to the Hindoo mind. From the beginning of the century, however, the dynasty of Oude had never been free from danger. The East India Company, which cared little for the Ramayana, began to declare to the King that his dominions were a garden of weeds, and that the seed came over the Company's partition wall. The nobles, more feudal than the most feudal nobles ever known in Europe, were declared to be robbers, who from their strongholds preyed relentlessly upon all the country round. Fertile land, it was said, had been purposely turned into jungle, and its inhabitants driven away, while a licentious imbecile king spent his days and nights shut up in his palaces, with wives, concubines, and entertainers. Some, at least, of the delineators of this picture were men of undoubted veracity; men too who had no wish to see a policy of annexation. In February 1856, Lord Dalhousie declared the kingdom of Oude at an end; and to one of the best men in India, and one of the best defenders of the rights of native dynasties, General Outram, was committed the uncongenial task of giving the edict effect. The King was pensioned, as we have seen, and the ancient kingdom of Oude became English property. We did more than merely dethrone a king; we degraded a whole nobility, as men like Sir Henry Lawrence and Mr now Sir Charles Wingfield pointed out, but pointed out in vain. All Oude was against us; but the germs of disaffection were as yet beyond ordinary observation. The "great pro-consul" had his will, and the men of Leadenhall Street theirs.[1]

Moreover, Oude was but the last of several annexations and forfeitures. The old Peishwa of the Mahrattas, Bajee Rao, had been dethroned in 1818, with an allowance for his comfort of £80,000 a year, and a jageer and fortified palace at Bithoor. In 1827, being childless, he, according to Hindoo custom, adopted as his own the son of a Brahmin of the Deccan, a boy named Dhundoo Punt, and educated him as a Mahratta nobleman and heir to Bithoor. This boy became the Nana Sahib. Bajee Rao died in 1853, and the pension was stopped by Lord Dalhousie. The Nana

[1] In referring to Lord Dalhousie's policy of annexation, I of course mean the policy of the India House, accepted by the nation, and have no wish to attempt to make one of the most powerful men ever sent by England to India the scapegoat for a policy which both the Directors of the Company and Parliament shared, and in the former case had indicated. Three facts remain in Lord Dalhousie's favour. First, that the time had come when some stern policy was needed. Secondly, that the abuses and dangers against which the annexation policy was directed were admitted by men who nevertheless opposed the policy. Lastly, that Lord Dalhousie, wearied and sick, was not able to apply the remedial measures which his strong hand might have applied to temper a policy which, in spite of all special pleading, history will sternly condemn. Yet if there had been no Mutiny, the policy would have been deemed the greatest political success.

swallowed his anger as best he could, gave dinners and entertainments to the neighbouring English "Station" at Cawnpore, smiled upon the English ladies and their children, and nursed his hate the while to white heat.

I met in Cawnpore with people who believed, of course absurdly, that in reality the Nana never met or was seen by the people he invited; but, so deadly was his concealed hate, dressed up a low-caste person to represent him, and so to degrade the Sahibs and Mem Sahibs without their knowledge. The Nana left no stone unturned to win back the pension. He sent as his agent to England the clever, and afterwards relentless, Azimoolah Khan; and the agent, although he failed in the main object of his mission, brought back with him letters which proved to our enraged soldiers, who found the letters at a maddening time, that while in London he had stood high in the favour of some titled English ladies. He also, having returned by way of the Crimea, brought reports of what he deemed the absolute collapse of the military power of England before Sebastopol. On both sides of the Ganges, therefore, there was bitterness intense enough to rouse a whole country. The Nana, in spite of the loss of his pension, was still rich. That he spent money like a prince the English of Cawnpore could testify. He was still, too, chief of the Mahrattas; and if he had a wrong, it was the wrong of a warlike race, remarkable for cunning and the power to strike swift and sure blows.

The year 1853, when Bajee Rao died, was rendered still further memorable by the death of the Rajah of Jhansi.[1] It was then discovered, and cleverly proved by clever men, that Jhansi, having originally belonged to the Peishwa, was English property, which the Rajah had held on sufferance. The right of adoption in his case, therefore, certainly could not be allowed. Since 1818 the Company had been kept out of its just rights in Jhansi. The Rajah had, it is true, adopted a son, and so had received in the

[1] See Chap. VIII.

last hours of his life the spiritual blessings which only a son can give. Here, however, the privilege must end. The right of the rulers of Jhansi to adopt, it was also found, had previously been disputed, and that the latest ruler had himself owed his sovereignty to that dispute in 1835. It was not discovered with the same unerring ability that when the right of adoption was set aside in 1835, it was for the exclusion of a stranger and in favour of the real heir of Sheo Rao Bhao, with whom we had in 1804 made a treaty declaring the territory hereditary in his family. It was very clever, but India saw the real fact, and when Jhansi was annexed the Government of Lord Dalhousie might have saved itself the trouble of defending the annexation on any other ground than that they had taken who had the power. The Ranee's property was sold, and bought under circumstances of distressing high-handedness. She too nursed her "burning wrongs."

In addition to these and other complications, there were the royal family of Delhi, the descendants of Timour the Tartar. The nominal sovereignty of Delhi had been left, with a pension, to the old King, Bahadur Shah, and his heirs. A dispute as to heirship having been removed by the death of one of the claimants to it, the whole question was very satisfactorily settled in 1856. Then the princes of the royal house travelled, by permission of the great pro-consul, winning sympathy and sowing animosity to the English. Nothing could well have been more remarkable than that all these elements of disorder —germs of mutiny—should have found their way to the eyes and understandings of India on the eve of the hundredth anniversary of Plassey, the date which prophets had assigned as the end of the reign of "John Kompany." In 1857, the little cakes, the chupatties, which an eloquent writer, Mr Trevelyan, terms the red cross of India, were carried from village to village by sure hands. All that was needed then was some unmistakable signal that the hour to strike had arrived.

Such was the dread situation early in 1857. Enfield cartridges arrived from England in January, and ominous whispers ran from rank to rank and from regiment to regiment that the cartridges were greased with cow's and pig's fat, to break the caste of the soldiers, as the first step to making them Christians—a powerful witness to the wisdom of the Company's "latitudinarian" rule in matters of faith. Alarming news came rapidly of cartridges having been refused by the men at Dum-Dum and Barrackpore, and indeed no one knew where, and of a dreadful feeling of uneasiness from Dacca to Peshawur. March came, and there was seen in Barrackpore that strange thing, one of the faithful sepoy regiments (the 19th) disbanded in face of European artillerymen, match in hand. Mungul Pandy, too, had stepped out of the ranks of the 34th at Barrackpore, had wounded two officers on open parade ground, and would be hanged. Where, then, had those disciplined men of the 19th gone in boats by the Ganges and along the great trunk road? To Oude, some said, where disaffection could be felt in the very air; to Bundlecund, where the Company's rule of annexation had made every man an enemy of England. To disband a regiment for misconduct would have been little—regiments had been so disbanded before. But here was a common cause never before seen. The 34th, immensely the more culpable regiment of the two, followed the 19th. The first regiment had gone away with some signs of penitence; the second went away exultant. Sahib was now powerless, was told in the bazaars and at the Ghâts of Lucknow and Cawnpore and Delhi. Sahib too knew, as the native prophets knew, that his year and almost his hour had come. One more step and the veil might be thrown aside. The native troops at Meerut did what the 34th had proposed to the 19th. They murdered their officers and all

English people who could be safely murdered. Then (May 10) they marched off to Delhi.

General Hewitt commanded a strong English force at Meerut, and had power to give a good account of the mutineers; but General Hewitt was paralysed with the weight of his responsibility, and the mutineers had a pleasant night march, their cavalry trotting jubilantly into Delhi a little after daybreak next morning. Delhi rose to the grand news. The King was saluted. The Europeans, men, women, and children, were dragged to the great street of Delhi, the Chandnee Chouk, and there, in the presence of some of the Princes of Delhi, were murdered. The royal city of the Moguls was no longer British. The last point—the arsenal—had been blown up by its eight heroic defenders, some of whom escaped; all of whom, living or dead, told of the true, and only true, refuge of England in this her time of mortal extremity—her fearless spirit, her unyielding resolution to death. Men who shuddered at responsibility might return home, if not too late. Those who remained, women as well as men, must gird up their loins for such a fiery trial as only comes at rare intervals to any race of mankind.

General Anson, commander-in-chief, hurried from Simla to recapture Delhi, which Sir John Lawrence, Chief Commissioner of the Punjab, had telegraphed him must be taken. General Anson died at Kurnaul on the seventeenth day after the outbreak at Meerut. Sir Henry Barnard assumed the command, and, joined by Brigadier Wilson from Meerut, marched direct upon Delhi at the head of 4000 mostly British men. The two brave Lawrences, sons of a gallant soldier, had differed strongly in the Punjab in a bygone time, and Lord Dalhousie had supported Sir John. They would differ no more, even to the end. The Commissioner in the Punjab, finding his sepoys dropping off, enrolled Sikhs. Chiefs and people, they flocked to him, the man whose pulse beat as calmly as ever, now that the clouds were black as pitch. Sir Henry had been a short time at Lucknow, Chief Commissioner of Oude, Lord Canning's selected man; designated, too, if he lived and Lord Canning died or was incapacitated for work, to wield the highest power in India under the Queen.

No man had done more than Sir Henry Lawrence to improve the position of the sepoys, and to rectify the injustice that fell alike upon nobles and private persons with the annexation of Oude. He had a handful of men and a few guns in the cantonment. He fortified the Residency, and a building above it, the Muchee Bhawn. He would not, he said, fall back upon Allahabad; he would defend Lucknow. The month of June came. Sepoys from Aligurh, from Mynpoorie, from Nusseerabad, from Bareilly, from Peshawur, were converging joyfully upon Delhi, to serve "the King." At Futteghur, a great station, 166 persons, merchants, civil officers, and others, including many poor ladies and children, embarked (June 4) for Cawnpore; sure to be well received—the Nana was so princely and so kind. About 126 of them reached Cawnpore on the 12th; four days after the Nana had opened fire on General Wheeler's entrenchment. The poor fugitives felt then that they had come to doom, as they had. Those left at Futteghur prepared for a siege, the memory of which would remain to their honour and the honour of the English name.

Sir Hugh Wheeler was at Cawnpore, confident in the Nana's loyalty, and trustful to the last to the faithful sepoys, to whom he had been as a father, and a daughter of whose race he had married. On 4th June the faithful sepoys prepared for a gladsome march to Delhi. They had even begun their march, when the Nana, who now saw the possibility of a Mahratta dynasty, stopped them, and brought them back, together with the human scum of many districts, to where General Wheeler was entrenched. The entrenchment was 250 yards square, surrounded by a mud wall, over which children might have leaped at play; a wall which you still may trace, and which, with the trench behind it, only gave a cover of five feet. There were now nearly 1000 people with Sir Hugh Wheeler, including 200 soldiers, gallant men of the 32nd and 84th Foot, and of the Royal Artillery. Three hundred women, children, and sick persons were crowded into two small buildings at the middle of the entrenchment, and which had been entered on the 21st May, amid fearful forebodings which one poor lady in her agony chronicled for all time. The combatants remained under canvas. All, civilians and soldiers alike, were combatants. Fire was opened by the Nana on 8th June. Attempts to break into the entrenchment were beaten back, and the assailants scattered like chaff before the wind. Provisions, however, would not last long; and for water the gauntlet of musketry must be run to a well at the far side of the entrenchment, over an open space which, long before the end, could only be traversed by night. Ladies who a month previously had been in possession of all the luxuries of Indian life were now exposed to an Indian June sun, and in sight by day of a maddened mob, like the sea in number, and all night through in the hearing of ceaseless cries for vengeance.

Walking over this sacred ground in company with an officer fresh to India, but not to the service, it was a matter of after remark between us that conversation had unwittingly fallen to a whisper. "There they went for water." "There they conveyed their dead by night." There they stood—200 fighting men—ever growing fewer, against, in the end, 10,000 men who had been soldiers, yet who never once dared to charge this forlorn hope of England. "Here they came out for the last fatal march." The women, one writer says, suffered terribly. "Some went mad, some sought death, some behaved like angels." The noise and revelry and musketry ceased not day nor night.

General Wheeler and the men learned by degrees the hopelessness of their isolation. The banks of the river above and below Cawnpore were so carefully watched, that even if Sir Henry Lawrence could have spared help from Lucknow, and the relief could have reached the Oude side of the river, the attempt to cross must have been fatal. Lucknow was itself besieged. Mr Colvin, Lieutenant Governor of the North Western Provinces, was shut up in the old red sandstone fort at Agra. The Ranee of Jhansi, after besieging the European residents of Jhansi for four days in the palace fort, had induced them to surrender, and then (June 8th) had cut them down, seventy-five in all, to the last man, woman, and child. The Gwalior contingent, young Maharajah Scindia's force in aid of the British, was either in mutiny or on the eve of mutiny. The fugitives from Futteghur and elsewhere who had fallen into the Nana's hands numbered about 136, who had been slain in some cases, and "reserved" in others. The King of Delhi had been proclaimed successor of the Moguls. The Nana had assumed the headship which he claimed of right over the Mahrattas. Such was the intelligence carried in, scrap by scrap, often with exaggerations, to the doomed garrison of Cawnpore.

On the 24th June, Mrs Greenway, a poor lady, wretchedly clad, and with a baby in her arms, arrived at the entrenchment with a message from the Nana. She was one of a family who were said to have paid the Nana £30,000 for their lives, which after all were sacrificed. She was the bearer of the Nana's offer to permit all of the garrison who were not concerned in Lord Dalhousie's proceedings to go to Allahabad; and the offer was accepted. On the 26th a few officers strolled down to the river side to see that the promised boats were ready. On the 27th a long line of tattered woe-begone people wandered in the same direction, with such precautions as could be taken against treachery. They entered a shallow gorge, now like a small dried-up watercourse, and were pressed upon and separated by a vast crowd, conscious of some great treat in store. Some were at once slain. General Wheeler, who had come down wounded in a palanquin, was ordered to leave it, and was murdered, perhaps in mercy, before he had well touched the ground. The head of the line reached the Ghât, to find the boats aground, and the people around eager and laughing. Women and children, all must wade through the mud and water; a slight trial compared with many, but dismal nevertheless. They waded. Some reached the boats, some were in the water, some at the Ghât, when the thatched roofs of the boats were seen to be on fire. At the same time volleys from carbines, muskets, and guns planted on the river bank were poured upon them. About 450 had marched down to the river that morning; in the evening 163 women and children remained close prisoners of the Nana. Four men only—Captain Mowbray Thompson, Lieutenant Delafosse, and Privates Murphy and Sullivan—after perils of a hundred kinds, escaped by the river and the river banks to tell the sad story of Cawnpore. To Captain, now Colonel, Thompson references are made in other chapters. I had some difficulty, when I saw him, in fully understanding that the quiet gentlemanly officer was the hero of these fearful adventures, the story of which will be read in generations to come in his own narrative.

The Nana had now in his possession 163 women and children of the survivors of Cawnpore, and about 47 left of those from Futteghur and elsewhere. The men had been at once put to death. The prisoners were confined in one house, close to another in which, from the 27th of June to the 15th of July, the Nana at intervals held high revel, with music and festivity, fancying himself a real king. The known horrors of that imprisonment were dreadful. Havelock, however, was at hand, sweeping the rebel forces before him; and in the dusk of the evening of the 15th, five men entered the prison-house sabre in hand, and did not leave it again till dark. For a time, Mr Trevelyan tells us in a story which no one ever need re-tell, there were screams and the sounds of struggling. When the ruffians had left and closed the doors, nothing was heard but a low dismal moaning, which continued all night through. Three hours or so after sunrise next morning, the bodies were dragged over a piece of waste desert ground, and thrown into an old well. On the same day the Nana was defeated by Havelock. On the following day (the 17th), Havelock entered Cawnpore. I have not related these bare general facts from any morbid wish to dwell upon them or revive the sad story, but because it is necessary to account for the spirit which for several months from this time animated both the English army and the English nation.

On a part of the site of Wheeler's entrenchment there is now a beautiful Memorial Church; and near to where our countrymen and countrywomen strove in that mortal agony which God alone fully knows, I heard an earnest and good sermon from the words, "When ye pray, say, Our Father;" and a choir composed of soldiers and their little boys sang the hymn "Abide with me." The preacher explained that "our" was all humanity, and "Father," the Father of all. Near to where the women and children were slain the Bank of Bengal now stands; and there, with the Memorial Gardens in front, on my last visit, I wrote out some of these notes of Cawnpore. The gardens which cover the once desert, weed-grown piece of ground are preserved in admirable order, and you are informed as you enter that you must drive slowly. No rule is needed to remind any one that it beseems the place to speak in a low tone, to forget for the time to smile, or that it is incumbent upon men to stand bare-headed at the sacred well. It is good also to remember, standing there in view of Baron Marochetti's great creation—the sweet mournful face of the angel in whose hands are the crossed palm leaves of peace over the dead—in view too of the many well-chosen texts, entwined as it were around the monument, from the Book of the Christian's God, that there was a noble faithfulness never properly recorded on the part of many of the Hindoos; that the rising was military, not popular; and that when the story can be told from the point of view of Native India, for every act of barbarity there will be set off many acts of mercy, devotion, and loyalty even to death on the part of the people,[1] and acts also, on the part of Englishmen, in which innocent persons were made to pay the penalty for the guilty.[2] Passing from the now sacred well, you might visit other equally sacred parts of this God's Acre; some places where bands of heroes died; several where heroes are buried.

Cawnpore is once more a flourishing station, with fine markets for the produce of the North Western Provinces, and a trade representing great wealth. I crossed the river therefrom one morning with a party of people on their way to a ball at Lucknow, forty miles distant. The toll of the bridge of boats was a rupee. We had then a railway train, which travelled at the rate of fifteen miles an hour through some very peaceful scenes, and there was ample time to remember that it was the self-same ground over which Havelock, Neill, Outram, and Sir Colin Campbell passed in 1857–58. The contrast was sufficiently striking—"the relief of Lucknow," and a Lucknow ball.

To illustrate the existing native life of Cawnpore, and with it one other feature of Indian native life generally, I recur to what I saw in Cawnpore of a great cotton market, one of the most notable in India. The market was held in an immense square, which at an early hour

[1] I do not here refer merely to the conduct of princes and chiefs, of which something has been said in previous chapters, but to that of numbers of the people whose names never were heard of. The Mutiny was military; but around the sepoys clustered all the floating vagabondism and rascality of the districts, with a certain amount of real worth which race feeling or our own unwise action had carried into rebellion. The people generally, however, were certainly not barbarous. No feeling of nationality ought to prevent an Englishman from stating this, or Englishmen from facing it as a sober truth. If any one would write a faithful military history of India, with a special view to showing on how many fields and under what circumstances of danger Englishmen and natives of India have stood shoulder to shoulder, and how loyally the latter had acted, England would be surprised at the facts adduced.

[2] I know a Mohammedan gentleman, now high in the favour of the Government, who was within a hairsbreadth of losing his life in 1857.

in the morning was almost densely crowded with men and women, donkeys, horses, bullocks, camels, and gharries or other conveyances; a scene of barter of all manner of commodities, on every side, and on a large scale. Around the square were those low warehouses, the Indian "go-down," filled with cotton, the property, in some cases, of very wealthy persons, whom, however, it was impossible to distinguish, by their dress, from the poorest clerk. An eagerness for barter in some cases, an apparent carelessness as to sales in others; purchases made by the manipulation of fingers without speech; a market containing what many districts of the North Western Provinces could produce, and of what the representatives of one of the greatest industries of England, and one of the growing industries of India, were there to buy. Of course one felt certain that in that great mass of human life there must be many persons whose memories carried them back to 1857; but the subject is little talked of. The busy life of to-day covers the deeds of the past; and the residents of Cawnpore seem scarcely conscious of the feeling of relief with which a stranger turns away to other scenes.

CHAPTER XX.

LUCKNOW DURING THE MUTINY AND AFTERWARDS: THE LESSONS OF 1857.

WHILE General Wheeler and his little band were struggling in Cawnpore, like a crew of castaway sailors on a frail raft in a tempestuous sea, Sir Henry Lawrence was defending the lives of many helpless people, and the honour of England, in Lucknow. On the last day of June he advanced from the city to meet a large body of mutineers, reported to be approaching. At the moment of action his native artillerymen cut their traces, and went over to the enemy. The day was lost. The commander, prostrate, but not wounded, was carried away on a gun-carriage to the beleaguered city. The Muchee Bhawn was now given up; the Residency itself was the utmost that could be defended. On the 2d July Sir Henry was struck by a shell, and mortally wounded. From that time till the 4th his words were treasured up by brave men, whom he besought to hold out to the last, and never to make terms. To the Nana, however, must be ascribed the production of the weightiest argument for no surrender, when he ordered the politically insane massacre at Cawnpore. No one could resist that argument. "God help the poor women and children!" and then, in a low voice (and as if in self-communing), "Here lies Henry Lawrence, who tried to do his duty; may God have mercy upon him!" are among the sentences which remain as pictures of this one more of the favourite heroes of England. These last words were accepted as his epitaph, and written upon his tomb. Colonel Inglis, Mr Gubbins, Lieutenants Hardinge and Charteris, Dr Fayrer, and others, were left behind, to also make for themselves monuments in Lucknow. But to where Lawrence received the Lord's Supper, amid a storm of shot and shell, an Englishman looks as he looks on the cockpit of the "Victory."

In the Punjab, meanwhile, a mighty power—heroism, too—was rising, as the Brahmapootra rises in the rains. Sir John Lawrence was marshalling the Sikhs, and pushing them onward to Delhi. General Sydney Cotton, Colonel John Nicholson, Brigadier Neville Chamberlain, and others, had decided upon a movable column, destined to be memorable. Brigadier Chamberlain, under whom the column was at first placed, was required at Delhi, and John Nicholson had the command. On the 14th August Brigadier Nicholson, having previously scoured the country, and made his name as terrible in war as it had been loved in peace, marched into the camp at Delhi, with flags flying and drums beating; very cheering, it is recorded, especially to those of the men who had arrived before Delhi on the 4th June, and on the 8th had won that position behind the famous Ridge, from the shelter of which great deeds had already been done, but which, after all, had appeared not unlike a place besieged rather than the camp of the besiegers; save when Captain Hodson had undertaken to clear the country, or when an action had been fought to secure some military end, or as a warning of what was to come. General Barnard had at this time been dead more than a month, and Brigadier Wilson commanded.

At three o'clock on the morning of the 14th September, three columns stood ready for the spring. Brigadier Nicholson to attack the Cashmere bastion; Brigadier Jones, the water bastion; Colonel Campbell, the Cashmere gate. Other columns were in reserve. For six long days the fighting continued in the narrow streets. No quarter was given to men with arms. The enemy fought desperately, and cleverly left liquor in the men's way as a snare.

Delhi, however, was won. Hodson had made his way to the Jumma Musjid. The strongest bastions and gates had been stormed. Not an armed mutineer was to be seen within the city. But John Nicholson, among other brave men, had fallen. Wounded on the 14th, he lived till the 23d, and was then laid with mournful solemnity in a new burial-ground near the Cashmere Gate of Delhi. An intelligent native guide who went with me over this burial-ground, and who had given to every other of the renowned dead the proper designation of his rank, said, "That is John Nicholson." It was the most touching of all, for one had learned before this that "John Nicholson" was a name beloved by many of the native peoples.

About three miles from Delhi on the Agra road is the tomb of Humayoon, the father of Akbar; a fine domed building, and, like nearly all great Mohammedan palaces and tombs, standing in a spacious walled enclosure, almost like a city, and laid out as a garden. To this tomb the King and his family had fled. On the 21st September Captain Hodson appeared at the gates with fifty men, and in the end took away the King, Queen, and a young son, whose lives he guaranteed. Next day he repeated the daring act with a hundred of his own troopers, and took away the two princes, the murderers, unless history is at fault, of the Chandnee Chouk. The road was crowded with armed mutineers, and Hodson, believing, as he said, that he never could take his prisoners into the city, shot them. Sir John Kaye in his latest work asserts that they could have been taken into the city. Hodson and Lieutenant Macdowell solemnly affirmed that they could not, and one would not like, without direct proof, to disbelieve them. If the act were other than purely military, it was undoubtedly wrong; but Sir John Kaye gives no reason why Captain Hodson's word should be disbelieved.

Of Delhi itself a volume might be written. As a mere sight it is marvellous. Looking from the Ridge you have spread out before you a city with bastioned walls which have a circuit of seven miles, and with many gates, in almost each case memorable for something; and with a forest of cupolas and minarets, the white and red stone intermingling, and in both cases relieved by the never-failing dark or bright-green foliage. A little outside you are pointed to the Flagstaff Tower, where the magazine was blown up in May 1857, our first victory, because the first marked indication of our resolve to die rather than surrender to the mutineers. Inside is the beautiful mosque, the Jumma Musjid, and the royal palace, with the fort, the scenes of the glories of many generations. The fort has one of its sides to the Jumna, and from another looks upon the Chandnee Chouk, a street which, in its width and the almost illimitable variety of trades, private houses, shops, gardens, tombs, temples, and assemblages of all manner of men, may be said to stand alone among thoroughfares. The palace is a little city, with walls, gates, and other defences. In it are those wonders in marble of which travellers love to tell—the hall of white marble, inlaid with curious devices of precious stones, the filagree work and perforated walls, dumb witnesses of those times when the renowned peacock throne was the judgment-seat of the Moguls.

Ascending a long flight of broad and imposing steps, covered with worshippers, you come to a rocky plateau and a large quadrangle, at one side of which stands the great mosque, relieved by chaste little buildings of white marble, which in turn are relieved by red stone. Looked at either within or without, the Jumma Musjid is beautiful. A marble fountain without for the ablutions of the myriad worshippers corresponds with a marble pulpit within, on a floor of white marble with jet borders. The general effect is most imposing, and it is not difficult to see, from the mere presence of the countless worshippers, that the Mussulman faith, in a land where it has been conquered, has still a use for its great churches.

Four days before the assault had been delivered at Delhi,

Brigadier Greathead, with another memorable column, had dispersed the rebels in the neighbourhood of Agra; but a day earlier Lieutenant Governor Colvin had died. It has been questioned whether Agra was ever in any serious danger so long as Lucknow and Delhi were the centres of operations which kept the rebels so fully employed. But in the great fort there is a tombstone testifying, on the word of "a devoted wife," that Mr Colvin died from the effects of his unremitting labour. I asked a gentleman who was in Agra during all the period of the Mutiny, if other evidence agreed with this. He said, "Yes, thoroughly. Mr Colvin was one of the finest men I ever saw." The fort of Agra is, as we have seen, of red stone, and, like that at Delhi, it commands both the river and the town. In front of it, on one side you are pointed to a busy crowded street, at the end of which the King of Delhi was proclaimed while English children were playing on the marble floors of the palace of Akbar. The throne of Akbar, the grandest judgment-seat in the world, is here the central object among the treasures of a marble palace, or rather, as it seems, of a series of marble palaces, which compare with those of Delhi as the bright streets of Paris compare with the solid, sombre streets of London. Whether we take the palaces, or the Tomb of Humayoon and the Tâj Mehal, the contrast is the same: in Delhi, solid beauty; in Agra, a fairy creation, or, as some one has said, "poetry in stone." Among the other treasures of the fort are the sandalwood gates which Lord Ellenborough removed from Ghuznee to restore to the temple at Somnâth, but which he was glad at last to leave at Agra.

There is one exquisite little palace, with a temple also, built by the Mussulman Emperor Jehângir for a Hindoo wife—a lesson in toleration from a time when Europe could no more have comprehended such an act than it could have laid an Atlantic telegraph cable. A Christian king would have insisted on his wife becoming Christian. The Mohammedan—the "idol-breaker"—was content that his wife should remain Hindoo. The streets of Agra are crooked, narrow, and crowded, and the lofty houses are, in many cases, especially of the old ones, elaborately carved. The skilled artisan is there at his work, as his forefathers were at their work, in the same kind of shops, on the same spots, generations ago. The verandahs, from which people look down upon the Englishman to-day as he drives slowly through streets which could only be driven through more rapidly at the risk of life, are the same as those from which other people looked upon very different scenes when very different races ruled in Agra.

At a little distance from the city is the Tâj Mehal, which every one who has visited it has described, and in which so many different persons have seen so many fresh beauties. Twenty thousand workmen are said to have been twenty years building it, at a cost of £750,000, the tribute of Shah Jehan, who had fabulous wealth, to his beautiful wife. Outside is a plain, intentionally, perhaps, kept as a miniature desert. Then you enter an enclosure, the walls of which are red stone, and the interior a choice garden. In the centre is the Tâj, a palace of red stone, inlaid with marble and precious stones, and surmounted by a dome, the grace and proportions of which, and the reliefs of which, have, as far as I know, been generally pronounced matchless. Seen from the fort, the Tâj, with the bright sun shining upon it, cannot well be better described than as a fairy palace. When nearer to it, the view formed at a distance is confirmed. When within, and you see beneath the graceful dome, itself spangling with precious stones, the inlaid tombs, whatever doubt you might have of the first conception vanishes. The more the points of view from which you look at it, the greater number of beauties you perceive, Analyse it, and perhaps you might be a little disappointed. It is like the peculiar sweetness and beauty seen at times on a female face, and which you cannot reduce by any analysis to its component parts. Compared with the Tomb of

Humayoon, the Tâj presents a contrast in some respects as if the two were of different lands, though not so great a contrast as either presents to the Egyptian pyramids.

Delhi and Agra are alike Hindoo at the base, but Mohammedan in what are now known to Europe as their leading characteristics. Their fate, often diverging, often united, became one under the greater of the great Moguls. A heavy intellect was displaced by a lighter, and the purely reflective and self-communing spirit by one which rose buoyant to every fresh impulse in East and West, from as far westward indeed as the extreme limit of the conquests of the Moors. That India gained by the terrible inroads of the Mohammedans, the Hindoo is hardly yet prepared to admit; and no wonder, when he sees every footstep marked with blood; but that such is the fact no candid outside observer can doubt. The Mussulman, not the Englishman, or the strictly European of any name, broke the spell of ages, and laid India open to the march of new ideas; redeemed her, in fact, from the isolation of China. And he received intellectual benefit from her in return. The Mohammedan, moreover, though a foreigner and an intruder, strove to become native. He built as one rooted to the soil. The Tâj and the Tomb of Humayoon will, judging by human principles, survive all such works as the "Arthur Crawford Markets" in Bombay, or the Law Courts in Calcutta, though they may not, and we may well hope will not, survive the civilisation which these represent. What, however, is the impression the reader would gather from a comparison of the massive pyramids as the type of Egypt, the Buddhist topes and monasteries, as a type of the age when Hindooism was threatened with reform, and the Tâj Mehal, representing the impulses of a hotter blood and a graver purpose than that of India, in that great dawn of a new popular life in the age of the Commonwealth in England? At this stage of this simple recital of facts, not, I hope, overweighted with reflections on facts, perhaps the reader may see far more than the writer of the inner part and thing signified in the contrast of the pyramids and the Tâj Mehal.

Recurring to the Mutiny, we shall not be likely to overlook the fact that while to Delhi the attention of England was directed as the backbone of the rebellion, on Lucknow it was fixed with the still deeper interest of women and children whom any hour might consign to the fate of those of Cawnpore. On the 12th August, a month before the assault on Delhi, and a month after the massacre of the women and children at Cawnpore, Colonel Inglis stated his force to General Havelock as numbering 350 Europeans and 300 natives, in charge of 220 women, 230 children, and 120 sick. His provisions might last till September; but the enemy, he said, "are mining in all directions; their eighteen-pounders are within 150 yards of some of our batteries, and from their position, and our inability to form working parties, we cannot reply to them." The Gwalior men were also in the field. Let us now see how and from whence the relief was coming.

The Mutiny found Colonel Neill in Madras, newly arrived from England, and preparing to follow Sir James Outram, under whom was Havelock, to the war in Persia. This, however, was now countermanded, and Colonel Neill was ordered with his Madras Fusiliers to Calcutta, whence he started at once with a column for the scene of danger. On the 3d June he was at Benares—the first indication of help from outside of the mutinous districts. Benares was at the time in imminent danger, but Neill saved it, and made his hand so heavily felt that the heart of the Mutiny was as it were plucked out so far as related to the sacred city of the Hindoos. He then marched direct to Allahabad, and in a series of fierce and almost unceasing actions, from the 9th to the 13th June, effectually crushed out the rebellion in that capital of the North Western Provinces. There had a short time previously been a cruel massacre in Allahabad, and Neill therefore gave no quarter to men in arms. Having rescued this important military station, he (June 30th) despatched Major Renaud, with 400 Fusiliers, 300 Sikhs, and two guns to the relief of Cawnpore, intending himself to follow speedily.

Havelock, returning (May 29th) from the Persian expedition, at the head of which Outram remained, received at Bombay the first intelligence of the doings at Meerut, and of the ride of the mutineers to Delhi. On 1st June he embarked for Calcutta. He was shipwrecked at Ceylon, then very narrowly escaped being promoted back to Bombay. He did, however, escape—thanks to the Madras Commander-in-chief, Sir Patrick Grant—and went on to Calcutta. On the way he expressed a calm but strong opinion against disbanding any more mutinous regiments. He would attack, and, if necessary, annihilate them. Appointed to the command of the movable column at Allahabad, he pushed on at once to his duty; and on 30th June, almost immediately after the departure of Major Renaud, General Neill was superseded, and an order sent after Renaud directing him to halt and await the main force at Futteghur. This order, the beginning of a painful misunderstanding between Havelock and Neill, was much criticised at the time, and has been so ever since; but subsequent events showed to all fair reasoners that it was the right course. If Renaud had advanced on Cawnpore, his little force almost certainly would have been cut to pieces, as a force sent a little later from Dinapore to the relief of the House at Arrah, defended by sixteen Englishmen and fifty Sikhs, was destroyed.

In 1872 I heard the story of this siege related by one of the besieged, with some interjectional help from the narrator's wife, who had been sent to Dinapore for safety. The gentleman himself (prior to the Mutiny a schoolmaster) had elected with others to wait for the mutineers at this house at Arrah, which they fortified as best they could. At Dinapore the lady learned, truly, that 400 men sent to the relief of the little party had been almost annihilated. At Arrah the schoolmaster learned, untruly, that Dinapore had been captured and all the Europeans massacred. The garrison at Arrah, commanded by Mr Boyle, an engineer, slept in turn, and maintained so strict a watch and so hot a fire that the mutineers were arrested in their progress for a full week. The gallant little garrison was relieved by Major Vincent Eyre, who, starting with a mere handful of men, augmented to 200 on the march, defeated 2500 of the disciplined men of three native regiments. Major Renaud would probably have shared the fate of the force from Dinapore. Still he was an able soldier; and looking on his force as an advance one, Neill following speedily, the plan, as against that of Havelock, involved a mere difference of opinion; and, as far as any one could determine at the time, either plan might have succeeded or failed, though to succeed the man who planned would have had to carry the plan into effect. It was only by the light of what occurred afterwards that a conclusive opinion can be formed, that if Renaud had not halted at Futteghur he must have halted somewhere short of Cawnpore.

The march of General Havelock began on 7th July, with a force, including Renaud's, of 2000 men, Europeans and Sikhs, a company of Royal Artillery, and fifty horse. In eight days he marched 126 miles, and fought four engagements, driving the enemy everywhere before him. On the 17th he made that mournful entry into Cawnpore, to find only an empty house of death and a terrible grave. Neill, with about 200 men, arrived on the 20th, and was left in command at Cawnpore, while Havelock himself (25th July) crossed the Ganges. He advanced five miles on the Lucknow road to Mungulwar, and halted to secure his supplies. On the 29th, after a march of three more miles, he met and defeated the enemy crushingly at Oonao. Another march of six miles brought him (the same day) to Busseeruthgunge, a walled town, where the mutineers had halted. The road lay direct through the town. The gate was battered down by artillery, and the way cleared by a charge.

The force, however, was now reduced to 1200 men, and hearing that the Nana was advancing to cut of communication with Cawnpore, Havelock fell back on Mungulwar. He wrote in explanation to Neill, and urged him to spare no effort to send forward fresh men as fast as they arrived, and to keep the bridge open. Neill, who had been investigating the circumstances of the massacre of Cawnpore, and, half mad with rage, pouring vengeance like molten lead on the heads of all guilty and of many suspected persons, replied in a sharp letter, urging an immediate advance. Havelock wrote back very sternly, and did not move till August 4th. On the 6th he again defeated the enemy at Busseeruthgunge. Cholera now appeared in the relieving army, and the Nana threatened a flank attack, while the Gwalior men, with great reinforcements, not merely bade fair to overwhelm Neill at Cawnpore, but, by an advance on Calpee, to cut off the communication with Allahabad. The position was terrible, and Neill saw it. He was threatened from Bithoor, twelve miles distant, and from Futteghur, seven miles distant, besides in his communication with Allahabad. He frankly admitted his inability to hold the position. Havelock again, therefore, fell back upon the river; but finding that he could not cross it with an enemy on his flank as well as in his rear, he fought another battle, and, driving the enemy back, recrossed to Cawnpore. He had been nineteen days on the Oude side of the Ganges, and had won eight battles. He now won another at Bithoor, and put a final end to the Nana's reign there. Returning to Cawnpore, he found in a copy of the "Gazette of India" a notification that he was superseded in the command by Sir James Outram, who arrived on the 16th September with 1400 men, but refused the command till Lucknow had been relieved.

On the 19th and 20th the river was recrossed with an army of 2500 men. On the 23d the army was at the

Alumbagh (palace and garden), in sight of Lucknow. A fierce battle cleared the way; and on the 25th the assault was made through two miles of narrow lanes, Neill leading with his headlong valour. He had waited for the signal of battle like a war-horse, and had, it was afterwards told, laughed a beautiful laugh when he heard Captain Olpherts call out to his men, "The sound of your guns is music to the ladies of Lucknow." Close to the Residency Neill fell, a glorious victor that day. He was buried at night, and the whole army mourned for him as for a fearless loyal soldier. It will be observed here that while Havelock, Outram, and Neill were crossing the Ganges, Nicholson and those other bands of heroes were storming Delhi. On the capture of Lucknow Outram assumed the command, and was himself besieged by the men through whose vast numbers Havelock and he had cut their way.

Sir Colin Campbell, however, had now arrived, and had hastened to Cawnpore. On November 9th he advanced on Lucknow with 5000 men of all arms and thirty guns, leaving General Windham of the "Redan" to guard the bridge over the river. Part of the troops were of the men intended for China; part were of Greathead's column from Agra; part were Peel's Naval Brigade. Sir Colin reached the Alumbagh without much difficulty; and a civil officer, disguised as a native, running the gauntlet of the enemy with the key to a semaphore telegraph, a communication was at once opened. On the 14th November Sir Colin's march began. By means of a detour through some of the beautiful groves of Lucknow, the sepoy defences were avoided. A park and a fortified building, the Martiniére, were captured after a fierce fight. Then Sir Colin rested for the night, to the dismay of the garrison, who had expected an assault like an avalanche. In the morning the men were under arms betimes. The Secunderbagh crossed the path or threatened their progress. It was a garden with lofty loopholed walls, flanked with towers, and in the centre of the enclosure there was a house of two storeys, in both cases loopholed, and filled with sepoys. The fight raged here for three hours with small advantage. At last two breaches were made at two opposite angles, and the 93d Highlanders and the 4th Punjabees were ordered to storm. They stormed—the men who had seen the well of Cawnpore—and when they left that awful garden, 2000 of the mutineers lay dead on the ground. Hardly a man escaped—one of the fearfulest deeds of any known to modern times. When I saw the Secunderbagh, it was covered with weeds, and was very desolate looking.

A little further was the Shah Nujeef, a domed mosque in a garden. The place was immensely strong, and was gallantly defended, but it must be taken. Sir Colin himself led the 93d, after Captain Peel had cannonaded for two hours with the guns of his Naval Brigade close to the very walls. The Shah Nujeef was stormed with tremendous slaughter. Another day's work was done. Next day the guns from the relieving force and from the Residency blended in one united roar, till the garrison and their deliverers met in a scene which will remain one of the grand tableaux of English history. The city, however, remained in the hands of the enemy; and Sir Colin was compelled to leave it so. Affecting to assail the Kaiserbagh, he quietly removed the women and children to the Secunderbagh. Then he retired successfully on the Alumbagh, and leaving Outram there with 4000 men, directed his steps once more to the Ganges' bank, He arrived at Cawnpore in time, but only in time, to save General Windham, who, with 1200 men, had been defeated by Tantia Topee, with a great army, of which the Gwalior's men were the nucleus, and whose little force was on the way to being as effectually fastened and destroyed as ever fly was in a spider's web. The enemy was dispersed in headlong route, and the Nana's property at Bithoor was then utterly swept away by Brigadier Hope Grant. Sir Colin proposed now to conquer

Rohilcund, but Lord Canning, who was at Allahabad, urged the moral effect of the complete conquest of Lucknow.

On the 1st February the Ganges was again crossed, now with 18,700 Europeans and native troops, while Sir Hugh Rose, with his Bombay column, was advancing on the way to Jhansi. Lord Canning, to Sir Colin's disgust, was anxious that Sir Jung Bahadoor of Nepaul, who had promised to assist with 10,000 men, should share in the attack. This caused delay, without much satisfaction to any one. Outram, during the absence of his chief, had had hard fighting at the Alumbagh, and Havelock was no more. Attacked with dysentery soon after the second relief of Lucknow, he died on the 24th, just as Sir Colin was leaving for Cawnpore. He was buried in the Alumbagh, in a spot now very green and very peaceful, and no English traveller entering the great garden will easily leave again without being offered a flower "from Havelock Sahib's grave." In my own case the gardener, "all eyes," but gentle withal, waited till I had read and re-read the rather too long inscription, written when every heart was full to overpouring, then he offered me the eloquent little flower.

I have little more to say of the Mutiny. The final attack on Lucknow began on March 6th. The capture of the Begum Kotie, of the Imambara, and the Kaiserbagh, presents a series of scenes of which no drama ever could give the slightest conception. In the attack on the Begum Kotie, directed by Brigadier Robert Napier, the gallant Hodson fell, and died on the following day. Sir Colin Campbell attended the funeral, and said with tears over the grave, "I have lost one of the finest officers in the army:" and he had. The Kaiserbagh presented, and still presents, a marvellous scene. It is a network of palaces interspersed with little gardens; but all, palaces and gardens, within one great garden. From the roof of the palace certain of the great men of Oude, in the crisis of their danger, had been flying kites in sight of the avenging army. That and all other amusement was very soon and very roughly checked by the sack of the palace, and the destruction of nearly all that could be destroyed. The palaces of Lucknow are now in many parts inhabited by soldiers and soldiers' wives, but as the traveller wanders through the portals and long avenues, it must be hard to forget the splendour of the noble capital of Oude. There is in those beautiful palaces something voiceful as to English errors of policy; something too of wrongs inflicted on the people of Oude. If any one supposes that we were a guiltless people in 1857, I would refer him for evidence to the contrary to the work of Mr J. Bruce Norton.[1] The statements given of the ruthless confiscation of property, and of deeper wrongs, would startle many who fancy that it was a rule of unalloyed justice against which the sepoys rebelled.

To the collapse of the Mutiny in Central India by the campaign of Sir Hugh Rose reference has been made in an earlier chapter. Of his chief antagonist, Tantia Topee, it may be said that he was greater in defeat than in the days when he had seemed on a fair way to victory. Defeated at Gowlowlie (Calpee), compelled to stand by while Jhansi was stormed and no quarter given, defeated with the Ranee under the fort of Gwalior, bereft by death of the support of the Ranee's indomitable courage and name, and with Oude and the North Western Provinces subdued, he still gathered men around him, threatening Jeypore, plundering Tonk, stopping in his flight to exact from an important town a heavy tribute in the very face of our own troops, directing his flight towards the Nerbudda and the Taptee, with intent to rouse the Deccan and fire the Rohillas to a new struggle, till at last he was betrayed, caught in his sleep, and executed. A few Tantia Topees would have told a different tale.

I desire to apply very briefly to existing facts this story of the Mutiny. Leaving altogether the question of what

[1] Topics for Indian Statesmen (1858), pp. 163–177.

preceded 1857, let us ask what the Mutiny signified politically. If we take it as a general revolt against English rule, the reply to it was a series of victories till the last embers of the flame were trampled out. If we take it as a revolt against annexations which threatened to sweep away all native states and confiscate private property, then the policy of Lord Dalhousie had its completion in the victories of the very different viceroyalty of Lord Canning. That this issue was forced upon us matters little if it really was the issue. I believe the people of Oude meant it to be so; but do we? The Queen's proclamation says, no; and the words of many wise statesmen both here and in India say no. Is there, then, no means of giving effect to the benign proclamation of the Queen? Could not some Commission specially devoted to the work go through India to examine all private claims in the place of the judgment-seat of the Moguls?

Secondly, and with a view to this suggestion, is it not worth our while to consider how much we owed in 1857 to adventitious circumstances? We had, prior to the Mutiny, concluded the war in the Crimea, and had had a finer army when we ended than when we began. Some of our best troops and officers were also set free at the critical moment by the peace with Persia. We were at peace with all the world except China, and that was one of the most favourable events of the whole, since we were able to intercept the troops intended for China and direct them on India. Then the mutineers had no real head of princely rank. The King of Delhi was an imbecile. The Nana was no soldier. The best soldiers of India and the ablest chiefs were on our side. Many readers will, I am sure, see in all this the silver lining to the dark cloud.

If, however, this was God's mercy to England, what was the mercy for? Assuredly it was not that Englishmen might with greater facility lay up stores of money, or the nation maintain its high prestige. I do not see that we have any special claim to God's favour in India, unless we can claim it on the ground of upright aims; and we had some of quite a different kind. I believe there are high-minded men in India ready to redress real wrongs, to push aside that dishonest self-seeking which never will be wanting while there exist such interests as Englishmen find in India, with such opportunities as Englishmen possess for making those interests paramount considerations. There are men working to educate India to self-government, to bring about that day, the dream of many an ardent spirit, when England, having at last done her duty in the greatest trust ever given to a nation, may retire from India with honour, and with the esteem of the nation, which she may, if she will, build up for a quiet future among men.

Finally, there is the vast important question of the duty of England to her own people in India. Are the securities for them greater than in 1857? We have seen that certain favourable circumstances existed in that year. In reference to those circumstances I have heard people say, "If ever there is another mutiny, the mutineers will be better prepared and more united;" and I have heard others reply, "Yes, and so shall we." Is this last assertion as certain as the first? Englishmen are in India one year and in England the next. Lord Napier, for instance, could not now be spared to India in case of a European war. The chiefs of India can study the history of the Mutiny at home. If Scindia or Holkar have not a complete strategetical plan of the country from other than British hands, it is his own fault. Our soldiers and civil officers pass away; Scindia and Holkar, and the interests they represent, remain. They might provide for this or that eventuality. We can only wait, because, though we govern as a despotism, we govern with a commonwealth, and the uttermost ends of the earth from India are our home.

If, however, India is fairly dealt with, very few chiefs, or educated men of any kind, have any motive to mutiny. The chiefs, for instance, to whom reference is made in an earlier chapter in relation to the Star of India, what have they to gain by an outbreak if England is just? An attempt perhaps to found another Empire; war that would once more transform the map of India, perhaps of Asia. They see, however, as clearly as we see, that the collapse of the Mutiny of 1857 was, in the first instance, the triumph of the annexation policy. What remains is to show them that it means, in the second instance, the honest carrying out of the proclamation of the Queen.

CHAPTER XXI.

NATIVE WORK: EAGERNESS OF THE PEOPLE FOR EDUCATION: EMINENT MEN: MATERIAL AND MORAL PROGRESS.

Of the hand-work of native India much has been said in the foregoing chapters, but very much more might be said without having indicated even the general features of trades and industries in which the natives of India excel. Looking at a large building—say, the new Law Courts in Calcutta—in course of erection, and while the scaffolding is up, you see a mass of stone-work in a bamboo cage, as intricate as the ropes of a ship. View it before the work begins, and you see some hundreds of men, with clothing of the scantiest, engaged in gossip. You will find it exceedingly difficult to believe that they are skilled labourers. View the building during work hours, and you find those men perched on bits of bamboo, carving stone here, laying stones there, busy as bees everywhere without and within; women, I am sorry to say, working as labourers, carrying the "hods." A workman in Europe would think the man mad who asked him to stand on such a scaffold. Yet these men stand on it, and sit on it; and in both cases the work goes on, and is often very good work. If you send for a man to mend a floor, he sits down composedly, with his knees as high as his chin, and saws and planes in that posture. If you watch him, you grow irritated; if you leave him, you find the work done in fairly reasonable time, and at a very reasonable rate. The one sight an Englishman never ought to see in an Indian printing-office is the lifting of a "form" of type, if he also have seen the fastening of it in the "form." The wedges (quoins) are always too large or too small, and the frame is sure to be so much too large that a tilt or a touch would seem sufficient to send the whole into chaos. When the type is lifted, an Englishman's best course is to close his eyes; when he opens them again, he is sure to find the type all right. The hand of an Indian workman, if not interfered with, is as sure as the foot of an Alpine mule. The first week of my own experience was that of a strike for wages. I tried all manner of reasoning, but to no purpose. The men pleaded a prior promise, and insisted upon the advance now. I was compelled to let them go and engage strangers, and, as a result, to stay in the office all night through each night before publication. I found it was an error. The men, timid as fawns in most cases, were disturbed by being overlooked. I gave it up, save at intervals, and the whole affair improved. The type is set up by workmen who, in many cases, know nothing of English; yet a sharp boy will in three months learn as much as an average English boy in three years. At about fourteen they are called "men," a very amusing term when applied to a delicate little fellow with a wrist about as thick as a man's thumb. The first "proofs" are dreadful; but the readers are patient men, and, after the third correction, you have a proof reasonably good.

If you tease a carpenter or a blacksmith, he will look at you in helpless bewilderment; not angrily, say what you may, but helplessly. If you let him alone, he will, in a very strange fashion, with strangely imperfect tools, give you satisfactory work. A gardener at work seems playing, but then his play never ceases while there is any light; and either he, or some Indian Robin Goodfellow for him, will keep a garden well trimmed, and have vases of fresh flowers on some table, or tables, every morning. So also in carving, weaving, writing, everything that one could name of light work. In engineering I should be doubtful of the Indian workman, at least till a race of engineers has been systematically trained. Exceedingly exact in weaving and penmanship, he would perhaps find a difficulty in the exact work of a steam-engine. The most finely-carved boxes are generally deficient in locks and hinges. In penmanship, as in chess or card-playing, the Hindoo is a master where his mind is really engaged. The clerks write beautifully, and often are born accountants. The little fellows in the jute-mills take the reels from the spindles like magic. If you give a labourer a wheelbarrow, and he prefers to carry it on his head instead of wheeling it (a fact, it is said, in the early days of railways), it must be remembered that he has hereditary claim to work as his fathers worked before him. If he is proud, and leaves your service rather than be compelled to work in a new way, he also will often be proud enough to leave his wages behind him, and never once ask for them. In fact, the Indian workman is often a skilful man, and if the paths were open to him, it would be difficult to mark a limit to his powers.

Moreover, there is everywhere in India a real deference paid to the man of skill and piety, as well as to caste. I was very soon attracted by the fact that while wealth nearly always is the chief means of distinguishing man from man in England, it has no such exclusive power in India. There are few sights more pitiable than the devotee. His whole life is to outside beholders one of misery. But what is he honoured for? Not wealth; for he is often wretchedly poor. He is honoured for his presumed piety, for his devotion to the Creator. He has subdued the flesh with its affections and lusts; has brought the body into subjection to the spirit; has risen above time, and lives in eternity. For these he is honoured. In a like but different way the true workman has his rank, while the Brahmin, however poor, has a right to sit among princes. When he is a learned Brahmin, you undoubtedly have the highest product of Hindoo life. Millions would bow to such a man, whom many rude Englishmen ruthlessly push aside.

Never was there a people more eager for education, or who deserved to be more leniently and kindly dealt with in that eagerness. "Give us knowledge," is the cry, at least throughout Bengal. A certain class of Englishmen in keen ridicule reply, "Go to your work; what has your M.A. degree done for you?" The Bengalee turns away from such men, with his insatiable craving only the more whetted by the repulse. He will work night and day, and will endure much persecution, if only he can have that upon which he has set his heart, the knowledge that will enable him to rise in life. "Yes," it is said, "that is all he cares for—to rise in life;" a rejoinder which comes badly from Englishmen, who in most cases are in India for that special purpose, and no other. The native of India, Hindoo and Mohammedan alike, where the latter is not altogether reckless or despondent, wishes to better his condition in life. Apart from all questions of right and wrong, is it not England's high interest to afford him that opportunity, and to encourage him to the grand race with Englishmen? He will in any case, and do what England may, enter the race heavily weighted. He must pass examinations in themes of foreign thought, in a foreign language, and in a foreign land. He must go, at immense cost—and not mere money cost, for he breaks his cherished caste by the voyage—to England. Often without a friend in London, these brave lads cross the ocean, and are thrown into the great dangers of a life whose pitfalls are on every hand. They face English tutors, mix with English competitors, brook English snobbery, and bear away from Englishmen the prizes of England's competitive examinations. The thorny path is in nowise smoothed for them by the common sense of the examiners, but is often beset by absurdities. I once sent home a list of questions and answers which I copied from the papers of the entrance examination for the Calcutta University, and some time after I found a gentleman attacking me in a book for ridiculing the young men. I was ridiculing the men who drew up the questions. Here are a few, with the answers :—

(*Q.*) "Dapper man?" (*A.* 1.) "Man of superfluous knowledge." (*A.* 2.) "Mad."—(*Q.*) "Democrat?" (*A.* 1.) "Petticoat government." (*A.* 2.) "Witchcraft." (*A.* 3.) "Half turning of the horse." —(*Q.*) "Babylonish jargon?" (*A.* 1.) "A vessel made at Babylon." (*A.* 2.) "A kind of drink made at Jerusalem." (*A.* 3.) "A kind of coat worn by Babylonians."—(*Q.*) "Lay brother?" (*A.* 1.) "A bishop." (*A.* 2.) "A step-brother." (*A.* 3.) "A scholar of the same godfather."—(*Q.*) "Sumpter mule?" (*A.*) "A stubborn Jew."—(*Q.*) "Bilious-looking fellow?" (*A.* 1.) "A man of strict character." (*A.* 2.) "A person having a nose like the bill of an eagle."—(*Q.*) "Cloister?" (*A.*) "A kind of shell."—(*Q.*) "Tavern politicians?" (*A.* 1.) "Politicians in charge of the alehouse." (*A.* 2.) "Mere vulgars." (*A.* 3.) "Managers of the priestly church."—(*Q.*) "A pair of cast-off galligaskins?" (*A.*) "Two gallons of wine."—(*Q.*) "Vis inertiæ?" (*A.* 1.) "Flesh of swine." (*A.* 2.) "Sweet milk."—(*Q.*) "The mule was well broken to a pleasant and accommodating amble?" (*A.*) "The mule was entirely covered with mud."—(*Q.*) "Columbus rode out the storm in safety under the lee of the island?" (*A.*) "Though there was a violent storm, yet Columbus, by riding on horseback, reached under the lee of the island in security."

Do not these answers at least show us how difficult is the course of the young men of Indian race who compete with Englishmen for the prizes of public employment? No ingenuity in the world could divine the meaning of phrases like several of these questions. They must have been heard, and in the language in which a person thinks, before they could have meaning to any human soul.

Again, I have heard it said that a native of India goes as far as he is taught, and can go no farther. I deny this thoroughly and entirely. It is a gross misrepresentation. The native of India is an essentially capable man, and he is often badly used. I have seen Englishmen going through crowds of the people of native India, as at the Calcutta and Howrah landing-stages, elbowing their way as through a herd of cattle, and the people, as a rule, falling back on all hands. Sometimes the rule is broken, and the brutality meets with its match; but as a rule it selects the poorest people, and rarely is met with real determination. We count men as of an inferior race, deny them careers, and then talk of them as incapable of a higher life. When the Catholic in England was shut out from public life, what did he become? Some sank, for want of society, to a low state; some went abroad; some, like Mr Charles Waterton, the naturalist, found a need for all their innate gentlemanliness and loyalty to preserve them from intense hatred to the nation that had proved to them so hard a step-mother. Yet no Roman Catholic ever knew aught so disheartening as the lot of the native of India.

Let them go to work and leave the colleges, it is said. Let those who say so set the example. It is not a mere question of public office, but of status in the place of a man's birth that is at issue. The native of India is, I have said, a thoroughly capable man. He is also a man by nature polite. Yet the most gentlemanly man, and the man of the highest social position in a district, may be made to feel, and feel sharply, that he is subordinate to some young officer fresh from England, and ignorant of all life save that of schools. It is very hard. It is also far from uncommon. "Why is this?" the people say. "Is it that you think you have only a life-tenure in India? Akbar governed on principles applicable to a rule which he wished to continue. You govern as if you felt that any day your rule might end." In a paper read in London, in 1874, by a native gentleman from Bombay, there is a black-list of cases of oppression and maladministration, and the native journals in reviewing the paper added to the list. One case mentioned was that of an attempt to intimidate some influential persons who wished to petition against the union of Oude and the North Western Provinces. Do not let anybody say here that I am making the interest of India to take precedence of that of England, or the interest of natives of India to take precedence of that of Englishmen in India. I am doing nothing of the kind. As between England and India, every Englishman would be for England, even if in consequence we had to leave India to-morrow. The interests of England and India are the same. It is simply that, as between justice and injustice, I am pleading for justice; and that, as between England's high permanent interest and the low interests which may be characterised by selfishness, I am pleading for the high and permanent. The Indian Civil Service contains some men of the highest character; but their efforts are thwarted and their safety endangered by lower aims and acts. We have opened to India a new door, a new life of knowledge, and the strongest arms in the world never again can close the door. We cannot follow the rule of Akbar, because the rule of England is really that of a democracy. The Queen herself must perforce view India in the light of affording careers to her subjects at home, while India adds nothing to the special revenue of the Crown. English interests will have influence, do what the greatest Viceroy may, and desire what he may. But English interests, to endure in India, must be interwoven with the interests of India.

In preparing the materials for this chapter, it occurred to me that some good might accrue if examples of the character and ability of some eminent men of native India, and not Christian, were given, as showing not merely what India can produce of intellect and manhood, but what a native of India may, in the face of all obstacles, achieve. To Sir Dinkur Rao reference has already been made. His distinction prior to the Mutiny rested on his great administrative ability, by means of which he pacified a number of disturbed districts, trampling down oppression, and uprooting a system of taxation by which the people had been very nearly goaded into rebellion. And while he reduced the taxes he increased the revenue. When the Mutiny came, and the die had to be cast for Maharajah Scindia,

Dinkur Rao said firmly, "for English rule." The Maharajah, however valid his grounds of discontent, has had reason to think with gratitude of that wise and far-seeing advice. Since 1857 it has been the delight of many English statesmen to honour Sir Dinkur Rao, and when the trial of the Guikwar of Baroda was decided upon, his name, as that of one of the judges, was the best proof of all to native India that the motive of Lord Northbrook was an upright one. That the native view delivered as a verdict was subsequently set aside, was not, I should say, a fault of Lord Northbrook, as it certainly was not that of Sir Dinkur Rao.

For the scene of action of Sir Mahdava Rao we must go southward, to a different and yet a not dissimilar field of labour. Sir Dinkur Rao began without a knowledge of the English language, and in learning it was his own teacher. Sir Mahdava Rao, in the year 1849, had completed a very distinguished career at the Madras High School, and on the strength of that, as well as of his family loyalty, the post of tutor to the young princes, nephews to the Rajah of Travancore, was offered to him. The story was well told, but without a signature, in the "Calcutta Review," in October 1872. Few people could have dreamt that the author of it was, as he was, one of Sir Mahdava Rao's pupils, the present first Prince of Travancore. Of Mahratta family, the Prince wrote, the ancestors of Sir Mahdava Rao had for several generations held offices of trust both under native chiefs and "the rising British power." His father was Dewan (prime minister) of Travancore, and was highly esteemed by Lord William Bentinck, and by the British officers with whom he came into official or other relations. Sir Mahdava Rao was the youngest of the Dewan's three sons.

He held the office of tutor for four years and a half, the affairs of Travancore going meanwhile from bad to worse in every way. The law courts were infamous; the police did what was right in their own eyes. Public works there were none; public spirit there was none; and at last the dreadful eye of Lord Dalhousie fell on Travancore, and one of those warnings not to be neglected was given. Lord Dalhousie, however, was called home, and the Mutiny gave Travancore a breathing-time. In 1855 Mahdava Rao was made Dewan Peshkar (next in rank to the Dewan), but there were other Dewan Peshkars—from two to four at different times—and the newly appointed officer claimed to have a certain number of Talooks placed under his own charge. His wish was complied with, but the worst Talooks—those from which complaints were most common—were selected for him. Within a year, Mr Norton said, in a most appreciative reference, the new Dewan Peshkar called order out of disorder. The law courts were reformed, and made to hold up the scales of justice with an even hand; the police were paid, dacoits driven away, and the revenue raised. "Here," Mr Norton added subsequently, "is a man raised up, as it were, amid the anarchy and confusion of his country to save it from destruction."

In 1857 the Dewan died, and the post was given to Mahdava Rao. He was then in the thirtieth year of his age, and might, his pupil and friend said, have been considered too young for the post, considering the sad state of the country. The dacoits (robbers) were all-powerful, and were only less dreaded than the police, who were robbers of even a worse kind. Robbery and oppression were the rule of the life of Travancore. The young Dewan required all his energy, ability, and address, but they were equal to the need. His influence was felt everywhere. A caste dispute, called into prominence by the Queen's Proclamation in 1857, he met with firmness and conciliation, and it was extinguished. The Maharajah died in 1860, and the Dewan had then the advantage of serving a Prince whom he had educated. For nine years the revenue steadily rose; yet, at the same time, the two great sources of income, the pepper and the tobacco monopolies, were sacrificed, and the police and all other officers were paid, instead of being allowed to pick and steal as formerly. At the time when Lord Dalhousie's dread warning arrived, the debt of Travancore was £50,000, with interest amounting to half as much more. In 1862–63 Sir Mahdava Rao paid £15,000, the last of the debt and interest; and he then said, with noble pride, "Tranvancore has now no public debt." This would have been little, however, if the public debt had been cancelled at the cost of private happiness, if trade had been fettered, and the means of comfort taken from the people; but such was not the case. In 1861–62 Sir Mahdava Rao had spent £30,000 in public works, and he increased the amount every subsequent year while his rule continued. Large sums were also spent on education. Yet, in 1864–65, without adding a penny to the taxes, save in the single case of salt, for which tax the British Government was responsible, and after abolishing two specially productive monopolies, he had in the Treasury a balance of £20,000. The Prince concluded:

> "We are tempted to dwell upon many more interesting features of Mahdava Rao's glorious administration of fourteen years, but want of space forbids us. However, we must make one more quotation from the last of his administrative reports. He says: 'In conclusion, it may be briefly observed, that it is the cherished aim of His Highness's Government to provide for every subject, within a couple of hours' journey, the advantages of a doctor, a schoolmaster, a judge, a magistrate, a registering officer, and a postmaster. The various departments concerned are steadily progressing towards this consummation.' Indeed, he found Travancore in the lowest stage of degradation and political disorganisation. He has left it a 'model Native State.' He has done a great work. He has earned an imperishable name in India."

Well, he may have "earned an imperishable name in India," but it is a name, I am sorry to say, very little known in England. In 1872 Sir Mahdava Rao resigned his post, and was offered a seat in the Viceregal Council; but he declined it, feeling, no doubt, that his strength lies in his individuality, and that to work in grooves would be to work in vain. He therefore accepted the office of Dewan to the Maharajah Holkar.

When I first read the story from which this is taken, I concluded that it was the work of some calm and conscientious officer of Madras. The idea of a native Prince writing such an article was quite beyond my range of vision, though I had read, and not a little, of the first Prince of Travancore. What was most apparent from the article was that we have no place for men like Mahdava Rao and Dinkur Rao, distinguished at once for their ability and their honesty. Let us face the fact—Why have we no place for such men? That they would make revenue to exceed expenditure, and at the same time relieve and foster trade, no one can doubt; but then they would demand the reduction of expenditure; and who knows where the reduction would first appear? This is the whole truth. While we cannot fathom the life of native India—and, perhaps, far less so now than when men remained in India for thirty years without ever seeing England—the very deepest depths are not unfathomable to those who, in addition to genius, possess a knowledge of the habits and a key to the sympathies of the people.

I brought with me also two lectures of this first Prince of Travancore, who is himself notable in various ways, and worthy of esteem. The one is on "Our Industrial Status," the other on "Our Morals." In the latter he says, with a generous boldness:

"I am *not* a Christian. I do not accept the cardinal tenets of Christianity as they concern man in the next world. On these matters I have my own beliefs. But I accept Christian ethics in their entirety. I have the highest admiration for them. Speaking of Christianity as it concerns this world, it has effected a wonderful moral revolution in Europe. I can imagine the question, 'Does not vice exist among Christians?' I do not hesitate to affirm that vice, crime, and immorality, exist in Christendom to the same extent as they do in India. Under the heading of 'Law and Crime' in the English dailies, you will always find abundant records of crimes of the worst description. Electioneering is, again, a mine of corruption. But yet there is a difference. That difference consists in the standard of morality which an average Christian and an average Hindoo respectively acknowledge."

Here is the "practical application:"

"My suggestion is, that those among my countrymen who, after mature consideration, can convince themselves of their ability to take the responsibility, should form themselves into a society or order. . . . It will be well that every candidate should continue to be a probationer for a time, say a year. . . . The society, as a whole, will possess the full freedom of reprehending any member for misconduct, and, if necessary, dismissing him from its body, without being amenable to the general public. I am convinced that some such plan . . . will prove a very effective means of promoting morality. With those who may wish it I shall be happy to confer further on the subject."

That is, the Prince would be glad to see his friends in the vestry after service to discourse on morals. Does this look like barbarism? I can convey no idea here of the varied character of the lecture on "Our Industrial Status." But the entire drift of it is to induce industry, enterprise, temperance, and public spirit. After a really clever description of the varied climates and productions of India, and especially of Travancore (as an epitome of India), he says:

"At the same time, I am strongly tempted to exclaim, in the words of the immortal Scotch novelist, 'Look at these barren hills, Mary, and at that deep winding vale by which the cattle are even now returning from their scanty browse. The hand of the industrious Fleming would cover these mountains with wood, and raise corn where we now see a starved and scanty sward of heath and ling. It grieves me, Mary, when I look on that land, and think what benefit it might receive from such men as I have lately seen.' We are not sufficiently industrious. . . . It never enters the mind of the peasant or those who are much wealthier and better informed than he, to endeavour to make two blades of grass grow where only one does now, or to make that one blade twice as valuable as it now is. The population has been rapidly increasing, while the cultivation of the land has been, out of all proportion, lagging behind. Paddy is the chief produce of the land; yet foreign paddy, worth several lacs of rupees, is annually imported. No attempt worth the name is made to increase the area of cultivation by reclaiming waste lands, of which we have abundance, or to enhance the yield of the existing lands by deep-ploughing, manuring, selecting the best and most prolific varieties of indigenous or exotic seeds; by irrigating where it is needful and practicable, and by carefully harvesting the crops. I think these are views worthy of the esteem of all men, and they are carried into practice."

Something of the lives of Rajah Ram Mohun Roy, and of his disciple Maharajah Romanath Tagore, we have already seen. Of the former much has been told in all civilised lands. As a product of the learning and meditation of Native India, he will remain one of the facts of modern times. His purity and calmness, his breadth and catholicity of view, were so marked, that he took up much of the ground previously occupied, as a special right, by Christian missionaries, and showed to his countrymen that moral truth and action do not belong exclusively to any form of creed.

One of his earliest and most attached disciples was Dwarkanath Tagore, the brother of Romanath. Springing, as the reader may have observed, from a race of Brahmins, the Tagores threw their traditions to the wind—not to become Christian, but to follow the first Brahmist. The story of the life of Dwarkanath Tagore was graphically told in Calcutta in 1870 by Baboo Kissory Chand Mitter; and it contains a fine moral. He was, his biographer says, "the first native gentleman who set up a banking-house on the European model;" and he was congratulated on the fact by Lord William Bentinck. His history as a banker is one of great forbearance and generosity, and of sterling probity and honour. He had factories for indigo, sugar, and silk. He worked coal and other mines, and did all that, and much besides, with a singleness of purpose which his countrymen deemed all but miraculous. As evidence of his tolerant spirit, it is said that when in the North West, he saw with enthusiasm the Tâj, the fairest monument of an antagonistic faith, gave a clock to a Christian church that needed one, and then bowed in the spirit of his own faith in the early home of Krishna, the god of the Hindoos. He gave freely to every charity, and every institution for the good of India, with the single exception of missions. Kissory Chand Mitter tells us of a district judge who arrived in Calcutta very sick, to embark for England, and was threatened with arrest and imprisonment for a debt of £10,000. Well-nigh in despair, he appealed to Dwarkanath Tagore, whom he did not even know. The banker made inquiries, paid the money, and received the bonds and notes. Then he called upon the judge, who began to show the sadness of his case. "But it is done," said the princely Hindoo; "there are the bonds." The judge wished then to give another bond, but Dwarkanath refused it. "If you live," he said, "you will pay me. If not, it would only be waste paper." The judge lived, and paid the money debt. The greater debt, one thinks, never could be paid. Nobody of the judge's own faith would have paid £10,000 for him. It was the Samaritan who poured in the oil and wine, who sent the sick Englishman to England free.

Ram Mohun Roy died and was buried at Bristol in 1833. Ten years later (1843) his body was removed from a shrubbery in which he had requested to be laid, and reburied in a beautiful cemetery of the town. This was done by his disciple, Dwarkanath Tagore, who also placed a monument over the grave. In England Dwarkanath was received in a kindly spirit by the Queen, and honoured by many leading Englishmen. He went to York, to Newcastle (to see the coal-pits, of which he made notes as a mine-owner), to Sheffield, and elsewhere. "At Smeaton," his biographer says, "he attended the kirk, but found a great difference between the Scotch and English services. 'Thinking one sermon,' says he, 'quite sufficient, I came away after the first, which was more like a lecture than a sermon.'" Probably he mistook a prayer for a sermon; an extempore prayer here has little in common with the devotional prayers of the Brahmist. At the Guildhall he spoke some loyal, earnest words. Finally, he died in England, and lies among Englishmen at Kensal Green. While, therefore, England has some sacred graves in India, the people of India are not without some claim to like sacred graves in England. No nobler dead lie anywhere than Ram Mohun Roy and Dwarkanath Tagore.

This notice seems to lead naturally to the name of Kissory Chand Mitter, who died in 1873. I believe he was a thoroughly brave man; I am sure he was very able. He had climbed his way from a lowly station to one of distinction in the public service, when he had the misfortune to quarrel with an Englishman above him in position, and the Hindoo, of course, went to the wall. He lost all the work of his earlier years. As a writer, however, he still had an open field which no man could close; and a very powerful writer he was. He edited the "Indian Field," afterwards incorporated with the "Hindoo Patriot." He contributed papers to the "Calcutta Review;" the fine paper on Ram Mohun Roy, and a series of brilliant sketches (1872) on "The Territorial Aristocracy of Bengal." As a Hindoo he was one of the most fearless I ever met, and I could see, though I only met him twice, one of the most scornful of all unworthy cringing to Europeans. He belonged to a brave little band of native men in Calcutta whom no Government can well afford to neglect, and whom no wise Government would wish to neglect. In November 1874, I sent home these few remarks:

"We have many stories of English lads who have made their way against all odds to honour and usefulness. Here is a story of a Hindoo lad—the late Mr Justice Mitter, Judge of the High Court. He was born in a little Hindoo village, and his parents were but poor. He received his education I know not where, but he came to Calcutta, as many a young man has gone to London, to carve his way to fortune; only in his case there was contention against a dominant race. He held his own, however, through good report and evil report, till the time when the poor Hindoo lad became a Judge of the High Court! He worked splendidly, subdued self, sat in modest dignity (I speak from knowledge, for I have seen him,) on the bench of the High Court, deciding intricate cases as a Judge and a gentleman. At last he was seized with a fatal disease. He asked to be taken to a sanitarium, and he was obeyed. Time went on, but he only became worse. It was death, the doctors mournfully said. Then he had but one request. He had sat on the judicial bench, had been a marked man at the levees and drawing-rooms, at public gatherings for institutions which sought distinguished names. Englishmen of the first position—notably Sir Barnes Peacock—did themselves honour by claiming him as their friend. Now had come the grand issue of all, and the dying Judge begged to be taken to the village, and, I suppose, the house, in which he was born. In this way the two ends of life came together—simply as in the play of children and grandly as in an epic poem. There, where the trees which he had loved in childhood waved before his eyes, the pure and noble Judge died. He had lived to make his countrymen proud of the Hindoo name, and he died in a path of duty which India, if it is wise, will not readily forget."

When the native papers were published at the end of the week, I found that there was much more to tell of the dead Judge. The "Bengalee," after stating that in early life Mr Mitter had been a zealous Hindoo, and a little later a "thorough-going sceptic," said that "from this anarchical state of mind he was roused by Positivism. Having accidentally come across a copy of Comte's Catechism, he was so struck with the novelty and profundity of its doctrines that he felt interested to read it through. Its effect was electrical; it transformed the entire character of his thoughts. When a student in the Hooghly College, the study of an annotated edition of Shelley's 'Queen Mab' made him a sceptic. A deeper insight into the philosopher whose catholicity is his most conspicuous merit, who reveres St. Paul as he is revered by the most bigoted Catholic, who has described the services done to humanity by the lowest fetishism, led to the gradual disappearance of this scoffing spirit, and at last he came to speak of even Hindooism and Brahman priests with respect." The "Patriot" said: "He was a voracious reader, but a very reluctant writer, and the only literary contributions he made were the articles on 'Analytical Geometry' in 'Mookerjee's Magazine.'[1] He was also a lover of science, and for some time regularly attended Father Lafont's science lectures at St Xavier's College. He marked his appreciation of science by subscribing the munificent sum of £400 to Dr. Sircar's projected Science Association. He was a man of open-handed charity." Was he not also an evidence of the yeast that is brewing, in God's good keeping, among the best of the young men of India?

The reference to Dr Sircar's Science Association leads on my little narrative to a living man and a great work. When I arrived in India in 1870, Dr Sircar's proposal had been a few months before the country, and already had some very honourable pecuniary support from his own countrymen, but very little from Englishmen. Dr Sircar explained his project at length, but with fastidious modesty. "I want," he said, "a purely Scientific Association, for the purpose of carrying on observation and experiment, and not for mere popular lecturing, though the latter will form a part of the programme of its working. Sight-seeing and sight-showing certainly ought not to be the objects of the Institution." To carry out all this, a house, books, a chemical laboratory, mechanical, electrical, and magnetic instruments, astronomical and meteorological instruments, a geological and zoological museum, a herbarium, and a thousand other things, "without which it will be a mockery to begin to work," were required. Altogether the scheme he considered, with salaries and costs, required at least a sum of £10,000. For a long time the sum stood at less than £5000, and the subscribers urged

[1] This magazine was set on foot, at an undoubtedly considerable money sacrifice, by an able man, and it bade fair to attract to it some of the best writers of the Hindoo race. Unhappily it was sent for review to a great English journal, and was mercilessly satirised, without the slightest consideration for the fact that it was a reflex of Hindoo life and opinion in an English dress. The review all but destroyed a fair and honourable attempt to do a public service.

Dr Sircar to begin the work. He did not, however, see his way; and what may surprise some people, till he could see his way he refused the money. Early in 1875, Father Lafont appealed to the public for help to build a spectro-telescopic observatory, and received the required money at once, cheerfully, and, of course, deservedly. Meanwhile, however, the modest, retiring, Hindoo scholar made little advance upon his £5000. At last the scheme caught the eye of the Lieutenant Governor, Sir Richard Temple. He contributed to it £50, and became a monthly subscriber. The subscriptions now rose to £8000, and the subscribers manifested as strange an inclination to pay down the money as Dr Sircar did a determination not to have it. At last he hit upon a notable device, which may perhaps be useful to the "Syndicates" of flash London companies. He would have an independent committee elected to receive the money and take care of it—the un-shop-like scholar! A meeting was held, and Father Lafont, who was chairman, said:

"I belong to a religion commonly, though erroneously, regarded as antagonistic to science, a religion whose priests are supposed to dread the encroachments of science for fear that their dogmatic teaching might suffer by this enlightened contact. Well, gentlemen, I declare to you, that though a Catholic and a priest, I hail with delight and pursue with love any advance of *true* science: the only thing that frightens me being the pretended discoveries of men who are not satisfied with facts, but put in their stead, and erect into scientific dogmas, the ill-digested lucubrations of their imaginations."

The following resolution was passed at a later meeting:

"We are of opinion that an Association for the cultivation of science by the natives of this country will be of incalculable benefit not to them alone, but may be ultimately to the world at large. We therefore strongly recommend that steps be taken at once for the establishment of such an Association."

Sir Richard Temple, when once he had entered upon the project, held to it in his characteristic, vigorous way. In February 1876 he stated in a minute that the Bengal Government would give a house for a term of years to the Association, on condition that £7000 were raised, and £5000 invested in Government securities, with subscriptions of at least £10 a month for two years. In this way the "Indian Science Association" was inaugurated in July last, with an admirable scientific lecture by Dr Sircar, and a happy and buoyant speech from Sir Richard Temple, who was the chairman. Europeans and Natives, of many different pursuits and of various positions in life, gathered that day around Dr Sircar, and claiming him as their friend and the friend of India, bade him God speed. I could say much more, but I must not add much to this recital of facts. The scholars of India are in all cases modest men—it seems to belong to their scholarship—and Dr Sircar is modest to an extreme. For himself he never would ask or accept aught that was like a gift. He bravely, however, asks for English help for his Association, that he may teach, in divisions now formed, "General Physics, Chemistry, Astronomy, Systematic Botany, Systematic Zoology, Physiology, and Geology," and extend his range of usefulness according to his means. He invites his countrymen to shake off the trammels of false science, and reason on exact facts. He is, in fact, a scientific missionary. If he had a scheme for fireworks or upholstery, India would support him; but as he has only science to offer, he will, in spite of all, fail, I fear, unless he has the support of scientific men in England, with some other generous help. Neither the Hindoo nor the Mohammedan cares much for science, and some Hindoos and Mohammedans oppose it as opposed to their faith. I sincerely wish that this little notice may lead some scientific men to lend to Dr Sircar a helping hand, and so to knit to England and mankind a generous and hopeful work.

I have referred earlier to a Free Library, at which I heard a reading of the "Ramayana." The owner of the library, a very able man, Baboo Joykissen Mookerjee, is stone blind. He is a thorough Hindoo, but his choice of books for his poorer neighbours is of the widest. Nothing is banished so long as it is not immoral. In connection with the library there is a lecture-room, and in a neighbouring village, under another and quite as public-spirited a branch of the same family, an institution of a similar kind. The villages are purely Bengalee, and apart from English society. I met in both some most intelligent and good, and, at the same time, very poor men, labouring for their bread by day, and to improve their minds in the evening hours. I saw them nearly all struck down at one time of fever, so that the one could not carry a drink of water to the other. This is one phase of the life of the poor—the deserving poor—of India. What little money is needed for their institutions, they easily obtain. For themselves they ask nothing. They are poor, they are Hindoo, and they are gentlemen. If an Englishman will lecture to them they are delighted. They ensure him a crowded room and a close attention; and when he has finished, they approach him slowly, diffidently, and say, "Thank you, sir: it is very kind." Would the reader regret to know more of these men?

Desiring in this chapter to say something of Hindoo humour, the untimely death of the author of the "Nil Durpan," referred to previously, came at once to my mind, as one of the best possible illustrations of the geniality of that humour. The humorist, Baboo Denobundha Mitter, was a post-office inspector of the first grade, and for good organising ability during the Looshai expedition was made Rai Bahadoor. He never, people said, made a personal enemy. Yet the "Nil Durpan," of which the "Patriot" affirmed that "it was a faithful transcript of the condition of the indigo ryots, and that it still charms crowded audiences," bade fair for the moment to wreck the author's prospects; and it is to his honour that he was willing for them to be wrecked if by giving up his name as author he could have saved Mr Long. He seems to have embodied and represented all the gentle humour, that real sense of the ludicrous, for which the Bengalee is remarkable; that love for teasing, not always, I must say, merciful, but never, it appears, unmerciful in his case. I may also mention the instance of a wealthy writer, the Rajah Kali Krishna, late head to the notable house referred to in Chapter xiv. He, besides producing work of his own, of the merit of which I know nothing, translated "Rasselas" and "Gay's Fables" into Bengalee, and in that way added to the stock of native literature.

I must mention also, however, with true regret, that when Sir Jung Bahadoor died, several of the native papers claimed him as a Hindoo worthy, and the "Patriot" even spoke of the *coup d'état* which had "not been followed by a Sedan." Jung Bahadoor was very able; he was the ally of England; but he waded through slaughter to a throne—not on the battle-field, but in ruthless massacre. The "Patriot" would say, "We are following English example;" but such is not the case with reference to any English example worth following. Few of us can read of Plassey without a flush of pride, but few of us also have a word of praise for the transaction with Omichund.[1]

Taking all these elements as working to one end, we see the educated, orthodox Hindoo, with his scorn for the men whose conversions can be bought; the elder Brahmist striving hard to proclaim the oneness of the Supreme God and still remain a Hindoo, cherishing, indeed, the old familiar name; the younger Brahmist advancing boldly beyond Hindooism to a philosophy and a faith in which Christ is one of the master-builders, and God all in all; the scientific student casting off the old figments of an absurd science mixed up with a huge superstition; the Mohammedan compelling attention to be paid to his long-neglected condition; the Parsee, claiming to possess all literature, yet still worshipping the life-representing fire; the Catholic proving that he still possesses the power to reach the "common people," and win by sacrifice their pecuniary support without even asking for it; the Protestant, under

[1] Appendix VII.

many various names, labouring by all manner of agencies, to establish higher standards of morals and education. Can we suppose that all this work is in vain?

Finally, we may notice the testimony of eminent Englishmen, or Englishmen of high place, to the value of native work. The Indian Association (in 1853), in aid of a petition which Mr George Thompson was to present to the Court of Directors, made a large collection of statements of opinion, from which I shall take these few:—

Mr Orme wrote: "The administration of justice has been almost universally, by the Mogul conquerors of Hindostan, devolved upon the Hindoos, the office of Dewan being generally conferred upon one of that people." And Mr Mill said further: "The conquest of Hindostan, effected by the Mohammedan nations, was to no extraordinary degree sanguinary or destructive. It substituted sovereigns of one race for sovereigns of another, . . . but the whole detail of administration, with the exception of the army, and a few of the more prominent situations, remained invariably in the hands of the native magistrates and officers."

English rule altered this, and for a long time the natives of India were refused admittance to any office of high trust. In 1802 Lord Wellesley circulated a series of interrogatories among his officers as to native efficiency, and had these among many replies:

Sir Henry Strachey, judge and magistrate: "I am inclined to think that an intelligent native is better qualified to preside at a trial than we can be ourselves; and a very few simple rules would perhaps suffice to correct the abuses of former times. The native commissioner decides with the greatest ease a vast number of causes. He is perfectly acquainted with the language, the manners, and even the person and characters, of all who come before him. . . . I cannot help wishing that these situations were more respectable in a pecuniary point of view, and that they were empowered to decide causes to almost any amount. . . . I confess it is my wish, though possibly I may be blamed for expressing it, not only to have the authority of the natives as judges extended, but to see them, if possible, enjoy important and confidential situations in other departments of the State." Mr Neave: "I am of opinion that the natives, in respect to integrity and diligence, may be trusted with the administration of justice. Still I would not commit exclusively to the natives any branch of the administration of justice on a large scale; I think we ought to keep the judicial branch to ourselves, as a sacred deposit to raise ourselves in the estimation of the natives. Let our judicial character counteract the evil impressions created by our financial system." Mr T. H. Ernst: "At present the natives have certainly more reliance on the uprightness of European judges than of judges appointed from their own people. But this distinction is chiefly to be ascribed, I think, to the unequal footing on which the natives are placed in all official situations compared with Europeans. The remuneration of the native judges consists of the institution fee, a miserable pittance, seldom amounting to more than £50 a year, and sometimes to less than half that sum; yet, with few exceptions, I have found reason to be satisfied with the conduct of the moonsiffs and commissioners who were employed in the districts of Burdwan and Hooghly." Mr E. Strachey: "Everything combines to make the European honest and independent, and the native the contrary: reverse their circumstances, and I have no doubt their conduct would be reversed. . . . For my opinion of the integrity of the natives, I beg to refer to my answer to the last question. In respect to diligence I think they are entirely to be trusted." Lord William Bentinck, Sir Charles Metcalfe, and Mr Bayley, in a letter to the judges of the Supreme Court, said: "You will thence observe that the native judges already dispose of about fifteen-seventeenths of the regular civil suits (original and appeal) tried and determined throughout the country; that it is chiefly in the Superior Courts that the suits in arrear are of long standing. . . . We are disposed to doubt whether natives could advantageously be associated with the European officers as judges in the zillah courts. Men of admirable acuteness and talent we certainly could command; and in a few years, probably, the prospect of honour and liberal emolument would produce an abundant supply of any species of knowledge. But moral character depends not less on the general sentiment of the community than on the workings of the individual mind; and its improvement, however ultimately sure to follow, will not necessarily keep pace with the progress of knowledge." Mr Sullivan, Coimbatoor, in answer to the question, "Would you not be disposed to place as much confidence in the natives of India as in your own countrymen?" replied, "Yes, if equally well treated."

The pamphlet from which these extracts are taken contains ninety-five closely-printed pages, but the gist of the whole is, that while some of the witnesses trust and some distrust the native character, nearly all agree that the remuneration of native officials is wretched, and the position almost a degradation. I am not, I repeat, arguing here so much for justice to India, as for justice to British rule. It is not possible to go on to all time governing India on English principles; and the first steps towards governing it on Indian principles is to govern it partly by Indian intellect. It may "pave our way out of India;" but it is infinitely better to pave the way out than allow it to remain unpaved, and so leave anarchy and ruin behind us when we bid adieu to India as conquerors. The time has gone when it could be justly said that if England left India, the sole monument of her rule would be pyramids of beer-bottles. She has connected Bombay with Calcutta, and Madras with both, by railway. She has lines to both the frontiers, west and east, and branch lines are numerous in British territory and in native states. The great colleges, secular and missionary, represent all that is foremost in Christendom, and offer to India those elements of safety and progress which would have saved Turkey from ruin. Finally, the land has peace. It may be said—it has been said—that all these things have the sore defect that they are of foreign growth. That, however, is nonsense. Christianity was of foreign growth to Britain. The civilisation of Rome was to Britain both foreign and conquering. But all the same the seeds were sown and the weird web woven; and when Rome was in ruin and decay, England stood with a robust young life, pushing her way into other lands, and impressing her genius and enterprise in perilous times upon all nations. What there is of good in the civilisation of England, India need not fear to take. It is merely the return of the tide of civilisation which India sent out to the West generations ago. It is harder and more brittle than when it first went out. It cannot so easily bend or so easily mould itself into new forms. But it may be to India like the omen of a great deliverance and a great future, tending God only knows whither, but assuredly in a right direction; beyond which it will be well for us to remain silent and blind. Sir Thomas Munro said:[1] "The main evil of our system is the degraded state in which we hold natives. We exclude them from every situation of trust and emolument. We confine them to the lowest offices, with scarcely a bare subsistence, and even these are left in their hands from bare necessity, because Europeans are utterly incapable of filling them. We treat them as an inferior race of beings." Sir Charles Napier said: "We must mix with the people, give them justice, give them riches, give them honours, give them share in all things until we blend with them, and become one nation. When a half-caste or a full native can be Governor General, we shall not hold India as a colony or conquest, but be part inhabitants, and as numerous as will be required to hold it as our own."

The Native Press of India has been undergoing a fiery trial little comprehended in England. Every word of comment it directs against any officer or any official act is construed by some one into disaffection; and by some into disloyalty. Even Mr Eden, who is as free as most persons from race and other prejudices, and who certainly is friendly to Bengal, has lately spoken with severity of the press. If I might venture so far, I would submit to the native press of India a receipe which I think would not fail to meet the trial, and make it the means of giving a great free life to India. I would say: 1st. Be rigorously just in criticism. Do not attack a man because he is an Englishman. Remember that an officer, especially of one race governing another race, has many difficulties. Give, therefore, to every man so placed credit for a right motive as far as charity can extend. Nay, strain the point in his favour to the utmost, and reason on just principles. 2nd. In criticising a man or an act, keep in view some number of Englishmen in England: say, Mr Gladstone, Lord Salisbury, Mr Bright, Mr Edward Miall, Mr Fawcett,

[1] Quoted in "Mementoes of the Government and the People," by a Hindoo (1858).

Lord Derby, Sir Alexander Cockburn, Sir Henry Maine, Sir James Stephen, and the higher leaders of the press, not in London alone, but in the great provincial towns. Ask the question fairly and with rigorous exactitude, what would these men think of the criticism? If they would condemn it, the chances are it is wrong. If they would approve it, fear nothing. But settle the point, that no such men ever would approve scandal or abuse, or anything tending to cause disorder. 3d. Send copies of the papers regularly, not to London clubs, which always run in ruts, but to the reading-rooms of London, Birmingham, Manchester, Leeds, Bradford, Edinburgh, Glasgow, Dublin, Belfast, Newcastle, and so on; and to a few upright journalists. Shift the venue to the great life of England, where justice can always be had in the long-run. Then, resolve to use as men, soberly and restrainedly, but firmly, the honourable right conferred on the press by Sir Charles Metcalfe, and supported by Lord Macaulay.

On behalf of the Indian press, I have no hesitation in saying that in its higher parts it is generally characterised by fairness, and that in the journals of a lower character, the strength of the language used is often miscalculated by the writers, while in neither case is it characteristically disloyal. Nothing of all that England has commended to India by precept and example is better worth preservation by India than a free fearless press; and any money spent in making that press known to the great towns—the popular life of England—would be a valuable outlay. While, however, combating all wrong, do not let it be forgotten that the press is a solemn trust, nowhere more solemn than in India, and that to aid the right is even more important than to denounce the wrong. To be on the side of law and order is infinitely better than being on the other side if conscience and the support of law and order can go together. I venture to throw out these few hints in the full light of English publicity, in the hope that they may contribute something alike to the security and sobriety of the powerful engine which, for weal or woe, England has placed in the hands of India.

Having said so much, it is only right to add also, that the native press should face the fact that no nation in the position of England in India could permit her people employed as officers to be unfairly dealt with even in the name of a free press. The native press has in some cases the faculty of pursuing a dispute to the end. I would suggest that the true principle of journalism—and the safeguard against many perils—is to fight a matter out, even to the last trench; but, for the sake of good neighbourly feeling, to pursue it no further. The one thing most dreaded in a newspaper in an English community is the habit of fixing upon a man or an act for everlasting reprobation. The fault is even commoner in English than in Indian papers. Still it is worth mentioning, if the native press of India would keep before it some such English names as those I have mentioned.

CHAPTER XXII.

TO ENGLAND BY BRINDISI, AND FROM THE HOOGHLY TO THE THAMES.

HAVING attempted in the first of these chapters to represent to some degree the impressions created on the mind by the voyage from England to India by Marseilles, I desire, in this concluding chapter, to complete the design of my notes by a partial picture, first, of the return home by Brindisi, and secondly, of that by the Hooghly to Madras and Ceylon, and so, by Gibraltar, to the Thames. From Marseilles the voyage was by the shores of Sicily. From Alexandria to Brindisi it was through the Isles of Greece; at the time I saw them, covered with snow—a very different scene from that in the Straits of Messina on that summer evening referred to in the earlier chapter.

In both cases there are the same historic pathways, and if any wonder had existed in the mind as to the intimate relations of Rome and Greece, and of both with Spain and Gaul, and Carthage and Egypt, it would probably before this have given place to a greater wonder, that at least the two first should have so long been separated and able to pursue different and independent lines of action. That the Romans could have crossed the Great Sea to Carthage, and the Greeks to Sicily, and even to Egypt, without materially interfering with each other's aims, is a fact the strangeness of which can hardly be lost sight of by any reader of history voyaging over the Mediterranean to Brindisi, after having voyaged over it from Marseilles. One perceives, as no book ever can teach, how intimately connected and yet how widely separated were the nations that had direct access to the Mediterranean, and by means of it to three of our four divisions of the globe. It is as if, while looking with the bodily eye upon the renowned sea, one found, with the eye of the mind fixed upon history, that the sea was a magnet which had drawn the most highly civilised as well as the most barbarous races to a common centre, where, as nowhere else in the whole world, a meeting ground, with, at the same time, impassable boundaries of separation, could be secured.

No one can form any, even the most general idea, of the future of India, who considers the subject without an intimate relation to the Mediterranean and the Red Sea. That the struggles of the Arian and Turanian led to vast waves of human beings eastward and westward from some part of Central Asia, or the high land beyond it, is one of the starting-points of our historical knowledge. If we can with the eye of faith and reason see one wave of the men of the past rolling on towards the Mediterranean from the east, and other waves rolling in the same direction from the north, and then the Mediterranean asserting its place to give laws to all the world around, we shall not merely not need food for thought on the voyage to or from Alexandria, but we shall find a key also to the relation of England to India.

It is not too much to say that that relation has rested primarily on the fact that the highway from Europe to India, from the beginning of the eighteenth century till a comparatively recent period, was by the Cape of Good Hope, and that England held that highway as mistress of the seas. The ridicule thrown upon Lord Palmerston for his opposition to the Suez Canal may or may not have been deserved, but at least the commonest point of the ridicule, the advantage that England before all other nations has received from the canal, represents a very short-sighted idea. Rightly or wrongly, Lord Palmerston was looking beyond a time of peace, to one when the Mediterranean Powers might be able to repeat the deeds of old times. We shall never be cut off from India while we are the first of maritime powers, and that we shall for a long time be so, at least, to sufficient purpose to prevent any other power from using the seas on both sides of the canal, is very probable. But that by some combination of powers, we might be compelled to use the Cape route to secure the Canal route to ourselves, or render it useless to an enemy, is quite within the range of possibility. One can hardly, on the Mediterranean and the Red Sea, miss seeing that the position of England in India is one of the boldest ever occupied by any nation. It is bold as regards India, and it is not less bold as regards Europe. It is so bold, indeed, as regards both, that it will some day be again challenged by both; and while it has often been a national virtue of England not to see too far into the future to forget to provide for the present, it is one of the highest qualities of statesmen to face all and provide for all eventualities. We may not always be able to command the canal route, but even if that should come, we still may be able to render the canal useless to an enemy.

From the day-dreams that pass through the mind after a sojourn in India, and during a voyage from the land of the Pharaohs to Brindisi, where we find a highway leading to imperial Rome, the traveller from India awakes to new scenes. Readings of early life—probably Gibbon and Volney, and Plutarch and Rollin—together with readings of later life—perhaps Grote, and Arnold, and Rawlinson—may blend in a picture of Greece, Rome, Egypt, Arabia, India, and Palestine.

What strange influences rest upon the mind as you bid adieu to India at Brindisi—see the last of it when you leave the Peninsular and Oriental steamer, and begin to re-read, amid the enduring monuments of Foggia and Naples, and Rome, and Venice, and Pavia, and Verona, and Florence, and Bologna, and Milan, and Turin, of the key to all modern history. You see an old life which nevertheless is young compared with the history of Babylon, and Nineveh, and Egypt. You see a young life responding to all the impulses of to-day. At Venice you, as it were, look from the Apennines to the Balkans, to Bosnia and Servia, and beyond them to Constantinople. On the shores of the Bay of Naples you may read, in the clearest book ever handed down to man in stone, the history of the pomp and luxury of the "choice spirits" of great Rome. Nothing that the traveller to India may have seen in India or Egypt, or anywhere, has the same handwriting on the wall that remains at Pompeii. Other relics of the past may have been preserved. This alone of all that belonged to the past is embalmed. The streets, the temples and palaces, and tombs, and taverns, the houses of pleasure and the houses of shame, are as distinct to the eye now as they were in the days before the Saviour of men was born. It is a great lesson, if it can in any way be rounded off in one view of ancient history and present times.

All other scenes, however, give place to those of Rome. You perceive at a glance what is meant by the "Eternal City." You perceive that, whatever else you may have seen, this is unique. You pass through miles of ruins. You observe the Seven Hills clad in a great measure with vineyards, and fields of corn and pasture. Yet nothing removes the impression that you are looking on the Eternal City. The Capitol and the Tarpeian Rock; the road along which the Apostle Paul travelled; the dismal Catacombs; the grandeur of the great Church of St Peter's, and the exquisite beauty of the Church of St Paul's, peerless as a whole among churches, are at once memorials of the most imperial of cities, and of a system by means of which, from that city, the world of men was more nearly welded into one than it ever was before or has been since. The Coliseum, with the palaces of the Cæsars close at hand, has a voice in every stone. You see whence the trumpets sounded when the Emperors went forth, with all the pomp of the empire of the world, to witness the doom of prisoners;

the seats of the Cæsars; the cells from whence the sounds of revelry in the palaces could be heard by the doomed; the gates through which the Emperor passed; the doorways through which the prisoners were driven to death, and through which their bodies were dragged out of sight. All is there, and almost as real as when the cup of the empire was being filled to the brim. If you turn from St Peter's in its grandeur, you may not be far away from the little workshops where Roman genius still reigns. You may drive from those awful lines of coffins in the labyrinth of the Catacombs to the beautiful English cemetery where Shelley and John Gibson lie, and where you may find perhaps as many vulgar epitaphs, on the tombs of lords and ladies, and shopmen and shopmen's wives, as could be found in any cemetery of the same size in the world. Everything in the English Cemetery at Rome is beautiful to the eye, if you can forget the tombstones.

In Rome a man may feel as a verity the greatest of the turning-points of history; the rise of the Church of Christ, when from the blood of the martyrs grew the freedom and the new life of nations. In this sense, coming from the images of Brahma and Vishnu, and the mosques, and the marble palaces, and the tombs of India and of Egypt, an influence more subtle than any of them creeps, one may say, into the very soul in Imperial Rome. You carry it with you to Florence and Milan, to the quiet beauty of Bologna, to Turin, to the unchanging beauty of the Alps, the survivor of all the dynasties and empires; the same, in much, yet not in all, as in the days of Hannibal. The Mont Cenis tunnel is essentially a new thing, telling of a different age, of a civilisation which has eaten up all others, and which still remains young.

The Alps are seen to advantage when you can compare them with the Indian Ghâts. In one respect they are similar. The scenery in both is as varied as the shifting slides of a panorama; now grand, now quiet and simple; now leading into an apparently bottomless gorge, clad with tangled many-coloured verdure; now looking upward to mountains similarly clad and towering to the clouds. But the Ghâts, with all their marvellous verdure, are like a section of chaos bordering on some of the dimmest if most restless of populations, while the Alps tell of bright and cheerful peoples whose industry has clad the mountain sides with vineyards, and built cottages like eyries in the far-up crags and crevices of mountains whose tops are in the snow. There are parts of the line along the Alps, as there are on the lines of the Ghâts, where timid people close their eyes. But he or she who can look calmly from a giddy height will not miss seeing a furlong of these scenes. Taking the whole from the landing at Brindisi to the entry into the cities of France as one picture, and comparing the picture with that of India from the landing at Bombay to the departure therefrom—the two ends of an interval which may seem to crowd a decade of years into one year,—I know not what may not be possible to be read by any one who can feel his own littleness in view of the wonderful works of God—the moon and stars which He created; the rolling seasons; the riches of nature; the dark problems of history; the fearful darkness that rests on the infancy and the lot of man.

From the Hooghly to the Thames is, as compared with the Overland route, like a dip into the life of another planet. Say that the health of an intended voyager has been shaken, and that he has been anxious as well as ill, the embarkation at Calcutta in a vessel whose direct destination is London may resemble a glimpse of paradise. Many a wearied Anglo-Indian has found that there are two sides even to "the comforts of the Peninsular and Oriental service." There are the changes, the examinations of luggage, the fresh life, gladsome enough to the fresh mind, the reverse of gladsome to the mind that is not fresh or free. In any case, the direct canal voyage is a new and altogether different experience.

The evening of the 24th November 1874 was just such

an one as a man, set free from India, might have chosen for his first step in the direction of home. The gladsome cool season had fairly begun, and when a few friends had departed, and the fine canal steamer had dropped down from the jetties of Calcutta to Garden Reach, and anchored in a quiet spot nearly opposite to the palace of the ex-King of Oude, the stillness on the Hooghly was almost solemn. Higher on the river there had been incessant turmoil. The great bridge talked of for a generation had at last been opened, quietly, by the modest engineer, Mr Lesley, whose only anxiety appeared to resolve itself into escaping display. He had connected Calcutta with the North Western Provinces, and with a great part of Bengal, from which it had been divided. When the bridge was opened, it was at once and henceforth crowded with people in conveyances and on foot, laughing and talking of the great new thing that the year 1874 would carry into history. The lights flitted backward and forward in the grounds of the ex-King, and only the song of a crew of boatmen, or the plash of a fish in the water, or the steady step of the officer on watch, occasionally broke the stillness which, in other respects, remained unbroken till nearly day-dawn.

All departures from the Hooghly in the same class of ships are much alike, and there are people who affirm that all scenes on the Hooghly are alike to all persons; but there they are mistaken. A duller river in some respects could not be conceived; but in charge of an intelligent captain, at once a good sailor and acquainted with books and life, and a pilot who can speak of what he has seen, much may be learned from Calcutta to the Sand Heads. With a captain of this kind, Captain Cosens of the "Hindoo," and two such pilots, the one in charge of the vessel, the other a passenger to the pilot brigs, we steamed down between the two low shores of the Hooghly, a distance of a hundred and twenty miles to the Sand Heads, the pilot station, where two pilot brigs (the "outer" and the "inner" brig) are anchored, and where also the river empties itself into the Bay of Bengal.

The Hooghly pilot in his own case represents a great history, dating from the old "Covenanted" days when he met the storied Indiaman at the end of her long Cape voyage, and perhaps learned that all Europe was at war, or told of dangers and difficulties and bloodshed in India. Those were great days, as a few old shipwrights, eking out the last embers of life on the banks of the Thames, can tell. The enterprise that set in at Blackwall when the Indiamen appeared at Gravesend had its exact counterpart in the scenes at Fort William when they arrived at the Sand Heads. The sailing vessels were to old times what the Peninsular and Oriental steamers are to these. They carried the most illustrious passengers—great soldiers and statesmen, ladies who had long been separated from their husbands, servants of the Company who left England young, and would not return to it again till they were old and grey. The Hooghly pilot in charge of such interests held his head loftily. He had not entered the service without great influence, but once admitted to it by covenant with the mighty gentlemen of Leadenhall Street, he could not be removed save for gross inefficiency, or something as important. He rose from grade to grade, till, after twenty-five or thirty years, he became a branch pilot, the top of his profession. He wore a gold-lace cap, and often kid-gloves, as beseemed a man who might have the honour to explain to a favourite of the India House some subject which the representatives of the Council of Fort William had not quite mastered. Moreover, he commanded the ship. Much of this has gone. Men high in rank, unless for the comfort or health of the voyage, return home by Bombay, and the "covenant" has been worn to a very thin resemblance of what it once was. Yet the pilot, if shorn of his more gaudy decorations, has still his old power. He is captain for the time. He has vastly larger vessels than of old, and though he has the help of steam, he has not always that help in steering, and sometimes with hand-steering is unable, as in our own case, to bring the vessel's head to a right course in a treacherous and uncertain river. Some of these are facts that can never pass away, and these always secure to the pilot his right place and dignity. The captain of a vessel, however, is either a more than ordinarily good Christian or a more than ordinarily apathetic sailor if he can without a gleam of pleasure view the pilot-boat pushed away from the vessel's side. It is a sad failing of most captains to prefer commanding their own vessels.

Half-way down the river there is a good anchorage ground at Calpee; and there, with a fine long night and a monotonous outlook, we learned somewhat of earlier times. We had passed near to Calcutta the "famine steamers," which had evinced the irradicable propensity to go only with the stream. Farther down we were pointed to a shelving sandbank, on which many a fine vessel had been lost with all on board. Of scenery, in the commonly understood meaning of the term, there is nothing. You see, however, that you have been skirting the vast rice-fields, terminating at the vaster jungle of the Sunderbunds, where, in spite of the deadly rifle, the Bengal tiger still rules as king. On a road through this jungle poor travellers in droves from the coast often began, and did not always end, a journey of sixteen days to Calcutta. The impediments were robbers, tigers, snakes, and a fever which hung, and still hangs, on the low land of the Sunderbunds. At last a tug-boat having been sent out from England for some purpose, for which she proved unfitted, it occurred to the owner, or the representative of the owner, to try to induce the walking traders to travel by river and steam. The experiment was a great success. To passengers were added cargoes—rice, hides, horns, and much besides; and the one vessel grew into an imposing fleet, which has now sharp native competition. Some of the vessels of both lines we passed. We were pointed also to several of the vessels of the British India Steamship Company, which has a suggestive history. Begun at first by a comparatively poor man, and upheld by his perseverance in the face of great difficulties, it had in this year (1874) more than forty vessels afloat, and its name was potent and respected on many seas. We passed, thirty miles or so from Calcutta, a steamer freighted with actors, actresses, and barmaids for the new theatre in which Calcutta was so interested. The theatrical people had the vessel, but with the proverbial generosity of their profession, and their well-known partiality to the pulpit, they had allowed, it was said, a few spare berths to missionaries. Considerably to the eastward was the Mutlah river, and the almost deserted site of Port Canning, one of the greatest failures of mercantile Calcutta.

I had visited and spent some hours at Port Canning in the season of 1872, and, by the kind help of a lady and gentleman who were so good as to accompany me, had learned the history of a project which, I fancy, is not yet irrevocably doomed. The idea of the projectors of the new port was to escape the difficult navigation of the Hooghly by discharging the vessels a little above the mouth of the Mutlah, and taking the freights to Calcutta by railway. They forgot or ignored the enormous vested interests of the capital of India. The town was laid out; the shares were taken at enormous premiums; the principal projector was for a time a miniature King Hudson, the very stones turning to gold at his feet. Then there came a reaction. The pilots who had been educated to the Hooghly did not know the lesser river, and there were some shipping disasters, which were laid to the charge of the Mutlah. Miniature King Hudson thereupon found the gold returning to stone.

The little party with which I visited Port Canning in 1872 started from a shed which served for a railway station in Calcutta, and on a line which was grass-grown. We accomplished successfully in two hours a distance of twenty-eight miles, gliding noiselessly through a district covered with paddy, a great, and, so far as we could see, boundless sea of rice. We found the "town" composed of a very few habitable houses; a number of abandoned new houses and warehouses; an exceedingly fine and finely fitted up rice-mill idle, the property of the company whose faith had been shown by these costly works; a good stone house for the manager of the mill; a magistrate's house, prettily situated; a fine river with a splendid anchorage; well-built jetties, deserted and railed off from the land side; in fact, a city of the dead. A new company, chiefly formed in Bombay under Parsee management, had re-bought the property; but the Lieutenant Governor of Bengal, Sir George Campbell, stepped in and closed the port, and took away the buoys. The company pleaded in vain. They had, they said, "taken over from the old company 351,146 beegahs of rice land (the beegah 1600 yards), had brought one-fourth of it into cultivation, and could cultivate the remaining three-fourths at a cost of from ten shillings to fourteen shillings a beegah. There was no mill in all India, they pleaded, so large and fine as theirs. Sir George, however, was inexorable. It remains for some future, perhaps for the present, Lieutenant Governor to say whether or no Port Canning shall die.

On the evening of the 26th our "king had his own again." The pilots departed to their brigs; two more added to about twenty skilled and in some cases educated men usually kept on the station, and the good ship "Hindoo" bounded into the Bay of Bengal. At noon on the 27th, Friday, we were 188 miles from the pilot brigs, the porpoises and other fish of the rolling and tumbling species accompanying us in countless numbers and never-ending gymnastics. On the 27th a plug was blown from somewhere in the ship with an explosion as of a mine, followed by a screaming of firemen, a storming of the captain, and a detention of three hours, the companionable fish making up their minds to wait for the repairs, and see their larger brother some distance further on his way. When the vessel started, so did the fish, in the best of good-fellowship, rolling grandly from the crests to the hollows of the waves, and rising again in the wildest and freest sport that ever the heart of man conceived. On the morning of the 29th, a beautiful Sunday morning, we anchored amid a fleet of shipping in Madras Roads, and remained there two full days.

I had seen much of India, but there was something in Madras which contrasted with what is found in other places. I thought, as compared with Calcutta and Bombay, it was homelier, more united, and more genial. In Calcutta there is often an ungenerous spirit of depreciation, as if every one but the person to whom you speak were a fool or a rogue. "The Commander-in-chief is all well enough, but—." "Sir Henry Norman has—yes, beyond doubt he has a wonderful memory, but—." "So-and-so is detestable;" and so on. I did not notice this in Madras. I had occasion to mention Sir P. Haines, the Commander-in-chief at Madras, now Commander-in-chief in India, and I heard nothing that was not in his praise. Dr Cornish, the sanitary inspector, was the best sanitary inspector anywhere; and Dr Cornish deserved the praise. But I wondered nevertheless, and all the more because I had heard the very opposite quality ascribed to Madras. "The missionaries!"—"Yes, what of them? we have been unusually fortunate in our missionaries." "The Catholic priests!" —"They have an immense influence and do great good." Perhaps my experience was exceptional, but at all events it was not an experience of wrangling, fractiousness, and calumny. The club at Madras I thought the most complete in some respects of any I ever saw. It provides for everything relating to business or pleasure, and the ladies have a special department, where they can see each other while their male friends are engaged elsewhere. The green hedges and hedgerows resemble those of Surrey rather than anything in Calcutta.

In topics of conversation, also, a Madras drawing-room

seemed to me to differ from the usual drawing-rooms of India; the conversation related more to permanent interests. The great struggle of several generations of English residents in Madras has been for a harbour. Year after year, with intervals of a few years, the destruction of life and property has been an ever-recurring calamity. It has of late become possible to forecast a cyclone, but even then the only possible signal is—"Put out to sea." There is no shelter; no chance but in meeting and breasting the storm. The Madras people argued the case of their harbour with great earnestness, and not as people there one day and removed the next. There was no good harbour, they said, from Comorin to Calcutta on the east coast of India, and none from Comorin to Cochin, where there was a natural harbour on the west coast. They pointed to the fact that Madras was the centre of the telegraph system to China and Australia; and they asserted that if they had a harbour, it would as certainly become also the centre of the China and Australian postal system —a not unreasonable assertion, when it is considered in relation to the fact that Madras and Bombay had a railway communication which can be made in about twenty-four hours, while from Bombay to Calcutta was about sixty-five hours. That Madras is the centre of the banking system of the south-east of India is equally beyond doubt. At the end of 1874, the conversations and projects of many years had arrived at a practical point, and a harbour was proposed to be made at once, and paid for by a tonnage duty.

I had observed long before this, in the Administration Reports, the peculiar position taken by the people of the Madras Presidency with respect to model farms, and the naturalisation of seeds and animals. The Indian Government, with a special view to the improvement of tools and implements of agriculture, and of all that relates to the cultivation of the soil, had formed an agricultural department which had done much good, but mostly with the initiation of district officers. In Madras, on the contrary, the improvement of agriculture is taken up by private persons, and fostered and encouraged both by precept and example. Cows, sheep, seeds, fowls, tools, all manner of living things for the use of man, and all the appliances whereby the earth is made to yield her increase, are subjects of interest altogether apart from Government action.

Connected also with social life and intercourse is the servant system. In Bombay the best servants are the half-caste men. In Bengal the house-servant is a Hindoo, and the table-servant a Mohammedan, and in both cases is often selected, not because he speaks English, but because he professes entire ignorance of it. Sahib feels more comfortable if he knows that his talk at dinner is not understood. The Madrassee is often engaged and taken to Calcutta because he does know English, and without that knowledge he would have a difficulty in being engaged in Madras. There a great number of the servants are Christians—mostly, I think, Catholic—and in any case are free from the caste difficulties which prevail in Bengal. They are generally excellent servants. The author of the "Folk Songs of Southern India" says that the people not Christians are not by any means what some missionaries have painted them; that they in many cases believe in eternal life, and inculcate purity as the chief duty of man. Several of the "Folk Songs" confirm the author's assertion, and some are very beautiful. I may say also that from all I saw I believe the author's views to be the truth.

The boatmen of Madras are a wild, hardy race, compared with whom the Bengalee boatmen are civilised. They speak English, and speak boldly, and soon convince you that the men of the river and those of this exposed coast are essentially different beings. Of the population as a whole Dr Cornish says in his Census Report: "There are in the Presidency about 11,610,000 persons who speak the Telugu language; Tamil, 14,715,000; Canarese, 1,699,000; Malayalum, 2,324,000; Tulu, 29,400; Ooriya and Hill languages, 640,000; and that of the whole population, 28,863,978 are Hindoos, 1,857,857 Mohammedans, 490,299 Native Christians, 14,505 Europeans, 26,374 East Indians or Eurasians, 21,254 Jains, and 6910 undistinguished as to nationality or religion." The Neilgherry Mountains I did not see, but Dr Shortt, in an admirable description of the "Hill Ranges of India," ascribes to these favourite mountain retreats almost every kind of fruit and vegetable, and a charming climate, in which Europeans can work outdoors all the day through.

I have referred in an earlier chapter to the dreadful calamity that has now fallen upon Madras, and which bids fair to devastate the Presidency. It would be foolish to take advantage of such a calamity as a peg upon which to hang any crotchets for the prevention of famine for all future time. Whenever news arrives in England that people are dying in thousands for want of food, immediately the columns of the newspapers are filled with suggestions as to how the famine might have been prevented, and how all other famines may be prevented. I think this course is worth very little, and is often baneful. The point now is to feed the people. The next point is to raise the general condition of the people. It is not by mere irrigation, or by railways, or by the extension of trade, but by all of them, and by a hundred nameless things that famines must be prevented. A skilful doctor will remove a local ailment by giving general tone to the whole system, and so will a sound statesman. More than this it is difficult to say reasonably at a time when thousands are dying. It does seem, however, as if these famines were likely to try British rule in India to the very core. They can, I repeat, be averted by honest and unselfish statesmanship; and honest and unselfish statesmanship would also be to England the highest self-interest.

Leaving Madras on Monday evening, the light of Colombo came in sight on Wednesday night, but it was too dark to anchor, and the vessel was kept well out to sea.

She was brought to anchor with the first streaks of dawn, and all who had no duties on board were soon in catamarans and outrigger canoes on the way to the shore. It would be difficult to conceive without having experienced the luxury of going to bed on board a fine steamboat, with the consciousness that by day-dawn in the morning you will, without any effort of your own, be carried into new scenes. You dine comfortably and rest cheerfully while the vessel's head is put off from land. Then you are rocked to sleep in the hope of such a treat early next morning as a home-staying man never knows. I suppose there is not in the whole range of creation any luxury to equal such a night and morning under such circumstances on the sea. All the tailors, and milliners, and perfumers of Bond Street, and all the cooks, and jewellers, and wine merchants, and shoeblacks, and footmen, and footwomen could not produce anything to give a spark of the gladness of spirit that these healthy scenes create.

From Madras to Ceylon is a transition greater than the mere distance in miles might seem to indicate. It is a change from an imperial to a strictly colonial government. Mr Gregory, of Galway Pacquet fame, was King of Ceylon. On this particular day the captain of an English vessel lying in the roadstead was seized by the Cingalese police, for, as we learned, an absurd debt, which he thought the agents of his vessel had paid, and the captain, in his indignation, knocked down the policeman, with the result of a great uproar, a nominal committal to prison, and a fine. While the peace of Her Majesty the Queen was being endangered, King Gregory passed by on the other side. Lord Northbrook, in Calcutta, would probably have stopped and asked what it all meant; but Lord Northbrook would not perhaps have dared to do so in Ceylon.

We had only a day in which to see the churches and institutions, the shops and people of Colombo, but it chanced to be a long day. The shops contain in many cases curious conglomerations of mixed goods, from ladies' embroidery to the tackle of a ship, and they were very extensive, as they are also curiously indicative of a colonial society, possessing all the wants of England, and compelled to supply those wants by importation. No person whose experience is altogether that of English towns can have an accurate conception of how much this fact involves. The tone of the conversation everywhere in Colombo revolved so materially on one subject, that before the day closed a stranger could hardly be blamed if he came to the conclusion that within the previous twenty-four hours all flesh, and every creeping thing, and all the beasts of the field had been turned into coffee. Of course a drive through a most beautiful country dispelled the delusion, but I refer to the impression created by what one heard inside. The first and the last word was coffee. Some Dutch conclave, at Rotterdam or somewhere, was keeping down prices, and bidding fair to ruin English planters. One grew angry with the Dutch conclave, and wished that it had but one neck, and that neck in Colombo. One heard, too, of the planter's "hard lot." How he personally mustered and set his coolies to work at five o'clock every morning, and then rode over his plantation till nightfall, runners preceding him with his luncheon. How the land had to be cleared and "filled in," and a house built, and a nursery made, and the vexatious markets watched, and the health and well-being of the coolies carefully provided for according to the law of India, and the at least equally keen law of the planter's own interest. The life is by no means an easy one certainly, but the property often becomes very valuable.

A frightful disease was at this time raging among the poorer natives (not coolies) in one part of the island, and had existed some years, it was said, before any European help had been sent to the district. One of the officers then reported that "the tanks or pools of water, of which there are many, emit a putrid smell; . . . that the water itself is black as ink, and teems with animalculæ." Reading this, one felt inclined, as was natural, to sing with good Bishop Heber of the "spicy breezes that blow from Ceylon's Isle—where every prospect pleases, and only man is vile." Yet that there are balmy breezes one felt at morning and evening, when the breeze was off the land. One was not suffered to miss the fact that Ceylon was "the first colony to relieve the mother country of the cost of defence;" that the revenue was increasing; that the railway from Colombo to Kandy—eighty-seven miles—paid eight per cent.; and that towards "the wilderness of Adam's Creek," fifteen years earlier accounted the great forest reserve of the Crown, you might at this time from one spot look upon 40,000 acres of land under coffee. On the water you had the primitive catamarans, or outrigger canoes—logs of wood hollowed, and prevented from overturning by spars being laid across the log till they rested on each side of it on the water. It was pleasant also, in a rather rough sea, to find that the boat could be effectually steadied by a man sitting on the far-off end of the spar, with his feet dangling in the water; and it was interesting to know that if the water grew rougher two men, and if it grew rougher still, three would take the place of the one; and that the war of the elements would be known as a "one man," "two man," or "three man gale."

In quiting Ceylon one really left India, for Aden is only India politically. The porpoises and bonito again awaited us in mighty hosts, and skipped away before and behind on the big waves that rolled down the Straits of Manaar. Steadily the good ship threaded her way along the north coasts of the Maldives, and through the maze of the Laccadives ("the hundred thousand") coral islands; mere rocks, bleak and barren in some cases, covered with verdure in others, governed by laws with which Englishmen have no concern. The large island of Minacoy, credited by Findley's "Maritime Directory" with a population of 3000, sends yearly to the Governor of Ceylon a tribute of cocoa-nuts and fish in return for his august protection. We passed very close to Minacoy, but saw only here and there a stray representative of the 3000 to whom belong this lonely southern isle. Three or four men, fishing in the quiet waters, rested on their oars to watch the leviathan steamer; a little farther three or four more did likewise; in a green creek a few little children were at play—one of the loneliest of all human scenes. Not a hut was in sight; vessels avoid, and rarely have need to touch land in this strangely studded part of the ocean, where a huge island, if not a part of the great continent, is slowly growing by the ceaseless toil of those inconceivable millions of tiny insects. The fish leap in the water in a silence as of eternity, and sea-birds of many names cover the surface of the ocean for miles. One pauses in such a scene—one may well pause in awe. One wonders what the world, and the things of the world, may be when these "hundred thousand islands" have become one—what civilisations may have been swept away, what new inventions may have come to light, what old inventions may have been lost, what progress may have been made towards that great time when the knowledge of the one Lord of all—the Father in every age adored—shall cover the earth as the waters cover the sea.

One wonders too what those lonely fishermen think of our big ship, and of the lands from whence she came; what possible conception one could convey to them of that great Thames to which we are every hour approaching nearer, and of which they probably never even heard the name; what they can think, if they do think, of the purpose of the large vessels they see driving eastward and westward, and northward and southward, on this great ocean highway to India, to China, to Japan, to Australia. Indeed, one may well pause. One hardly, if one desired it, could escape the solemnity of the scene. When the shades of night begin to fall the solemnity deepens. One sees the little islets wrapped up in the same great mantle that, at a different hour, will fold itself around London, and Paris, and Rome, and New York. Walk the deck long enough, and we see the rise of the Southern Cross, and the constellations only known by name in that distant northern land to which we are bound; and while the sea around is as one blaze of phosphorescent light, it may be possible to once again lose the mind in a dream, the spell and charm of which may remain for many years, perhaps for ever, as a childlike conception of the wonderful manifestation of life and death on earth.

Later in the voyage—the Maldives and Laccadives now far behind—our captain called me to see a curious spot on the sun—a remarkable spot, he said, which, often as he had "taken the sun," he never had seen before. And it was a really curious spot—moving, too, as if to tantalise us, and then be gone. Alas! for any claim we might have been disposed to make to scientific knowledge (and it is dignified to make such a claim, at least by silence), we had been looking upon the transit of Venus, yet had known it not till too late to share the pleasure with any other person. The captain brought out his marked almanack—when too late. Yes, it was all there, and the place clearly marked with a big black cross. We had seen yet not seen, observed closely enough yet not comprehended, that we were looking on a phenomenon that the silent and awful laws of nature never will afford us an opportunity of seeing again. It came to us as a mere chance, and then fled like a shadow, as it had come and gone in the generations of old, and as it will come and go in generations to come.

Passing over the lonely desert of the Indian Ocean—lonely alike by day and night, yet abounding in both with beautiful sights—we discerned in the broad daylight, and approached in a swelling but not boisterous sea, the bleak rocks and bare sandhills of Cape Guardafui, the dreary outlook of Africa to the East; the greeting also of Africa, but often as the greeting of an octopus, to the westward-bound vessel. "Is it not a real shame and disgrace to England," our captain said, taking his telescope from his eye, "that in spite of all the disasters and loss of life here, the Government will not go to the slight cost of putting up a light on Cape Guardafui? Sir Bartle Frere drew attention forcibly to the imminent danger and necessity, and his arguments were enforced almost immediately by some dreadful wrecks; yet nothing has been done." Since then, nearly three years later, the arguments have been still further enforced; this very year a long list of wrecks has been so far completed by the loss of the "Meikong" and the "Cashmere." Probably something may now be done. Cape Guardafui is on the direct highway of some of the most important trades represented by some of the largest ships in the world; and in certain conditions of the atmosphere cannot be seen till the ship is close upon land. On a dark night, in a stormy sea, there is no escape whatever for a vessel that has, by any of those chances for which no skill of seamanship can fully provide, been carried too near Cape Guardafui. Close upon Aden, yet far enough distant to render any ready help from Aden absolutely out of the question; on a coast where the people are thoroughly barbarous (though not always, it is said, unkindly, provided the person shipwrecked is willing to act on the principle of the Greek philosopher and claim no more of his property than he can carry about with him), the plea of our sailors, passengers, merchants, and all concerned, is irresistible; and if a bishop or a governor general were driven on the coast and lost, the light would be granted without any delay. After the lessons of this year it will indeed be a crying shame if the winter should pass over without a light on Cape Guardafui. Surely we will not any longer let it be said of us, that while we spare no cost to secure a military or naval station, we grudge the smallest outlay for one of the clearest duties of humanity. Of course the light would need protection; but it could have that protection; and no nation would be jealous of our new station.

Taking in coal at Aden, we voyaged once more along the Red Sea, passing a French man-of-war engaged in gun-practice, passing also ships of many nations, on peaceful voyages of many names; spending Christmas Day in sight of the coast of Arabia, the border-land of that wherein the mighty deeds represented by Christmas Day were done. In the canal we ran very closely past a Dutch troop-ship bound for Acheen, and noticed especially what a fine body of young and stalwart troops she carried. A little farther we were ordered to stop for the mail steamer to pass; the steamer, I found, in which I had made the out-voyage, and we exchanged cordial greetings, almost at speaking distance. At Port Said we had a view of human life at its lowest; I should say that no wickeder or more lawless port could be found. We voyaged along the shores of Tripoli and Algeria, and opened the year 1875 amid mighty big waves, which rolled the ship from beam-end to beam-end. In the darkness of a very dark night a sail was carried away in advance of the ship with a report as of a battery of cannon. Yet after a time use became "second nature," and people ate and drank, and laughed and talked, and tried to calculate the height of the big waves and the depth of the valleys beneath. From the turmoil of the storm we steamed into the quiet shelter of the Bay of Gibraltar.

And now, if an Englishman were at all given to enthusiasm, he might take for himself a wide and glowing retrospect of what he had seen and learned of England's rule in India, and her place among nations. Writing in sober prose, however, I shall aim at little more than to bring this narrative as speedily as possible to a close. No one of ordinary reading could well pass over the history of the Rock of Gibraltar; its relation of old to Phœnician and Carthagenian commerce, to Roman, Visigoth, Moorish, and Spanish deeds in arms. In India I had heard Gwalior spoken of as an inland Gibraltar, which indeed was not a bad comparison, though it is, after all, as if one compared the Caspian with the Mediterranean. The town of Gibraltar is chiefly remarkable for its mixed population, and the strictness of the military laws. There are an exchange, a club, a hospital, Catholic and Protestant cathedrals, a good library, and an interesting museum. Inside you can ride very speedily over the neutral ground to the Spanish lines. Seawards, you may cross to Ceuta and Tangier.

It is the Rock, however, rising from the Mediterranean on the one side, and from the Atlantic on the other, over a bay filled with shipping, and with an outlook, as it were, to both east and west—to Bombay even, and to New York—that gives Gibraltar its place in the history and interest of men. Towering 1250 feet above where your vessel lies, and with a surface, or series of surfaces, of about three miles, you find the Rock of Gibraltar to be one complete mass of stupendous fortification, and you can easily understand that nothing in the world compares with it for strength and completeness. The story of how this completeness was attained is simple. First, you perceive that the rock is admirably adapted for a concentration of engineering skill and ability, and that the fortresses stand alone, commanding everywhere, commanded from nowhere. Secondly, Gibraltar fell at last to a strong and warlike race, which knew how to go steadily on doing its work in its own way, and neither asking nor waiting for the permission of its neighbours to fortify afresh, and to continue fortifying year after year. Thirdly, it belongs to a people who not merely command the sea, but who also possess the largest amount of the most highly cultivated and perfected engineering skill of the time. Lastly, it has been made the sole business of able governors and selected officers to find new means of supplying strength to the famous stronghold—means which have been found from year to year, with slow, persistent, and continuous labour, and practically irrespective of cost. It would be a marvel and a shame if, with all these circumstances in its favour, the Rock of Gibraltar were not, as far as men can determine, impregnable. You wander through galleries and batteries in the solid rock, some closed, some open, all constructed in such a way that the assailants who captured one or more would merely find the way to certain destruction. Passing along a gallery, you come to a battery; inspecting a battery, you find an entrance to a gallery; climbing from gallery to gallery, and battery to battery, you reach some important summit. In all cases you perceive that there is no possibility for any lodgment for an invader unless he can, by some miracle of war, take the principal of the fortifications at once. In fissures of rock, in casemate chambers and halls, on plateaus and in galleries alike, you read the one lesson, that they who would wrench Gibraltar from British hands must command the sea. It is a fitting place at which to end the notes of a tour or a residence in India. The flag that flies here flies also at Aden, at Bombay, at Ceylon, at Madras, at Calcutta, over the marble palaces of Delhi, and over the graves of Lucknow and Cawnpore. It is the flag of the strong, and, when need arises, of the aggressive. When it is borne by men of another kind, men who doubt and hesitate in the face of an enemy, or talk of yielding to any power save that of justice, some other race may assert the right to hold the mightiest fortress in the world. That day, however, has not yet come. We are not educated to see too far, to provide for events too far in the future. The law of our warfare, if warfare is inevitable, can still be reduced to the simple principle, that where a captain has any doubt as to his orders let him run his vessel alongside that of an enemy and he cannot be wrong. Whatever the circumstances, moreover, under which certain deeds of war were done in the past, there can be no doubt that we hold Gibraltar to-day in the interest of civilised nations. It belongs, and will continue to belong, only to the strong. But there is more than strength needed and implied in the occupation. It must continue to be held for the general well-being of peaceful nations. One of the first conditions of unchallenged occupation is, that no one shall be able to show logically that Gibraltar could be in better—that is, more just and honourable—hands. I submit also to the reader that the same law underlies the rule of England in India. Some people tell us that there is in India no such thing as Native Opinion; but they are in error. There is Native Opinion, voiceful in some cases, dumb in others; in both lying at the foundation of English Rule. This fact may not always be apparent, but it will be recorded in history as one of the certainties of the present time. The greatest despots in the East have found in the end that they ruled by the strength of Opinion, and that when that failed, their sabres became blunted. How much more does the rule apply to a free nation professing to govern on just and righteous principles.

We steamed from Gibraltar as the sun was setting, but following him sharply by the Strait, we saw him set the second time in the Atlantic. Then skirting the coast of Portugal, and passing pleasantly through the Bay of Biscay, and round the North Foreland, and the Isle of Sheppey, we came to the old anchorage of the days of Clive and Hastings at Gravesend. A hundred and twenty years have gone since Plassey, and the habits of life are vastly changed. We can only now imagine the feelings of the people who landed at Gravesend after a Cape voyage in the renowned Indiaman. No telegraphic messages met them on their way. The king might have been ever so long dead, or the nation at war, for aught they knew, till the pilot arrived on board, and even then private news had still to be learned. Those hundred and twenty years since Plassey have brought other changes. British India is now an unnecessary term. The Empire extends from the mountains in the north to the Southern Ocean, and the ruling Princes of India pay tribute, and acknowledge the sovereignty of the Queen. Our telegraphic communication is such that, in my own case, messages from the interior of India to London outstripped the march of the sun; that is, leaving, say, at eleven o'clock, Indian time, they were in England at, say, ten minutes before eleven English time. Our steam-boat service, in case of war, is unapproached in efficiency by any in the world. The British army in India is allowed to be excellent. The native army is at once a strength and a weakness accordingly as it is dealt with. The interests and good faith of the Princes go hand in hand. Whether, with all these facts in favour of English rule, that rule is in itself more secure, is hidden in the darkness of times yet to come. Whether the officers who can run away to England for a two months' holiday are more efficient officers than those who could not take more than one furlough to England in less than twenty years, remains to be seen when the test again comes. It also remains to be seen whether the competitive examinations—the only possible rule now—secure men equal to those of the system of patronage, and whether the idea of creating "careers," to be opened by book knowledge, has or has not impaired the sense of responsibility? That rules of seniority would be set aside in time of danger is as certain as that I am writing these lines. Whether it ought not to be tempered even more than it is now—and it is tempered now—by selection, is a serious question? Probably the machine of Government, materially altered since 1857, will go on till it is again tried to the strain, and then will again be reconstructed. That it is a powerful and effective machine, every one knows. That it has fundamental defects no true statesman will forget, even though his recollection of the fact should compel him to lay his hand upon a thousand special interests.

I believe that the connection of England and India, viewed from the present time, represents a period of great and real progress; with drawbacks, it is true, but drawbacks incident to human affairs generally, under like circumstances. It is certain that England, in her true men, has infused a higher and more earnest vein into Indian life; has opened up to India the foremost civilisation of the present time; has secured to India strength in government, and comparative peacefulness amid which the arts of peace may grow. The tone of Anglo-Indian life also has undoubtedly improved; the pictures presented of it in days much later than those of Clive and Hastings would not be fair representations of Anglo-Indian life at the present time. There are, I repeat, and repeat strongly, unquestionable drawbacks, and some of them have been pointed out, in different ways, in the foregoing pages. There are wrongs, petty oppressions, aims, reduced to arts, of self-seeking. But if we view the picture as a whole, and imagine a like picture of India under any other rule, we may without any strain of conscience endeavour to do our best, loyally, and in the face of our own times and of history, to strengthen the rule of England in India. France would have created a grander military empire; would probably have welded the military races together for aggressive war. England, when the worst that can be said has been said of her rule, has certainly created a powerful machinery for peace, and in many respects for practical freedom. It is this machinery that India, for the present, has an interest in strengthening and preserving.

The advantages that England has reaped from her connection with India are also great, but also, however, with drawbacks. As a trading nation she has no longer, as Mr Goldwin Smith lately pointed out, any commercial advantage that is not shared by all civilised nations; and therein is one of the chief elements of the safety of her position. She holds India, as she holds Gibraltar and Aden, as the protector, not as the assailer of peaceful commerce. I would like, if I knew how, to make the letters which record this view deep and distinct, as an indication of the policy at once of safety and freedom in future times. If we stand on the insane policy of conquest, the policy will be rudely questioned some day. If we stand on the policy of doing the best that can be done for India, and of securing to all nations the trade for which several nations fought us, as for a special advantage, in old times, we remove many of the grounds of contention. If we can make friends of the people, we remove many more; but that unfortunately is what only a few Englishmen ever attempt.

In naming what I believe to be one advantage to England of her connection with India, my opinion will, I know, be questioned, and I confess that it is not an opinion at which I very readily arrived—I mean the imperial tone that accrues therefrom both to the acts of government and to individual life. Men may go out merely for careers, and come back without being any the more intelligent, and with much harder and more relentless views of the responsibilities of the rich to the poor. It is only very rarely that an Anglo-Indian ever again takes the slightest interest in purely English, which, after all, are world-wide, affairs. He may, as a sentiment, deliver a lecture, or, with a view to a place in Parliament, talk of education and the Established Church or Nonconformity, but in reality his views are confined to "the services," one of which has been to him the means of making a great position. In such Anglo-Indians there is little to interest England. They are worth much less to her than the same number of respectable artisans, and at times they are a baneful element in politics.

There are other Englishmen, who, going out at first simply for careers, return very different men. Joseph Hume and David Hare probably left England without any clear idea of duty. Both, however, did high duty, and assisted greatly to raise the standard of duty, in the case of David Hare, chiefly in India, in that of Joseph

Hume, in England. These are but two of a number of examples which might be given of how a stern faith and earnest purpose may become intensified by a residence in India, and how it may react on the life of England. An oppressor by nature will become more oppressive by being in India, but a lover of freedom by nature will probably love freedom the more with every year of his life in India. He will see more of the real meaning of those enduring interests which no mere personal selfish aims can affect. He will assuredly see human history from a loftier standground. Lord Macaulay owed much to India, and England owed much to that debt of Lord Macaulay's. Thus the life of India and of England act and react upon each other, with varied results, when considered in detail, but, I think, with clearly beneficial results when viewed as a whole. That is, England nationally, has a clear benefit in the connection, if it is made to rest in justice. Of the benefit to individuals, in the opening of careers, I have no object in writing at present, though in a just and honourable career, even the individual advantage must recur to the whole community.

When people talk of going to India for India's good, they in most cases talk hypocritically. It is not easy to go anywhere purely for the good of people of whom you know nothing. But Englishmen have risen, are rising, and will rise, into the duty of remaining for India's good. We were attracted at first by the renown of India's wealth. Our factories were for trade, for the benefit of individual Englishmen. This fact was marked by all manner of means, and especially by the laws against interlopers, including missionaries. We were to know nothing either of politics or faith save as they bore on trade. When the Company rose to sovereign power, whatever else it was, no one can say it was in any respect unselfish. Lord Wellesley, looking upon the past of a trading company, and on the fact of a company wielding sovereign power, said: "The duties of sovereignty must be considered paramount to mercantile interests, prejudices, and profit. In time of peace the happiness of its subjects, the permanent improvement of its dominions, the dignity, purity, and vigour of its government, must take precedence of commercial considerations." And again: "The civil servants of the Company can no longer be considered as the servants of a commercial concern. They are, in fact, the ministers and officers of a powerful sovereign. They are required to discharge the functions of magistrates, judges, ambassadors, and governors of provinces in all the complicated and extensive relations of those sacred trusts and exalted stations, and under peculiar circumstances which greatly enhance the solemnity of every public obligation, and aggravate the difficulty of every public charge." These words were written when Englishmen were first gaining perceptions of the real and vast change in the relation of England and India; and the policy of Lord Wellesley was that of a statesman to whom India has owed much. It was a policy worthy of the best of the Romans. Edmund Burke and Charles James Fox, however, rose higher than this. Lord Wellesley saw England's executive duties at their highest and noblest. Fox and Burke went deeper than executive duties—to the kernels of truths, to the relations of men to men, as well as of men to governments; and their words and their political action in the House of Commons will remain among the noblest charters that ever England gave to India. France, by the lips of Mirabeau might have made more fervid and thrilling assertions of freedom. But nowhere in the world in the years from 1789 till the principles of 1789 passed away could there have been produced anything in view of India to surpass in nobleness and value what Fox and Burke said and did during the earlier of those years. The trial of Warren Hastings was marked by many errors on the part of the prosecutors—by much personal enmity, and many unworthy aims. The enmity to Clive was even more so; but there was at that time a line drawn beyond which even genius of the first order must not pass; and what was done then has never since been pushed out of sight.

Returning to 1877, the foremost duties before an Englishman in India seem to consist in making friends of the people by justice, fair-play, and courtesy; by developing trade; by assisting individuals to usefulness in life; by upholding all truths, religious or otherwise, in the face of all falsehoods; and by striving to raise flowers in the place of weeds in social life. We may be assured that our first means of defending India will be found—not on, and certainly not beyond, the frontiers, but in India itself. We shall find those means in various ways; but the key to them all is, that they shall rest on a fair consideration for the just wishes, and even for the errors and prejudices, of the people. Englishmen have caused much suffering in India. But if India has suffered, England too has given some noble and generous blood to India.[1] Leaving, therefore, the things that are behind, and pressing on to those that are before, it is possible, I think, on right and just principles, even yet to establish an empire which may resist a hundred storms, and win the cordial affection of the people in future times.

[1] Appendix VIII.

APPENDIX.

No. I.—*Page* 43.

THE identity of the gates recovered with those removed from Somnâth was questioned at the time in the sharp satire directed against Lord Ellenborough, but I do not know any sound reason for doubting that the gates I saw at Agra were those taken away by Mahmoud of Ghuznee.

No. II.—*Page* 46.

It should not be forgotten that the passes of Afghanistan and the co-operation of the Afghans were essential to Napoleon's scheme for the invasion of India; and that when Lord Wellesley in the year 1800 sent Captain Malcolm on the famous embassy to Teheran—the first marked indication of the new frontier policy—it was with especial view to Napoleon's designs. A little earlier Lord Wellesley had planned an attack on the Mauritius, and in 1800 he carried out that memorable invasion of Egypt by a force from India; an event which may perhaps rank in political importance with the battle of the Nile as proving to Napoleon that the invasion of India, while India was governed by a man like Lord Wellesley, would be a desperate enterprise. The French had assailed England in several different directions with a view to India;—by means of Tippoo, whom in 1799 we conquered; by invading Egypt, which was even then (without either a Suez Canal or an Overland Route) the key to the operations of a ruler who, powerful on land, was impotent on sea; and finally, by a very subtle influence, directed to Persia and Afghanistan. There can hardly be a doubt that with Lord Wellesley at Calcutta we should have defied and defeated even Napoleon. How thoroughly he grasped the whole question with the intuition of genius, and provided for every possible chance, and even for what he deemed impossibilities, his recently published dispatches show. Instead of waiting for Napoleon to attempt the march from Egypt to Afghanistan, Lord Wellesley, with a daring equal to Napoleon's own, sent the force referred to above to dispute the first step of the invasion in Egypt, and he provided for failure there by influencing Persia and Afghanistan. He said: "This French state actually holds possession of the person and nominal authority of the Mogul; maintains the most efficient army of regular native infantry, and the most powerful artillery now existing in India, with the exception of the Company's troops, and exercises a considerable influence on the neighbouring states, from the banks of the Indus to the confluence of the Jumna and the Ganges. . . . Nor could an instrument of destruction more skilfully adapted to wound the heart of the British Empire in India be presented to the vindictive hand of the first Consul of France." That both Lord Wellesley and his brother, the future Duke of Wellington, were impressed with a belief that the invasion of India from the north west was practicable, cannot be disputed; and though they would have met it with high hearts and every hope of success, we must bear in mind that the rule of England at that time was in exceptionally able hands, and that if Lord Auckland had been in the place of Lord Wellesley, the entire conditions would have been different. That Napoleon could have marched from the Caspian to the Khyber we may deem impossible if the march had of necessity been through enemies, and with Nelson triumphant on sea. If, however, France could have held the Mediterranean, and Persia and Afghanistan had been conciliated, and the Indian princes influenced by the able and skilful French officers employed for that purpose, and, above all, if Lord Auckland, and not Lord Wellesley, had been Governor General, the face of the world might, as Napoleon delighted to say of many of his operations, have been changed from the day the French landed in Alexandria. Wellesley in India and Nelson on the Mediterranean destroyed Napoleon's chance of attempting to repeat for France the splendid drama that Clive had achieved for England. It will be perceived, however, that a "frontier policy" was necessary, and that the invasion of India was by no means the chimera that some people would have us suppose. To defy the danger is one thing. To deny the existence of the danger is to increase it many fold.

No. III.—*Page* 63.

The rumour of Yakoob Beg's death was afterwards contradicted, but incorrectly so. The latest intelligence up to the time these lines go to press is that the late Ameer's son, Beg Kuli Beg, has been defeated, the Dadkhwah's son killed, and the Dadkhwah himself taken prisoner.

No. IV.—*Page* 108.

I was much struck by the way in which some officers, whose memories went back for as long as perhaps thirty years, and were continuations of other memories, spoke of these frontier soldiers of adventure. Of Avitabile, and his unscrupulous seizure of any person, male or female, or any property necessary to his interest or personal gratification, there are many, and I should say, authentic stories.

No. V.—*Page* 134.

Mr Fawcett made this strong statement at Salisbury (September 9) this year :—"Our present income-tax of 2d. in the pound yields an annual revenue of about four millions; an income-tax of the same amount when imposed in India did not produce more than £400,000. Not only, therefore, is the income-tax a most feeble resource for adding to the revenue of India, but there are such manifold abuses connected with its collection, and the tax is so entirely unsuited to the Indian people, that nothing but extreme necessity can justify a resort to it. So strongly was this felt by Lord Canning, one of the best Governor Generals that India ever had, that he once declared he would far sooner run the risk of reducing the European army in India by one half than incur the danger which might result from the discontent which the imposition of an income-tax would produce." Mr Fawcett also said :—"In a volume issued by the India Office in 1873 it is said, 'In the 14 districts of Madras there are said to be 43,000 tanks, all of native origin, with probably 30,000 miles of embankments and 300,000 separate masonry works. The revenue dependent on tanks was £1,500,000, yet in 1853 not one new one had been made in Madras by the English, though many had been allowed to fall into disrepair.' Again, it is stated that under native rule, by well and canal irrigation, 'the district of Mooltan, between the Sutlej and Chenab, where rain hardly ever falls, is converted into a succession of beautiful gardens, shaded by date palms.'"

No. VI.—*Page* 218.

Mr Eden recently said of Lord Northbrook: "Some little time antecedent to Lord Northbrook's arrival, there had arisen from some cause or other a condition of coldness and restraint in the relations between Europeans and natives, and a general want of mutual confidence and good feeling, which was much deplored and regretted by thinking men of both classes. But I observed that year by year after Lord Northbrook's arrival this state of things vanished away; and I believe that this was mainly due to the personal example of courtesy and consideration which Lord Northbrook set in all matters of communication and intercourse with natives. I know, and I can say it most confidently, that the educated native gentlemen of Bengal were much impressed and influenced by the unvarying courtesy with which he treated them, and with the calm, patient justice with which he considered all matters connected with them."

No. VII.—*Page* 293.

After this chapter was in type I fortunately mentioned it to Mr Wilson, proprietor and editor of the *Indian Daily News* (now in England), who kindly sent me a note, referring to an Indian worker, Baboo Sasipada Banerjee. Mr Wilson wrote: "Baboo Sasipada Banerjee is, I believe, or rather I should say was, a Brahmin by birth, and resides at Baranagore, a village a few miles north of Calcutta. He is yet a young man. When I first became acquainted with him, he was engaged in earnest endeavours to improve the character of his neighbours and benefit the village. The jute-mill of the Borneo Company had brought to the village numbers of men who were rapidly becoming 'mill hands,' but who were very ignorant. Sasipada was, I think, at this time a member of the so-called reformers of the Brahmo Somaj, of which Baboo Keshub Chunder Sen is the recognised leader. But he is not a man to be held in iron-bound creeds. In opposition to the feelings and traditions of his race, he had the sagacity to perceive that future generations must be affected for good through their mothers. His means were limited. He was only a clerk in a magistrate's court; but he resolved to employ the hours not required for official duty in useful work. He laid his plans before the managers of the mills and other friends who sympathised with him. Schools were started for infants and for adults. To the latter he devoted his evenings, frequently not reaching home till near midnight. He started girls' schools, and the idea of girls' schools is, or was, a very revolutionary one in India. He established an improvement committee in the village, and was laying the axe so vigorously, albeit very unostentatiously, to the root of many long-standing evils, that some of his fellow-villagers, including members of his own family—taking that term in a wider sense than our English one of his own household—began to take alarm. He became subject to all sorts of opposition and persecution. He was put out of caste, intercourse with his fellows was denied him. His house was defiled at the instigation of men who professed to be not only gentlemen but religious. He showed no resentment. Greater trials were in store for him. His wife, devotedly attached to him, and taught by him the difference between real religion and ignorant idolatry and worse sham, sympathised with and encouraged him. The time of dire necessity was coming upon his wife, when she must experience the sorrow that precedes the compensating joy of maternity. The village doctor would not, or dare not, attend the wife of an out-caste; no midwife would or dare render her mercenary aid any more than she dare assist from sympathy. Here, it was said, we shall touch Sasipada to the quick, and bring him to bend beneath the yoke of Hindooism. Sasipada felt that in this extremity, as in others, he must trust in God and the intelligence which He had given him. He made the best use of his time in the study of a few physiological and medical works, and performed most satisfactorily the duties of family *accoucheur*. One day while he was at his daily duty some seven or eight miles away, his wife was taken from his house at Baranagore, he knew not whither or by whom; and of course none of the villagers likely to be concerned in the affair would give him any information. However, he was not to be baffled; and love, which laughs at locksmiths, somehow in this case opened a communication. Sasipada found that his wife had been spirited 500 miles away to Benares. He found her and brought her home. Some of these facts became known to European gentlemen in Calcutta, and one of the papers expressed itself in a style that was not calculated to flatter the self-love of Sasipada's persecutors. But he had almost beaten or wearied them out himself, and after this they modified their animosity. Sasipada had conversed with English gentlemen of institutions in England for working men. He had also read of various organisations of labour, &c. He wished to visit England to see these in operation. His work attracted the notice of Miss Carpenter on her first visit to India, and one of the results was an arrangement that Baboo Sasipada should pay a visit to England. There was some difficulty about it. Native gentlemen—even Brahmins—had been known to commit the iniquity of crossing the sea against the injunctions of their Shasters. He went, however, and Mrs Banerjee accompanied him. They were the guests of Miss Carpenter, and a son was born at Bristol and was named 'Albion.' Though this visit was not regarded with favour, the 'enemy' had seen sufficient. Some thought he might perhaps return a Christian; but I am not aware that he has ever been considered one, or has professed to be so. He is a Brahmist, and most assuredly a 'reformer.' Though he belongs to the 'Progressive Brahmos,' he does not accept implicitly the doctrines of Keshub Baboo; nor do I suppose he will accept those of any sect, of whatever denomination. Amongst other things resulting from his visit to England was the publication of a little work in the Bengalee language, upon the model of the *British Workman*, though, of course, at an infinite distance. The circulation has reached 8000 or 10,000 copies. Two or three years ago, the great sorrow of his life fell upon Sasipada. His wife, who had been the faithful partner of his sufferings and persecutions, whose devotion and affection sustained him in the most trying periods of his life, was taken from him. The management of the little paper for working men necessarily devolves largely upon him, but he has occasionally to be absent on duty, and on one such occasion a letter or paragraph based on a fact, though the fact was not accurately expressed, was inserted. His opponents charged him with criminal defamation, their object being to put upon him the indignity of imprisonment. They managed to get him convicted, and the native magistrate sentenced him to a heavy fine and to three months' imprisonment. Notice of appeal was given, but bail was refused, an act of malice that was defeated by a prompt representation to the sessions judge—an Englishman. On appeal the sentence as to imprisonment was reversed, and the fine was reduced to a comparatively small sum."

No. VIII.—*Page* 330.

Mr Wilson, in the course of conversation also said, with reference to the advantages and disadvantages of the English occupation of India: "Yes, the very same subject arose in conversation at Delhi on the occasion of the proclamation of the Empire. One of those present said it was true that some men made fortunes; that many received high pay and gained distinction; but we also gave to India some of our noblest blood, and paid for our occupation in lives that could ill be spared. 'The graveyards of India,' he said, 'sufficiently attest that. Whenever I visit Delhi, I never seem to have done my duty without going to the Cashmere Gate and to the cemetery outside, where lie the bones of John Nicholson and of many who fell with him. But it is not alone with the lives of the strong that we pay the price of our occupation. The other day I did my usual pilgrimage to the tomb of Nicholson, and what else did I see? On every side of the grave of the great man there were melancholy memorials of many who might have become great also under other conditions. Within a yard or two of Nicholson's tomb there is a newly erected stone with the inscription 'Sacred to the memory of our Sonny Boy' (a native phrase= "bright" or "golden"), 'who died ——— aged two years.' Again not more distant, 'In affectionate remembrance of —— ——, daughter of Captain and Mrs —— ——, aged one year and seven months.' These and many more very recent monuments of similar purport, attest in suitable inscriptions how parental hopes have been blighted, how passionate sorrow bewails the exactions of an Indian career. The young blossoms of hope scarcely bloom ere they droop and die: the young tendrils just learn to twine themselves round the hearts which they lacerate on being torn away. The bereaved parents leave a sad memorial over the graves which the instability of their position often forbids the possibility of their ever visiting again. These leave sad memories; and are a part of the price we pay for the occupation of India.' A medical gentleman present said: 'I am glad to hear you say that. It has been before me often in my experience, but I have never heard it so expressed before. I thank you much for saying that.'"

THE END.